THE PARADOX OF VULNERABILITY

Princeton Studies in Global and Comparative Sociology

Andreas Wimmer, *Series Editor*

The Paradox of Vulnerability

States, Nationalism, and the Financial Crisis

John L. Campbell
John A. Hall

PRINCETON UNIVERSITY PRESS

PRINCETON AND OXFORD

Copyright © 2017 by Princeton University Press

Published by Princeton University Press,
41 William Street, Princeton, New Jersey 08540
In the United Kingdom: Princeton University Press,
6 Oxford Street, Woodstock, Oxfordshire OX20 1TR

press.princeton.edu

Cover art: Willem van de Velde (II), *A Ship on the High Seas Caught by a Squall,
Known as "The Gust,"* c. 1680. Rijksmuseum, Amsterdam

All Rights Reserved

Library of Congress Control Number 2017945482

Cloth ISBN 978-0-691-16326-0
Paperback ISBN 978-0-691-16325-3

British Library Cataloging-in-Publication Data is available

This book has been composed in Adobe Text Pro and Gotham

Printed on acid-free paper. ∞

Printed in the United States of America

10 9 8 7 6 5 4 3 2 1

CONTENTS

PREFACE

The initial hunch that pushed us to write this book derived from our personal experiences, first as tourists in Denmark and then as visiting professors at Copenhagen University and at the Copenhagen Business School. The responses that one of us received in the 1970s when asking about the character of Danish politics all stressed factors having to do with social class, seen as the underpinning of social democracy. There is, of course, truth here, but the image that was often presented, probably as the result of Marxist influences in both Danish popular and academic life, suggested a society of great conflict, torn apart by visceral hatreds. It did not feel like that then and it certainly has not felt like that to us since the early 1990s when we both began spending more time in Denmark. Danes seemed to be Danes, highly similar and blessed with a huge consensual background that kept conflict within bounds. Perhaps this was our reaction because of our basic knowledge of the factors that created really vicious conflict within the deeply divided societies of Europe, such as Yugoslavia and Poland, during earlier times. What mattered in these countries was the layering of conflicts, to use Ralf Dahrendorf's expression— above all, the way in which class conflicts in combination with tensions among nationalities could create real social dynamite, as Ernest Gellner had so brilliantly demonstrated.[1]

It seemed that the Danes had forgotten the national homogeneity of their society and were unaware of how much this influenced their politics. The likelihood that a consensual background mattered then made us suspicious of the claim made in 1990 by Michael Porter, guru of the Harvard Business School, that Denmark was on the rocks, bound to decline, adrift in a sea of conflict.[2] There was certainly conflict, but one sensed that Danes would in the end pull together. After all, had not the dire economic crisis of 1933 been resolved among political rivals over beer and smørrebrød at Kanslergade, Prime Minister Stauning's residence in Copenhagen? We explored and subsequently confirmed this possibility through an intense collaboration with

1 Dahrendorf 1959; Gellner 1983.
2 Porter 1990.

several experts on Danish political economy.[3] This led us to think that Peter Katzenstein's superb early work on the way in which small states prospered in the world economy might be improved by adding an analysis of cultural homogeneity.[4] To that end, we began to ask whether our findings about this small culturally homogeneous society might be generalizable to other small nation-states in the advanced capitalist world.

There are several competing indices of country competitiveness and national well-being. Small and nationally homogeneous states continually feature at the top end of all such lists.[5] Two of our previously published statistical papers on the OECD countries in the late-twentieth and early-twenty-first centuries also suggested that there was something systematically at work here. Countries that were culturally homogeneous and vulnerable in terms of their openness to international trade, as small countries often are, tended to be the most successful.[6] But statistical associations alone may mislead. What matters is the discovery of mechanisms that show real causality to be at work. Concentration in this book on Denmark, Ireland, and Switzerland, the latter often falsely taken to be so culturally diverse as to lack a shared national identity, has allowed us to demonstrate that small nation-state vulnerability to external forces can strengthen national identity, social partnership, and institutions in ways that lead to resilience and prosperity. This is the paradox of vulnerability. By developing detailed historical case studies of these countries this book goes beyond plausible generalization to the identification of processes and mechanisms. It does so by focusing relentlessly on the ways in which these small nation-states responded to a single event, namely the international financial crisis that began in 2007. Analysis of their styles of crisis management, of their ability to navigate when hit by a sudden squall, has proved to be deeply revealing.

Even before we start, it is well to issue warnings. Nobody should think for a second that we wish to make all societies culturally homogeneous—or, for that matter, small. Switzerland demonstrates that cultural heterogeneity is no barrier to the creation of a strong sense of national identity that allows for high levels of cooperation. We abhor cultural "cleansing" of every kind, and know full well that a major problem facing the politics of the world is that of creating polities in which different nations and ethnicities can cooperate harmoniously. Neither should anyone imagine that we think that the only route to economic and social success is by means of this particular type of political economy. Capitalist society is diverse, and countries of very different charac-

3 Campbell et al. 2006.

4 Katzenstein 1984, 1985.

5 See, for instance, recent editions of the United Nations Human Development Report or the World Economic Forum Global Competitiveness Report.

6 Patsiurko et al. 2012, 2013.

ters within it have managed to swim successfully within its bounds. The claim that we will make is accordingly limited, namely that the combination of national homogeneity and vulnerability associated with small size can be a particularly beneficial recipe for success within today's world political-economic system. But much remains to be said about that "can be"!

The opening chapter is theoretical and conceptual. The core of the book comprises detailed comparative historical analyses of Denmark, Ireland, and Switzerland—all small nation-states but with important differences among them. The conclusion offers shorter examinations of further cases, before offering more general reflections.

ACKNOWLEDGMENTS

We have received many helpful comments on the arguments presented in this book. We thank the following, and apologize to those whose names we have accidentally forgotten: Michael Allen, Tassos Anastassiadis, Denise Anthony, Eddie Ashbee, Lars Bille, Mark Blyth, Martin Carstensen, Paolo Dardanelli, Francesco Duina, Brian Girvin, Niamh Hardiman, Eric Helleiner, Jason Houle, Jason Jensen, Erik Jones, Peter Katzenstein, Deborah King, Bill Kissane, Matt Lange, Kathryn Lively, Brendan O'Leary, Siniša Malešević, Janice McCabe, Seán Ó Riain, Ove Pedersen, Martin Rasmussen, Len Seabrooke, Kathy Sherrieb, Patrice Siegrist, Michael Smith, Thomas Soehl, Cathal Slack, Emily Walton, Andreas Wimmer, and seminar participants at the Copenhagen Business School, Copenhagen University, McGill University, Dartmouth College, the University of British Columbia, Hamburg University, the University of Salzburg, and the South China University of Technology. Special thanks go to Natalka Patsiurko, who contributed significantly to the analysis and data collection in work leading up to this book, and to two excellent anonymous reviewers from Princeton University Press. Eric Crahan, our editor, did a fine job ushering the book through the review and production processes. We are indebted above all to all those who agreed to be interviewed for this project, several of whom also offered comments on particular chapters.

Funding for this project was provided by the Nelson A. Rockefeller Center for Public Policy at Dartmouth College, the Department of Business and Politics at the Copenhagen Business School, Canada's Social Science and Humanities Research Council, and McGill University. The John Sloan Dickey Center for International Understanding at Dartmouth and the Saxo Institute at the University of Copenhagen held intensive workshops on the entire manuscript from which we benefited enormously.

ACRONYMS

Denmark

ATP Arbejdsmarkedets Tillaegspension (Labor Market Supplementary Pension)

DA Confederation of Danish Employers (Dansk Arbejdgiverforening)

DBA Danish Bankers Association (Finansrådet)

DI Confederation of Danish Industry (Dansk Industri)

DKK Danish krone

DNB Danish National Bank (Danmarks Nationalbank)

DØR Danish Economic Council (De Økonomiske Råd)

FS Financial Stability Company (Finansiel Stabilitet A/S)

FSA Financial Supervisory Authority (Finanstilsynet)

FSU Financial Sector Employees Union (Finansforbundet)

LO Danish Confederation of Trade Unions

PCA Private Contingency Association

SDP Social Democratic Party (Socialdemokratiet)

Iceland

FSA Financial Supervisory Authority

International

EC European Commission

ECB European Central Bank

EU European Union

IMF International Monetary Fund

OECD Organization for Economic Cooperation and Development

Ireland

AIB Allied Irish Bank

CBFSAI Central Bank and Financial Services Authority of Ireland

DSG Domestic Standing Group

ESRI Economic and Social Research Institute

ICTU Irish Confederation of Trade Unions

IBEC Irish Business and Employers Confederation

IDA Industrial Development Agency

NAMA National Asset Management Agency

NESC National Economic and Social Council

RTE Radio Telefís Éireann (Radio Television Ireland)

Switzerland

CCFM Conference of Cantons Finance Ministers

CHF Swiss franc

DRCM Dillon Read Capital Management

FDF Swiss Federal Department of Finance

FINMA Swiss Financial Market Supervisory Authority

SBA Swiss Bankers Association

SBF Swiss Business Federation

SP Social Democratic Party (Sozialdemokratische Partei der Schweiz)

SFBC Swiss Federal Banking Commission

SNB Swiss National Bank

TBTF Too Big To Fail Commission

THE PARADOX OF VULNERABILITY

1

Groundwork

When global financial markets crashed in September 2008 our countries—Denmark, Ireland, and Switzerland—were hit especially hard. They required substantial assistance from the U.S. Federal Reserve and the European Central Bank (ECB) because their own central banks did not have enough resources to shore up their financial systems. Policymakers and bankers felt vulnerable. Fear became general. "We did not know whether in the first quarter of 2009 we all were on our way to hell!" noted one Danish banker, thereby capturing the general mood of an unprecedented situation that nobody knew how to handle.[1] Yet Denmark as well as Switzerland displayed considerable resilience in the face of the crisis, thereby showing that the forces of globalization do not necessarily overwhelm small countries. They performed well thanks to thick political and economic institutions, best defined as professional, expert-oriented and nationally focused; politically inclusive; legitimate and trustworthy; and possessing well-developed organizational capacities. We will show that these institutions result from successful nation-building and state-building in the face of continual geopolitical and economic vulnerabilities. In contrast, Ireland did less well: the independence of the state is recent, its nation-building incomplete, and its institutions comparatively thin.

Much has been written about the policies that different countries adopted to handle the financial crisis. Far less has been written about the processes by which these policy decisions were made and the institutional contexts that shaped them. In particular, virtually nothing has been written about the ways in which patterns of national development affected these more proximate factors. We will show that one cannot fully understand what happened in the

---

1 Interview with Peter Straarup, former CEO, Danske Bank.

countries that concern us without appreciation of such historical patterns. It is as well to stress that this makes for an ambitious book. A brilliant paper by Charles Kindleberger that came to our attention as we were completing this book suggested that understanding trade and economic development across nations in the nineteenth century required "a rounded theory of social behavior [that] would include economic drives as only one strand in a broad web of social motivation," an argument interestingly reinforced by an incisive and accurate analysis of Danish economic development.[2] The general statement precisely captures our intent and the result of our research: economic performance cannot be understood without the contribution of sociology.

Some clarification of terms is needed immediately. What we mean by a small country is not as straightforward as one might think. Smaller countries typically have fewer people and less arable land than larger ones, which means in many cases that they also have fewer and less diversified resources than larger countries. The size of their domestic markets also tends to be small. Further, when it comes to international relations, their power is generally dwarfed by larger countries; they are often rule takers rather than rule makers. The implication of all this, discussed in detail later, is that small countries tend to be vulnerable to external forces to an extent unfamiliar to larger ones.[3]

The nature of the nation is even more complicated and the subject of intense debate—which, however, can be resolved for the purposes of this book. It certainly is the case that some shared sense of ethnic, religious or linguistic similarity can facilitate the creation of a nation. But total cultural homogeneity in terms of language, ethnicity, and religion is not necessarily required for the creation of a fully developed national identity. Despite linguistic and religious difference there was some sense of Swiss identity very early on, as we shall see, even though it was only at the end of the nineteenth century that various festivals and nationalist myths consolidated the nation. Crucially, nationalists are liable to mislead the unwary because they so often put forward the view that the fully consolidated nation was always extant, merely asleep, waiting to be awakened. In fact a nation develops over time, moving, to use Marxist terms, from something in itself to something for itself—or, to use different language, from merely nominal status to something substantively present in daily life. The same point can be made about the state, the centralized political apparatus responsible for providing order internally and protection against external threats. States develop gradually in response to modern social conditions. The strength of a state is enhanced when it is the home of the people: democratic, highly educated, and provided with welfare. This leads

---

2 Kindleberger 1951, p. 30.
3 The general point is now forcefully made by Abulof (2015).

to a very simple conclusion. The culmination of these two processes—nation-building and state-building—is the modern nation-state, the home of the people in every sense.

We have already claimed that our work will contribute to a broader and more complete view of the workings of economic life. But that aim might have been reached in other ways. So why should we care about a few small nation-states? One answer is simple: even the puny deserve attention! However, there is a larger theoretical issue. The theory that we offer about small nation-states suggests that the ability to act flexibly and quickly can help explain success within capitalist society. Earlier statistical papers certainly suggested that this is so.[4] The point is that there are also lessons here for larger countries. They may need to foster greater national unity and institutional resilience if they are to navigate effectively in an increasingly volatile world political economy. As small countries have been more exposed historically to international vulnerabilities than larger ones, the analysis of their social formations provides an especially clear view of the factors affecting resilience relevant nowadays to all countries.

There are additional reasons of a more academic sort that explain why this book should appeal to readers beyond those interested in small nation-states. First, it weds the insights of two very important social science literatures that rarely speak to one another, one on comparative political economy, the other on nationalism. Second, our arguments contribute to recent scholarship on how ideas as well as interests affect institution-building and policymaking, and they do so with a particular twist. The scholarship on ideas within comparative political economy focuses on the influence of economic frames and paradigms such as Keynesianism and neoliberalism while largely ignoring more general political cultures. Our emphasis on nationalism fills an important blind spot in the discipline.[5] Third, we offer a lesson about one economic paradigm in particular—neoliberalism—that went terribly wrong in some countries by convincing policymakers to limit government regulation of financial markets. As is well known, this led to disaster: the 2008 financial crisis. Although our emphasis will be on the ways in which thick and thin institutions affected responses to the crisis we show as well that institutions influenced the manner in which policymakers embraced neoliberalism in the run-up to the crisis. Finally the book speaks to the literature on the financial crisis from a new and broader perspective. Previous studies have tended to be

4 Patsiurko et al. 2012, 2013.

5 For a review of the literature on ideas, see Campbell (2002). Vivien Schmidt's (2002) comparison of different national-ideological styles of policymaking moves in our direction but does not focus on national solidarity. An important exception that does take nationalism seriously is Helleiner and Pickel (2005).

sector specific rather than taking into account the wider national political economy: Cornelia Woll concentrates on the organizational capacities of the banking industry in her analysis of crisis management.[6] Stephen Bell and Andrew Hindimoor analyze the industry's incentive structures, noting that they varied across countries.[7] Research on the U.S. financial crisis most often describes institutional and ideational factors specific to the financial services sector.[8] Our analysis situates such facts within nation-state–building processes that gave rise to the institutions characteristic of each country's social formation. So there are lessons here for the comparative political economy of advanced capitalism.

Vulnerabilities of Nations and States

Every small child knows what it feels like to be bullied by someone larger and stronger. Such a child feels vulnerable at all times, full of fear on occasion. Such sentiments are felt strongly in the international arena both by nations and states. The most obvious reason is that both entities know full well that they may cease to exist. The historical record is full of small states that have disappeared, gobbled up by their neighbors. Burgundy boasted the greatest court culture of the late Middle Ages, but is known to most today only as a center for wine production. Equally, cultural traditions, often based on distinct languages, disappear all the time, something of which we are reminded by attempts to revive Welsh, Breton, and Gaelic.

Small nation-states that have survived are well aware of these factors. They remember that their own survival has often depended upon forces that they could not control. Denmark is a clear example: none of the Great Powers wanted the entrance to the Baltic to be controlled by a rival, all thereby preferring control to be exercised by a smaller entity, and so sought the preservation of Denmark at various moments when its very existence was in question. Put differently, among the great vulnerabilities faced by small nation-states are geopolitical threats, the prospect of conquest by a larger state able to destroy sovereignty and to extirpate culture. Small states accordingly seek alliances and long for schemes of international order. Russia's recent military incursion into Ukraine shows just how real such vulnerability remains even today. For similar reasons, small nations seek their own states when possible, but otherwise work hard to gain cultural rights. Quebec provides a clear instance of the latter: fearful that its identity would be destroyed if its language lost salience, it has fought hard and successfully to protect it.

---

6 Woll 2014. See also Grossman and Woll (2012).

7 Bell and Hindimoor 2015. See also Kirby (2010a) and Kluth and Lynggaard (2012).

8 Campbell 2011; Ziegler and Wooley 2016; and many of the essays in Lounsbury and Hirsch (2010).

Economic vulnerabilities loom just as large as geopolitical threats. For one thing, as noted, a large state can set the terms of trade for the small states that surround it and bend the rules of the international political-economic game to its own advantage, forcing small states to maneuver as best they can within them.[9] For another, small states are likely to have relatively few natural resources, which makes them dependent on the external world. Still more important is the fact that small size entails a small domestic market—and this, as any reader of Adam Smith will realize, limits the specialization of the division of labor on which increasing wealth depends. Eras of protection and self-sufficiency have made small states poor. They long for agreements establishing openness in the international economy, for this allows the access to large markets on which their prosperity depends. Of course, nations can be just as vulnerable as states in economic terms. Palestinians in the occupied territories suffer from nothing less than economic persecution.

One very important caveat is necessary. A distinction should be drawn between vulnerability as an objective condition (easily recognized in hindsight) and the subjective perception of vulnerability. One may be in a vulnerable situation without necessarily being sensitive to it.[10] What matters is whether the perception of vulnerability is strong enough to trigger action. All else being equal, perceptions of vulnerability are more easily translated into a sense of solidarity or "we-ness" uniting people in small countries than in large ones; it is easier to energize and organize a few people in a small country than many, especially if they have diverse backgrounds, in a larger territory. This allows us to make a comment about the currently popular term "path dependency." Large countries are likely to be dependent on patterns established historically, finding repetition easier than change—and are able to behave in this way because of their large size. The pattern of small nation-states is different: at best their path is often one of flexibility, their path dependency being driven by the vulnerabilities that they tend to have at the forefront of their attention.

If vulnerabilities come in different forms, as we have seen, it is just as important to note that these change over time. One general point worth making about the contemporary world of advanced capitalism is that small nation-states have found it to be essentially benign. Order reigns geopolitically, and a marked degree of openness exists in the international economic realm. It is this background situation that serves as the condition of possibility for the success of small nation-states in the postwar world. This is not to say for a moment that vulnerabilities have ceased to exist; no set of institutions of a

---

9 Hirschman 1945.

10 The distinction we draw between vulnerability and sensitivity is similar to that discussed by Keohane and Nye (1977).

platonic sort is or ever will be available given changes in the international environment. This is obviously true in the economic realm. Capitalism changes all the time as do the rules that govern its workings, making it ever more important for the small—bereft of large domestic markets—to stay at the leading edge of the product cycle. Furthermore, the economy is not so to speak pure; to the contrary it is an arena in which power is exercised and occasionally shifts. Two particular elements of power, discussed later in this chapter, can be noted immediately. First, the geopolitical strength of the United States allowed it to borrow heavily from countries with financial surpluses, failing to balance its own books and thereby contributing to its Great Recession, which stretched from December 2007 to June 2009. Second, German surpluses have to be absorbed by countries within the Eurozone just as much, and this occasions vulnerability—despite the benefits of open markets—because the monies on offer have contributed to extravagant bubbles, particularly in housing markets.

There are additional complexities. Some nation-states are independent and exposed to the international political economy; powerful neighbors provide a measure of protection in other cases. In Ireland, for instance, exploitation by an empire was ironically followed by a measure of shelter for the new secessionist entity. Something similar is true of Eurozone membership. Nation-states are more vulnerable insofar as they relinquish control over monetary policy to the European Central Bank and agree to open their borders to flows of capital, people, goods, and services from other member countries. But at the same time they enjoy the protections and benefits of Eurozone membership—greater currency stability, lower interest rates and bond yields, and access to structural funds—that facilitate development that might not otherwise have occurred given their small size.

An interesting contrast neatly making our main point concerns the rather different trajectories of Ireland and Finland. Both nations at the start of the twentieth century were contained within great empires (albeit the Irish had suffered from this far more than had the Finns) before gaining independence followed by civil war. But the vulnerabilities of the new nation-states differed in the ensuing years. Communists had played a role in the Finnish civil war, and the very real possibility of Russian interference thereafter meant that the geopolitical threat was real and immediate. In contrast, there was very little likelihood that the English would try to reconquer the territory it had lost in Ireland; here there was the measure of shelter from the old imperial power already noted. Curiously enough, the greater vulnerability felt by the Finns led to greater national unity and political and economic institution-building. This discovery deserves a section to itself for the simplest of reasons: it contains the basic theoretical insight of the book.

The Paradox of Vulnerability

Two daily expressions allow us to explain the discovery with which the previous section ended: "necessity is the mother of invention" and "whatever does not kill you makes you stronger." That said, it is often forgotten that not every necessity leads to invention while some challenges do indeed kill. But the basic insight from which we start is that small nation-states do tend to rise to the challenge of the vulnerabilities that they face so as to become inventive and stronger.[11] This is our fundamental theoretical contribution, the paradox of vulnerability that gives this book its title. Consideration of the literatures on small states and on nationalism can explain what is involved.

Peter Katzenstein's contribution to the literature on small states is foundational. His central argument is that many small democratic countries, despite their lack of much natural advantage, were quite successful economically after the Second World War. He explains this in terms of their capacity to react to extreme vulnerability. The Great Depression and Second World War created a feeling of vulnerability for all states, but especially for small ones faced with the possibility of disappearing from the map. According to Katzenstein, small size bred the political ability to respond successfully to such feelings because all interested parties could be gathered around a single table to discuss problems associated with vulnerability and devise solutions for them. The ability of leaders to meet and draw upon these perceptions of vulnerability facilitated the development of an ideology of social partnership—a willingness to work together for the common good—and in turn helped produce much policy learning, cooperation, and flexible adjustment to the various challenges they recognized. Successful economic performance in the postwar period resulted. What mattered most was the capacity to coordinate: to limit internal conflict, to plot and plan, and to cope with international vulnerabilities by designing institutions and policies with which to contend with international forces beyond their control. This leads Katzenstein to appreciate corporatist institutions in small states. Corporatism, he argues, provided great capacities for learning and flexibility because it involved three things: a centralized and concentrated system of interest groups; voluntary coordination of conflicting objectives through continuous political bargaining among these groups, state bureaucracies, and political parties; and an ideology of social partnership expressed at the national level.[12]

Comparative political economists have written a great deal about the first two points, but have tended to ignore the third. For Katzenstein, small states

11 Of course, there are exceptions, such as East and Central Europe during the Cold War period.

12 Katzenstein 1984, pp. 26–30; 1985, chap. 1.

are successful in part to the extent that they can muster an ideology of social partnership and use it to help bring key actors to the bargaining table, coordinate negotiations, and reach consensus among these actors. He also shows that the ideology of social partnership and the institutions embodying it permeate all levels of society—national, regional, and local—and operate across industries. Swiss consociationalism is his paradigmatic case.[13] But where does such an ideology come from? To answer this question we turn to the national question, beginning by drawing on the work of Ernest Gellner not only for his understanding of the origins of national identity but also for his understanding of its consequences.

One can get at Gellner's contribution by noting simply that a common language is a useful resource for a modern society, not least as it allows those who sit down at the table specified by Katzenstein to understand each other, to communicate effectively and easily. Gellner claims that an industrial society is likely to be most successful when a common national culture is present.[14] He stresses homogeneity: each state should have its own nation, and each nation its own state. Societies that are deeply divided culturally often cannot cooperate and, thus, cannot coordinate policy because the different sides want different things. In contrast, the mobilization required for a coordinated response to vulnerability—that is, the willingness to sacrifice for the sake of the nation—often results from the sort of strong national identity found among people with a common culture. Gellner insists that rigid status barriers, such as ethnic, linguistic, or religious differences, that prevented occupational and social mobility in preindustrial times have to be reduced in order to facilitate economic flexibility upon which industrialization and socioeconomic development depend. Central to the reduction of these barriers, he believes, was the rise of state-supported mass education and the widespread cultivation of human capital. This was because a common educational background and elevated human capital enhanced the capacities for people to learn and respond flexibly to a wide variety of challenges. We would add that facilitating mobility and the formation of human capital in this way also has helped spur the development of a particular institutional form— Weberian-style bureaucracy where recruitment and advancement are based on merit and expertise rather than on patronage and clientelism, an important point to which we shall return.

But nationalist studies have gone beyond Gellner's position. Not every nominal ethnic difference leads to nationalist mobilization.[15] What really mat-

---

13 Katzenstein 1984.

14 Gellner 1983, chap. 3.

15 Gellner 1983, p. 7. See also Habyarimana et al. (2009), McGarry and O'Leary (1993), Min et al. (2010), and O'Leary (2001, 2003).

ters is not whether people have different cultural attributes per se but whether these attributes prevent some from enjoying the same rights as others. As was true of vulnerability, citizens do not always perceive nominal differences as being salient—that is, substantively meaningful—and they may accordingly not have important effects on political or economic performance. For instance, a country may have many ethnic groups, but if institutional arrangements are such that they are all included in political decision-making, then the possibility that divisive ethnic conflicts will materialize may be substantially diminished.[16] This is the Swiss case, a multi-ethnic nation-state. A deep and widely shared sense of national identity is present in Switzerland, a complex country in which people are blessed with multiple identities while also possessing a strong sense of national solidarity.[17] We can underline this point by invoking Benedict Anderson's notion of an imagined community: the term neatly fits Switzerland.[18] What matters is how people perceive the similarities and differences about which Gellner writes; whether they imagine themselves as having things in common with each other or not. Given this crucial caveat about perception, cultural unity is likely to matter in the ways that Gellner suggests. But it is equally important to note that a culturally homogeneous population can be divided politically. This has been true at times in Ireland, where the character of national identity has been deeply contested. The point, then, is that in order for a country to develop a strong sense of national solidarity it must first develop perceptions of a national identity (a sense of "we-ness") upon which solidarity can be based.

A strong national identity can have two types of effects, one is obvious, the other more subtle. The obvious one involves the presence of behavior: a visible willingness to gird the loins and withstand pain to preserve and protect the nation, such as citizens often do when their nation is at war. The subtle one involves the absence of behavior: the limiting of conflict because people take much for granted. In particular, Gellner argues that class conflict inside a common culture is relatively mild if, as noted, it is not conjoined with ethnic, linguistic, religious, or other forms of nationalist conflict.[19] Both of these effects ease—but do not eliminate—conflict and, therefore, facilitate cooperation, sacrifice, flexibility, and concerted state action in the national interest.

If we blend the insights from the literatures on small states and on nationalism we can construct an ideal-typical causal model about small nation-states

16 Posner 2004, 2005. Another factor that may mute ethnic conflict is the social construction of ethnicity itself—that is, whether people of nominally distinct ethnic groups consider themselves to be different from each other or not.

17 Wimmer 2011, 2012.

18 Anderson 1983.

19 Gellner 1983, chap. 7; see also Dahrendorf (1959, chap. 6).

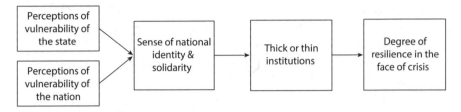

FIGURE 1.1. The Paradox of Vulnerability

represented in figure 1.1.[20] All countries face pressures and try to respond, but small ones perceive vulnerability most powerfully and often respond effectively, especially if they possess deep and widely shared national identities. We stress the following causal patterns. Perceived state vulnerability leads to an ideology of social partnership—that is, a sense of national solidarity—that contributes to the building of thick institutions that facilitate cooperation, sacrifice, flexibility, and concerted state action in the national interest. The result is resilience—the ability of countries to adapt effectively to new situations and challenges when they arise. Similarly, perceived national vulnerability facilitates a sense of national identity (a sense of "we-ness") especially when the nation is culturally homogeneous in terms of religion, language, and ethnicity, which may evolve into a sense of national solidarity. This too facilitates building thick institutions that lead to resilient outcomes. The creation of thicker institutions tends to benefit socioeconomic performance, particularly in today's fast-paced global economy.

Our notion of national identity and solidarity resembles what others have called social capital—a sense of reciprocity and trust.[21] Similarly, our notion of institutions is based on our understanding of Katzenstein but is similar to what historical institutionalists have in mind when they talk about the rules, norms, and compliance procedures that organize political economies, particularly through the administrative apparatus of the state.[22] One could rephrase our argument, then, and say that it blends an analysis of social capital and an analysis of administrative capital into a nation-state–building framework that

20 As noted earlier, it came to our attention shortly before finishing this book that Kindleberger (1951) made a very similar argument decades ago. He argued with particular reference to Denmark's response to changing international wheat markets in the late nineteenth century that small nation-states need to adapt flexibly to shifting international conditions, and develop the institutions to do so in ways that are influenced by nationalist feelings of social cohesion that emerge in response to economic vulnerability. Our argument differs from his by more clearly separating the vulnerabilities of the nation from that of the state, and stressing the difference between objective conditions of vulnerability and subjective perceptions of vulnerability.

21 Putnam and Goss 2002.

22 Hall 1986, chap. 1. See also Evans et al. (1985) and Thelen and Steinmo (1992).

explains the conditions under which some countries are more resilient in the face of crisis than others.

Remember that this is only an ideal-typical model. In real historical cases the manner in which these processes play out may vary in complicated ways. That is why this book is based on detailed case studies; we are searching for the causal processes linking the variables specified in this model.[23] Note too that our model is most applicable to independent countries rather than to those dominated or occupied by foreign powers that are able to stifle the sort of institution-building we have described even when the local population may perceive the need for it. As we will see, this is an important reason why Irish institutions were thinner than those in Denmark and Switzerland.

The three cases are presented in the next chapters, and then summarized and compared in the final chapter. We encourage readers to refer to table 5.1 in the last chapter as they read the case studies in order to see how the cases either conform to or deviate from our ideal-typical model. They will see that while the basic elements of this model explain much of what happens in every one of our countries, each case adds a bit of nuance and complexity to the basic model. The point is that there is nothing automatic about anything in the model: it is probabilistic not deterministic, stressing tendencies rather than inevitabilities.[24] It is not our intent to say that small nation-states always function perfectly, as if they were a piece of advanced German engineering. Very much to the contrary, we recognize that they can go off the rails in various ways, as will become especially clear when we discuss Greece and Iceland in the final chapter. Our precise claim is that those blessed with strong national identities often have the institutions with which to self-correct quickly and flexibly. Furthermore, their ability to cope may continue to be influenced to a degree by their vulnerability to external factors, such as a powerful neighbor or the Eurozone. Nevertheless, our claim is that of resilience over the long run, the ability to create, maintain, and adapt to external vulnerability and danger.[25]

By the same token, it is not our intent to deny enormous difficulties that arise when confronting vulnerability. How could we? All three cases that will

23 Bennett and Checkel 2015a, p. 12.

24 Lieberson and Lynn 2002.

25 Our view of resilience differs from the meaning that some comparative political economists have adopted. Vivien Schmidt and Marc Thatcher (2013), for instance, have used the term to explain why neoliberalism continues to be accepted more or less without question as the appropriate approach to economic policymaking despite abundant proof that it is both logically flawed and empirically wrong. See also Blyth (2013), Crouch (2011), and Hall and Lamont (2013). In contrast, our notion of resilience refers to the ability of small nation-states to respond flexibly and effectively to new challenges that confront them. Resilience for us refers to adaptability rather than persistence. In this sense our notion resembles Taleb's (2012) concept of anti-fragility—that is, the ability of a social system not just to survive shock but also to adjust so as to prosper in new ways.

concern us suffered from civil war! Denmark makes the case with great power. Vulnerability in the face of German unification during the nineteenth century led to nationalist pressures in Copenhagen that played a large part in war with Germany—war that led to the loss of a third of Denmark's territory! Crucially, the ideal-typical model faces challenges to do with immigration that may yet, as we emphasize in the conclusion, destroy it. Put differently, for a country to be closer to the model does not mean that it is ideal in a normative sense. Matters are more complex, life hard; advantages in one area can cause problems elsewhere, while a source of strength at one moment of time can turn into weakness in different circumstances. There is an additional reason why we do not take a Panglossian view of small nation-states: the propensity to engage in groupthink from time to time will be evident in later chapters.

Our earlier statistical analyses suggested that there is much to be said for this model. From the mid-1980s up until the 2008 financial crisis, countries in the OECD tended to experience stronger economic performance if they were culturally homogeneous and vulnerable to the vicissitudes of international trade.[26] This book starts where these earlier analyses ended, and it concentrates on cases rather than on statistics. This allows us to stress diversity among different countries, something that has always mattered not least because vulnerabilities vary, as noted, for particular countries. This matters enormously in terms of the claims that can be made; we are in a position to correct and add to the claims made by small state theory, and to subtly modify Gellner's view of nationalism.

Let us orient readers by hinting at some of our findings. Denmark comes closest to the ideal-typical model. This small and homogeneous nation-state has been blessed with a strong national identity and thick institutions thanks to a long history of geopolitical and economic vulnerability, which has been clearly perceived by Danish elites since the late nineteenth century. This stands at the back of economic and social success. Switzerland demands, as already noted, the modification of Gellner's work. The alpine country contains different languages and religions, but it is clearly an exemplar of prosperity. The different ethnicities live under a single political roof thanks to an institutional frame that is sophisticated and politically inclusive. But the modification is subtle. Switzerland is a multi-ethnic nation-state, in the end corresponding to the insights at the heart of Gellner's view of nationalism because it does possess a strong, fully developed national identity. This identity derived from perceiving vulnerability and then forging institutions that gave all cultural groups real political voice.

Ireland's social formation is less settled. It is a younger country, necessarily lacking institutional development while part of the British Empire. Here the importance of a country's independence or lack thereof becomes clear. It

26 Patsiurko et al. 2012, 2013.

behooves us to listen to Irish voices on the national question. The first is Bernard Shaw noting before Irish independence that

> [a] healthy nation is as unconscious of its nationality as a healthy man of his bones.... But if you break a nation's nationality it will think of nothing else but getting it set again. It will listen to no reformer, to no philosopher, to no preacher, until the demand of the Nationalist is granted.[27]

Thus, when nationalism is buried and consensual—that is, when nation-building has taken place—it can help nation-states cope with the challenges of vulnerability. But if nationalism is closer to the surface and contested, it can have such nasty consequences as political division, acrimony, corruption, and sometimes violence. This is a brilliant observation. On the one hand, Denmark and Switzerland prosper in part because their national identity has long been settled and taken for granted. On the other hand, as Shaw helps us understand, nationalist quarrels ensured the end of British dominance and the creation of a new nation-state. However, what is especially important for our account is that even after independence Ireland was for a while sheltered by Britain from the outside world and, as a result, not as vulnerable to geopolitical threats as Denmark or Switzerland or as vulnerable as Finland after its own independence. This meant that in Ireland national quarrels did not have to be quickly forgotten. This led to the dominance of a single political party and hence to thin institutions, notably clientelist practices, with the result that Ireland remained poor for a whole generation. As W. B. Yeats observed, "great hatred" with "little room" did much to "maim us at the start."[28] But once British protection ceased, vulnerability eventually became so pressing that it could no longer be ignored, old nationalist divisions were transcended, and at least some institutional thickening ensued before the financial crisis hit. The nature of the Irish case can be summarized very simply: it is mixed in the sense that the nature of vulnerability and nationalism shifted significantly over time. Its institutions were thinner than those in the Danish and Swiss cases because it faced less pressure and achieved independence much later. Consequently, its response to the financial crisis was rather weak. It is crucial to realize that the variability in the Irish case lends powerful support to the argument of this book.

Institutions, Thick and Thin

Let us explain the distinction between thick and thin institutions that lies behind the findings just noted. Institutions are formal and informal rules, including monitoring and enforcement mechanisms, and systems of meaning,

27 Shaw 1907, pp. xxxiv–xxxv.
28 Yeats 1933.

including identities that define the context within which individuals and organizations operate and interact with each other.[29] States contain institutions including constitutions, electoral systems and bureaucratic procedures that facilitate political decision-making. Nations rest on cultural and educational institutions that facilitate identity formation and solidarity. Institutions need not be static, partly because they are often ambiguous and subject to interpretation; partly because they are settlements forged through struggle, bargaining, compromise, and brute force; and partly because people often try to change them as circumstances change. There is considerable research showing that one such circumstance is the onset of a major economic crisis—a finding corroborated by our case studies.[30] These points must be borne in mind throughout the analysis that follows: a thick institutional portfolio is seen here as one that allows for nimbleness and adaptability, that is, for resilience.

Institutions typically operate as sets or configurations; something can be said about both thick and thin sets immediately. Thick institutions are similar to Max Weber's notion of legalistic and professional bureaucracy. They have four important features. First is expertise. Crucially, bureaucrats are recruited on the basis of expertise rather than patronage or clientelism. This is especially important for states so that policy—particularly policy that involves technically complex issues like banking and finance—is influenced by people who are able to judge objectively and in a relatively effective manner the likely effects of policy options.[31] The second element is inclusiveness. States also need transmission belts linking them to society in order for effective policymaking to take place. Civil society must have institutions based on well-organized groups representing group interests capable of engaging in what Richard Samuels calls the "politics of reciprocal consent" with their states.[32] Yet the balance must be right. States must not be so close to organized interests as to be captured by them and succumb to corruption, nor must they be so far removed from these interests as to be cut off from the vital information they can provide. In the words of Peter Evans, states should enjoy "embedded autonomy."[33] The degree of legitimacy is the third factor. When experts and others recruited on the basis of merit are responsible for policymaking, and

---

29 Campbell 2004, p. 1. Gellner and Anderson have much to say about systems of meaning, in particular the manner in which nationalism is defined, the degree to which it is taken for granted, and whether it is viewed as legitimate. Nationalism is not quite the same thing as an institution. But it is closely related. Any national identity includes rules of behavior associated with it. As Anthony Smith (1991, p. 9) explains, "National identity involves some sense of political community, however tenuous. A political community in turn implies at least some common institutions and a single code of rights and duties for all members of the community."

30 Eichengreen 2008; Gourevitch 1986. For a theoretical discussion, see Campbell (2004) and Fligstein and McAdam (2012).

31 Evans and Rauch 1999.

32 Samuels 1987. See also Berger (1981), Evans (1995), Pedersen (2006), and Streeck (1997).

33 Evans 1995.

when policymaking is inclusive and consensus oriented, then people are apt to view the policymaking process as trustworthy. This is especially so when people believe that policy is oriented toward advancing the country's best interests—something that is most likely to be found in countries with powerfully held notions of common culture and national identity, able in consequence to create ideologies and institutions favoring social partnership. In this sense scholars generally agree that a developed professionally oriented bureaucracy geared toward enforcing sound property rights and the rule of law is necessary to promote prolonged economic growth and social stability.[34] For our purposes, then, legitimacy, trust and consensus are more or less interchangeable terms. The final element is that of the degree of organizational capacity—that is, a well-developed set of rules, procedures, prescriptions, and policy tools established to organize policymaking and implement policy not only in routine situations but also during times of crisis. It stands to reason that older states with longer institution-building histories and more crisis management experience are more likely than newer ones to have these capacities.

The alternative set of thin institutions is wholly different and bears some resemblance to Weber's notion of patrimonialism. To begin with, recruitment is not based on expertise and professionalism but rather on tradition, patronage, or clientelism. Patronage involves the face-to-face exchange of favors, such as a job or zoning variance, between people of different status and power, often so that the patron gains political support and loyalty from the constituent. Clientelism is patronage on a larger scale, often involving the provision of favors through ward bosses, campaign workers, precinct captains, or other intermediaries. Patronage and clientelism are often based on racial, ethnic, or linguistic divisions, such as the ethnic political machines in nineteenth-century American cities. In other words, they are more likely to be found in heterogeneous societies lacking a strong, unified sense of national identity and social partnership. States based on patronage and clientelism provide privileged rather than equal access to the policymaking process for some groups but not others. In turn the absence of both expertise and inclusiveness undermines legitimacy—people do not believe that policymakers are acting in the best interests of the country. Finally, influence peddling and the lack of policymaking expertise often means that the state's organizational capacities are not well developed: policymakers are so absorbed with self-serving rather than nationally oriented purposes that they do not dedicate sufficient resources to sound institution-building—a problem that is especially acute in many corrupt postcolonial states.[35]

---

34 Barzel 1989; Fukuyama 2014; North 1990; Weiss 1998.

35 Our view is consistent with research on much larger nation-states conducted by Peter Hall and his colleagues, which showed that the ability of countries such as the United States,

Three final points have great importance. First, as noted, a strong sense of national identity and political stability can arise even in countries with significant racial, ethnic or linguistic differences if the institutions are right. This is why nominally heterogeneous societies sometimes perform quite well. Thanks initially to the insights of Arend Lijphart we know that constitutional design can mollify and contain antagonisms between different cultural groups. In consociational systems elites representing different cultural constituencies eschew decision-making by majority and instead seek compromise or amicable agreement. Proportional representation, federalism, and power sharing can help quite as much. Countries such as the Netherlands, Austria and Switzerland are often cited as examples.[36] The conditions under which constitutional innovations emerge and prove to be effective are the subject of much debate. This need not concern us here other than to say that solutions that have been tried have a mixed record of success. There is certainly no guarantee that any arrangement that works for a while will continue to do so. This has become particularly clear in the Netherlands and Belgium as economic and demographic conditions have undermined long-standing consociational compromises.[37]

Second, the institutional terrain of any political economy is uneven. Even in very well-developed countries institutions in some areas are thicker than in other areas. For instance, during the late twentieth and early twenty-first centuries in the United States a relatively thick set of institutions governed the stock market and banking system, but those governing the trading of derivatives in the shadow banking system, which is where the 2008 financial crisis originated, were so thin as to be virtually nonexistent. Institutional unevenness is one reason why all three of our countries suffered financial crises in the first place—parts of their institutional portfolios were thin, particularly in areas responsible for regulating the financial sector, as we will show in later chapters when we briefly discuss the origins of the crisis in each case. But when it came to coping with the crisis Danish and Swiss institutions were

---

Britain, France, and Germany to adapt successfully to the economic vulnerabilities associated with the Great Depression and the aftermath of the Second World War depended on their institutions, particularly those that influenced the ability of policymakers to rally around trusted experts from outside as well as inside the state and incorporate their views into policymaking. Those that did so were more resilient in coping with these vulnerabilities thanks to their embrace of what was then the emergent Keynesian economic policy paradigm (Hall 1989). However, our argument significantly expands upon their research by drawing attention as well to the importance of nationalism and national solidarity as a contributor to institutional resilience. This is another reason why our model has implications for nation-states of all sizes.

36 Lijphart 1999. For a review of the vast literature and debates on consociationalism, see Andeweg (2000) and O'Leary (2005).

37 Jones 2008.

thicker than those of Ireland. Hence, as noted, Denmark and Switzerland managed their initial crises more effectively than did Ireland.

Finally, although we are interested in the general institutional development of the state and civil society, and the connections between them in each country, our concentration is on particular actors. Economic expertise, especially in the area of macro-prudential regulation that is concerned with systemic problems in the banking and financial services sectors, mattered enormously. So too did the style of political decision-making, above all the manner in which state regulators, the legislature, the central bank, and stakeholders in civil society were organized and involved in crisis management. We will see that there was variation across countries in the relative thickness or thinness of these institutions, and in the specificities of the organizations themselves. Such variations are summarized in the last chapter in table 5.1.

Cases and Comparisons

Our earlier statistical analyses showed only correlations. These can mislead, as noted, suggesting causal patterns where none exist. Only when we identify underlying causal processes can we be sure that we have a true account of real relationships.[38] Locating the actual processes reduces the risk of lapsing into either erroneous functionalist accounts in which outcomes are explained by their consequences, or spurious accounts that mistake correlations among variables for real causal connections.[39] The latter is an especially thorny problem when we are trying to sort out causal relationships among many variables but have only a relatively small number of cases with which to work, as is the situation here.[40] This is the reason why we have chosen to turn to the examination of particular cases.

Ours is a comparative historical approach, seeking to understand the pattern of institutional development in one country by contrasting it with that in another. Some reflections on what this methodological approach can bring, both in general and for our analysis, can usefully help specify the character of the whole inquiry. A negative consideration comes to mind immediately. One hardly ever finds that cases are similar in all regards, differing only at a single point—thereby allowing for very tight analytic conclusions. But one can try to correct for this difficulty. We do so by focusing on a common crisis. All three of our countries experienced severe banking crises in 2008, each linked to the broader world financial crisis.[41] The countries affected had to scramble

---

38 Campbell 2004, chap. 3; Hedström and Swedberg 1998; McAdam et al. 2001, p. 30.
39 Elster 1989; Mahoney 2000; Pierson and Skocpol 2000; Sørensen 1998b.
40 Scharpf 1997, p. 16
41 Fligstein and Habinek 2014, p. 653.

quickly—most immediately with packages to rescue banks—to cope or face the very real possibility that their economies would implode in ways not seen since the Great Depression of the 1930s. It is very important to realize that at the time nobody knew how bad things really were, especially because events everywhere were unfolding very fast. Consider just the last two weeks of September 2008. Several big U.S. banks failed and disappeared. Problems metastasized so rapidly worldwide that the U.S. Federal Reserve bolstered bank liquidity by extending (and often soon expanding) swap lines to the European Central Bank and the central banks of such countries as Denmark, Switzerland, Japan, England, Canada, Australia, and Sweden so that they could begin to stabilize their financial systems. The entire Icelandic banking system collapsed. The point is that in autumn of 2008 and early 2009 all three of our countries faced what seemed at that time to be potentially devastating crises that called for immediate action. The situation was unprecedented as clear and definitive road maps out of the crisis were not available.[42] Fear was in the air. To this day people still disagree about what caused the crisis and what should have been done to cope with it.[43]

What interests us most are the processes by which policymakers made decisions when trying to handle the crisis. We used a variety of data sources in developing the case studies that follow, including interviews conducted with politicians, regulators, central bankers, and journalists involved with or intimately familiar with the events in question. Given our interest in process, interviews were especially helpful, because people talked to us about the ways in which policymakers decided to handle the crisis. In this way we were able to piece together the decision-making that transpired at the time and discern whether it was influenced by the key variables that concern us. Further methodological detail is provided in the appendix at the end of this chapter.

The bulk of our data powerfully captures the institutional portfolios that were in place when crisis struck. However, we also engage in historical process tracing—a methodological approach that is necessary for explaining the big, slow-moving causal processes that generated these portfolios in the first place through nation-state building.[44] But why should we worry about these histories at all? Without this history it is impossible to understand where the thin and thick institutions came from that affected the onset and subsequent management of the crisis. These historical sketches will help readers understand why these institutions worked as they did in ways that led to more successful outcomes in Denmark and Switzerland than in Ireland. In particular,

---

42 Bernanke 2015; Cardiff 2016; Woll 2014. The difficulties of decision-making amid uncertainty are discussed more generally in March (2010) and Borrás and Seabrooke (2015).

43 For a review of these debates, see Davies (2010).

44 Bennett and Checkel 2015b; Pierson 2003; Tilly 1984.

each country's prolonged historical experiences shaped the cognitive frames and other taken-for-granted assumptions that affected decision-making at crucial moments. For example, understanding the development of national identity and solidarity helps explain why Danish and Swiss bankers kept the national interest in the forefront of their minds during the crisis more than did key Irish banks, with one bank deliberately misleading the government. Understanding the origins of corporatist and parliamentary institutions helps explain why Danish policymakers turned more quickly to a wider range of experts during the crisis than did either the Swiss or, especially, the Irish. Understanding Irish state-building in the shadow of former British rule helps explain why policymakers did not seek more assistance from experts when the crisis hit. In short, analysis of the unfolding of the financial crisis and of its management requires analytic sensitivity to events in the past that sowed the seeds for more recent styles of behavior. Nevertheless, our discussion of these histories is necessarily brief and selective. To do otherwise would require that we write a much different—and much longer—book. So for each case we provide a thumbnail sketch of the country's relevant nation-state–building history as it unfolded as a result of peoples' perceptions of its vulnerabilities. These sketches act like bridges linking the distant past to the financial crisis in insightful ways.

Also, these historical sketches reveal the idiosyncratic events that occasionally influenced crisis management, such as the fact that Denmark faced a mini–financial crisis in the late 1980s, developed some institutions in consequence, and thereby found itself better armed than did Ireland in 2008 when the global financial crisis hit. Further, the crises were not identical, and therefore required somewhat different responses. Denmark and Ireland faced the collapse of domestic housing bubbles but Switzerland suffered from poor bank investments in the U.S. subprime mortgage market. Acknowledging these idiosyncrasies returns us to the prior consideration that historical comparisons are rarely as tight as one would wish. Nonetheless, our analytic approach does allow us to say something important about the eventual resilience of all three countries, and to note the dangers that lurk on the horizon of their respective futures.

We can add a little here to what has already been said so as to hint at the arguments to be made. The contrasts between Denmark and Ireland dramatically highlight the variation in responses to the financial crisis. Denmark is small, homogeneous, and blessed with thick institutions that fit our ideal-typical model like a glove. Denmark managed the situation well. Politicians deferred to the experts and eventually passed a series of bank packages that provided a privately funded state-backed guarantee for all troubled banks. It also included the imposition of haircuts (i.e., financial losses) on investors in the troubled banks. Ireland is a harder case for the model. Ireland is also one of the smallest and most culturally homogeneous countries in the OECD, yet it has comparatively thin institutions. It is often called a liberal market economy where there is much less state intervention, corporatism, and consensus-making in policy.[45] Yet in Ireland when the crisis hit, the state stepped in almost immediately and guaranteed all the banks at tremendous expense to the public purse and without demanding any haircuts. The putative costs were so great that a fiscal crisis of the state ensued. This required a massive bailout orchestrated by the ECB, the European Commission, and the International Monetary Fund—the so-called Troika—in order to avoid national bankruptcy! Finally, Switzerland is also a tough case for our model. Though small, it contains different linguistic and religious groups. Yet its nominal heterogeneity did not prevent it from creating a strong national identity that then allowed it to develop a sophisticated system of corporatism, proportional representation, and federalism in which technocrats dominate policymaking. This thick institutional portfolio allowed the financial crisis to be handled with relative ease: state funds quickly bailed out the biggest bank, and two commissions were established to ensure that the proper steps were taken to manage the crisis and to guard against any recurrence. Experts inside and outside the state acted in a highly professional manner, and as in Denmark this generated political consensus for the decisions taken. But let us remember the warning issued earlier about the dynamic nature of history. Despite the successful ways in which Denmark and Switzerland handled their crises compared to Ireland, there are some recent signs of rot in the state of Denmark, and in that of Switzerland too, while Ireland in contrast is not without some elements of real strength. We will explore these differences in the conclusion.

Precursors to the Crisis

Denmark, Ireland, and Switzerland each in their own way were in difficulty by the time the 2008 financial crisis erupted and world credit markets suddenly froze. The root of their vulnerability stemmed to a significant degree from the fact that banks in each one were able for a time to gain access to massive amounts of credit on very easy terms, thanks in large part to the financial maneuvering of some much bigger nation-states. How this happened deserves explanation.

The crisis began in the United States thanks in part to the tidal wave of foreign money that poured into the country helping to push up house prices. In the couple of decades preceding the financial crisis, America's appetite for

45 Ó Riain 2004, 2014.

borrowing money became nearly insatiable as illustrated, for instance, by the federal government's persistence in running budget deficits. In particular, China held over $1.3 trillion of U.S. debt by the time the crisis hit.[46] Furthermore, beginning in the 1970s U.S. financial markets were gradually deregulated.[47] This resulted in consolidation in the financial services industry.[48] But more importantly, deregulation contributed to the availability of cheap credit by enabling the securitization of mortgages and other forms of debt—an activity that turned out to be enormously profitable and financially dangerous. Securitization involved slicing up debt for mortgages, cars, and credit cards, bundling these slices into complex bonds called asset-backed securities or derivatives, and selling them to investors. This had become a multi-trillion dollar business worldwide by the early 2000s.[49] Coupled with money from abroad, the securitization of mortgages helped generate a massive real estate bubble in the United States through the provision of enormous amounts of credit because the originators of mortgages could quickly sell them to banks or brokerage firms for securitization—and, therefore, not worry about whether the people taking out the mortgages in the first place could actually pay them. Suddenly, nearly everybody could get a mortgage as the market for these so-called subprime and Alt-A mortgages grew rapidly—due as well to the shady lending practices of key mortgage companies. Many of these were adjustable rate mortgages with initially low interest rates. Adding fuel to the fire, issuers of these securitized bonds could buy credit default swaps—a kind of insurance policy—that would cover their losses in the event that the bonds failed, which created an additional incentive to ignore the possibility that the mortgages underlying these bonds might be prone to default.[50] Foreign banks jumped into the U.S. market for mortgage-backed securities. Between 2001 and 2007 foreign holdings of these securities jumped nearly 600 percent to over $1.2 trillion.[51]

Events outside the United States, particularly in Europe, also made credit easier to obtain. First, thanks to skyrocketing oil prices the world was awash in petrodollars after the 1970s, especially from the Middle East. Holders of petrodollars were eager to invest them in the West thus providing a growing source of easy credit for those who wanted it.[52] Second, Germany's postwar success in export markets elevated its savings rate, which enabled it to invest

46 Bernanke 2015, pp. 91–92; Campbell and Hall 2015, p. 105.
47 Davis 2009.
48 FDIC 2005.
49 Fligstein and Habinek 2014, pp. 641–42.
50 Campbell 2011.
51 Fligstein and Habinek 2014, p. 642; BIS 2008, p. 118; Morgan 2008.
52 Kapstein 1994; Simmons 1999.

increasingly abroad. In 2007 German foreign direct investment abroad was about $91 billion, highest among the Eurozone countries.[53] Its portfolio investment abroad in foreign securities and derivatives, specifically bonds and notes, in December of that year was roughly $130 billion.[54] Third, by joining the Eurozone countries with weak credit profiles, like Ireland and Greece, suddenly found instant access to cheap credit. Germany was one of the strongest economies in Europe when the euro was first introduced and, as a result, had one of the lowest debt yields on its government bonds of all the other members.[55] Throughout the 1990s yields on ten-year government bonds, which at first varied widely among European countries, began to converge toward the low German rate. This meant that the other countries were effectively endowed with Germany's very favorable credit rating. Ireland, for example, had much higher yields on its bonds than Germany before it was announced that it would join the Eurozone, but once the announcement was made those yields fell nearly as low as those paid by Germany. It was assumed that the ECB would back all outstanding government debt regardless of the country issuing it. After all, everyone was now using the same currency.[56] Finally, European interest rates were low thanks to ECB monetary policy.

The upshot of all this was twofold. On the one hand, banks were able to borrow increasingly on international capital markets to finance deposit deficits, leverage lending, and make other investments.[57] The abundance of credit helped pump up housing bubbles in European countries like Denmark and Ireland as well as the United States. In part as a result, by early 2010 Eurozone banks had a collective exposure in Ireland of $402 billion.[58] On the other hand, securitization put European banks, such as UBS and Credit Suisse, at risk as they invested heavily in U.S. mortgage-backed securities and often borrowed heavily in order to do so.[59]

All of this seemed to work. But in 2007 interest rates in the United States began to rise, which suddenly made it difficult for those with adjustable rate subprime and Alt-A mortgages to make their monthly payments. People rapidly began to default on their mortgages, and the U.S. real estate bubble began

---

53 Indexmundi 2013.

54 Deutsche Bundesbank 2013.

55 The "yield" is the difference between what someone pays for the bond and what they receive when it is redeemed at maturity. Low yields indicate low risk of default.

56 Blyth 2013, chap. 3.

57 Ministry of Business and Growth 2013, p. 7.

58 Blyth 2013, chap. 3.

59 Blyth 2013, p. 85. Irish and Swiss banks ranked first and eighth, respectively, worldwide as holding the most U.S. mortgage-backed securities. Swiss and Danish banks ranked seventh and ninth, respectively, as those holding the most U.S. asset-backed commercial paper (Fligstein and Habinek 2014, p. 648).

to collapse.[60] Banks and mortgage companies were suddenly in serious financial distress. Countrywide Financial, an enormous mortgage firm, went bankrupt. Bear Stearns, a large Wall Street investment bank heavily invested in subprime mortgage securities, nearly collapsed but was purchased by J.P. Morgan after much arm-twisting and financing from the U.S. Treasury. Lehman Brothers, another big Wall Street bank with large holdings in securitized mortgages, filed for bankruptcy on September 15, 2008, when the government refused to bail it out. The government feared that covering the losses of Lehman's investors would send a terrible signal to the financial markets that people would not be held accountable for their bad decisions and thereby create incentives for more bad behavior in the future, the "moral hazard" so feared by economists. At this point American International Group, one of the world's largest providers of insurance including credit default swaps, was faced with enormous liabilities and had to be saved by the government, which effectively nationalized it in order to cover its liabilities—but not before panic gripped the entire financial community. Repeated iterations of securitization meant that nobody knew who was holding the toxic mortgages. The credit markets froze. Without access to credit, even businesses that were in good financial shape had trouble getting and refinancing loans. The economy plummeted.

The international reverberations were swift and furious. The crisis metastasized to Europe. Housing bubbles in Denmark and Ireland were pricked; in consequence, some very prominent Danish and Irish banks that had invested in these real estate markets faced disaster. So did UBS and Credit Suisse, which had invested in U.S. mortgage-backed securities and suddenly faced enormous liabilities, perhaps leading to bankruptcy. Trouble was felt across the continent. By mid-2009 the United States and Europe were in the grips of the Great Recession—the worst economic calamity since the 1930s. In many countries unemployment soared, economic growth slumped badly, many people were unable to afford their mortgage payments and lost their homes, and personal savings were seriously depleted if not obliterated entirely. In response, many European countries heeded the advice of the ECB and pursued austerity policies in the hope of rectifying the situation. Following neoliberal theory, austerity was based on the idea that the best way to facilitate economic recovery and restore national economic competitiveness was to reduce wages, prices, and public spending and to raise taxes. In theory this would allow governments to cut their budgets, deficits, and debts. Business confidence would rebound, job-creating investment would pick up, and all would be well again. Such hopes have yet to materialize.[61]

60 Bernanke 2015, p. 165.
61 Blyth 2013.

Conclusion

Let us be clear about the scope conditions of our argument. First, as noted, our model is most applicable to independent nation-states rather than to nations controlled by an imperial power. Second, our claims, like those of Katzenstein, are specific to advanced capitalist democracies in Europe. In particular, while small size can lead to patronage, clientelism, and other forms of corruption that may undermine socioeconomic performance, this usually only happens in less advanced societies with little democracy, where political processes are not especially transparent.[62] Third, we recognize that the survival strategies of small nation-states vary according to the condition of the world political economy within which they have to live. The widespread protectionism of the 1930s was disastrous for these countries, which have ever since argued for free trade regimes. Fourth, the institutional benefits associated with a history of nation-state vulnerability are likely to be greater the more unpredictable the world gets due to growing international trade, capital mobility, and market volatility. In this regard, countries with such histories are lucky insofar as their historical efforts to develop institutions for coping with vulnerability happen to be particularly well suited for today's global economy.[63] In this regard the key variables with which we are working, especially the various dimensions of thick and thin institutions, are increasingly relevant nowadays for all countries regardless of size. Finally, and so crucial as to bear repeating, we fully understand that cultural homogeneity is a very tricky variable. All sorts of differences can be passively present in a society. What matters is the degree to which inhabitants of a nation-state perceive that their differences are salient politically.[64] Nonetheless, culturally homogenous nation-states are more likely, all else being equal, to develop the strong sense of national identity and ideology of social partnership with which we are concerned and in turn cultivate thick institutions than are culturally heterogeneous nation-states. It goes without saying that what also matters is the degree to which inhabitants of a nation-state perceive vulnerability.

We are not arguing, however, that culturally homogeneous countries have all the advantages that result in successful socioeconomic performance. Nor are we arguing that culturally heterogeneous countries are doomed to failure. There is not always one best or most effective route to resilience and success.[65]

---

62 Kang 2002.

63 Schwartz 2001. The advantage that large countries enjoy of having large domestic markets withers away with economic globalization as all countries share the same world markets (Alesina and Spolaore 2003).

64 Posner 2004, 2005.

65 Alesina and Spolaore 2003; Bennett and Checkel 2015a, pp. 19–21; Hall and Soskice 2001; Hollingsworth and Streeck 1994; Kenworthy 2008.

But we do maintain that national solidarity, whether based on cultural homogeneity or on institutional design able to counter cultural heterogeneity, is an important advantage that has been neglected for too long in the comparative political economy literature.[66] It is this that helped Denmark to right the ship of state when hit by the squall of financial crisis. Still, these considerations bring us back to the absolutely crucial warning issued at the end of the preface: we abhor every sort of ethnic cleansing, and are most certainly not calling for and indeed condemn all such actions.

Appendix: A Note on Method

Data for this project come principally from four sources: documents, including government reports; official online data sources, such as those from the OECD; secondary literature and histories; and interviews with policymakers, central bankers, regulators, academic experts, and others knowledgeable about the cases we studied. We selected people for interviews based on the recommendations of experts on the political economies of each country. We conducted thirteen interviews in Denmark in April 2012, fourteen interviews in Ireland in June 2013, and fifteen interviews in Switzerland in May 2014. Each interview was conducted following the same set of open-ended semistructured questions but varied somewhat depending on what we had learned in previous interviews. The interviews averaged seventy-two minutes in length. Nearly all were recorded digitally and transcribed professionally. We coded them using Atlas.ti (version 7) using two coding schemes—one deductive and one inductive.[67] The purpose of coding was simply to expedite data retrieval later on.

Our concern is with tracing the causal processes linking a series of variables. This is why the close historical examination of a few cases is of social scientific value. In this regard, process tracing is "the analysis of evidence on processes, sequences, and conjunctures of events within a case for the purposes of either developing or testing hypotheses about causal mechanisms that might causally explain the case."[68] The great benefit of this approach is that it avoids a preoccupation with surface phenomena and potentially spurious associations as, for example, in conventional statistical analysis that can cause us to overlook the deeper and more fundamental causes of the phenomenon of interest. Identifying these deeper factors is crucial for understanding big, slow-moving developments in a social formation.[69] This is also

---

66 The outstanding recent exception to this generalization is Singh (2015).

67 The rationale for developing the two coding schemes is based on Campbell et al. (2013).

68 Bennett and Checkel 2015a, p. 7. Bennett and Checkel (2015b) provide an excellent set of discussions of process tracing.

69 Pierson 2003; Tilly 1984.

a methodological approach particularly well suited for developing and testing new theoretical arguments on a small number of cases.[70]

In order to check the validity of our interpretations of the data and establish the integrity of our case studies, once we had written polished drafts we sent them to everyone we had interviewed in the first place for the respective chapters. We asked them to read them and provide us with whatever comments they wanted, including especially comments on mistakes that might have been made. We were unable to reach everyone we had interviewed initially. Some had moved to other organizations or retired, and some did not respond to our request. But many did respond, and each of them graciously offered comments and suggestions that were helpful. Virtually everyone agreed with our overall descriptions of the cases. Some suggested minor corrections. Nobody raised significant issues or disagreed with the basic story lines. Some told us that they learned new things by reading our material. As a result, we are confident in the validity of our case studies.

70 Rueschemeyer 2003.

2

Denmark

Being a small society, we have to look out for each other.

The causal path at work in our Danish case is relatively straightforward; a punctuated summary can easily be given so as to orient the reader. The country was once much larger, indeed an empire ruling over different nationalities. Defeats in war and the rise of nationalisms led to the creation of the rump state that we know today, one still fully aware of its history of exposure and vulnerability to outside forces as an independent nation-state. If cultural homogeneity facilitated nation-building, as important is the fact that social forces from below rather than above formed the thick institutions that characterize this country. Policymaking is generally inclusive, consensus oriented, and pragmatic, based increasingly on expert advice. As a result, most people view the policymaking process as legitimate and trustworthy. All of this served Denmark well in managing the 2008 financial crisis. But so did some additionally unique organizational capacities, notably blueprints for crisis management devised in response to an earlier bank crisis as well as dedicated funds provided by the banking community earmarked for that purpose. As a result, Denmark's response to the 2008 financial crisis was a model of nimble adaptation that received broad-based political support.

We begin by describing four legacies of Danish history—Lutheranism, statism, the solution of the national question, and the construction of layered homogeneity—that created modern Denmark. It is as well to highlight what is involved in our account. The historiographies of many countries—perhaps above all that of the United States—witness division between intellectual schools stressing consensus or conflict. This division is most certainly present in Denmark, with those who treat conflict often dismissively referring to the "myth" of consensus. There most certainly was and is dissension and conflict in Danish society, although one must also note that myths can have real consequences. Nonetheless, the account that follows stresses consensus, or at least the search for consensus, more than it does conflict. One reason for this is noted in the preface. Conflict gets out of hand, becoming violent and unrestrained, at times leading to catastrophe, most often when different sources of conflict—religious, national, and class—are layered on top of each other. There was little such layering in Denmark in modern times, effectively making conflict limited, with such dissension as there was taking place within manageable bounds. One should remember that Georg Simmel, the great sociologist of early twentieth-century Germany, explained that conflict—the process of claim-making, bargaining, and compromise—helps to establish social solidarity.[1] A truly brittle social order is one in which no conflict is allowed; regulated conflict allows problems to be expressed, and to be handled. It is this sort of conflict that characterizes Danish history.

From Empire to Nation-State

The first legacy can be dealt with quickly. The Reformation of 1536 established Lutheranism as the religion of the Danish monarchy. Then the Treaty of Augsburg of 1555 determined that the religion of the ruler should be the religion of the state. Accordingly, Lutheranism consolidated its hegemony within the lands ruled by the Oldenburg dynasty, which ruled the Danish kingdom from 1448 to 1863. Denmark became homogeneous religiously as a result. Recent studies show the importance of such homogeneity in early modern history: shared faith was often a precondition for shared national sentiment, confessional practices helped create newly disciplined social behavior, and the catechism created a disciplined Danish population, driven further toward asceticism and literacy by the spread of Pietism in the eighteenth century.[2] This does not mean, however, that religion was a force opposed to the state. To the contrary, Luther's insistence on loyalty to princes contributed to the second element that concerns us—a statist tradition.

The Danish state once resembled many in Europe in having a composite form whereby the prince was bound to different laws in the various areas over which he ruled. At the end of the sixteenth century, King Christian IV ruled over a medium-sized empire including Denmark, Southern Sweden, Norway, the Duchies of Schleswig and Holstein in what is now part of Northern Germany, three North Atlantic territories of Iceland, the Faroe Islands and Greenland, and colonies in the West Indies, West Africa and India. The com-

---

1 Coser 1956.
2 Marx 2003; Gorski 2003; Korsgaard 2004, pp. 35–103.

plexities of composite rule were particularly clear in the Duchies of Schleswig and Holstein; the latter was part of the German Confederation and was ruled for a long period by a junior branch of the Danish royal family. The state was relatively weak, extensive rather than intensive, lacking in centralized territorial coordination, and sitting atop peoples of different backgrounds and languages. Nevertheless, due to the fiscal benefits Denmark gained by controlling the entrance to the Baltic Sea, it had certain comparative advantages, including a magnificent navy—at its peak the third largest in Europe—which served as the military, technological and political backbone of its multinational composite state. Ironically, this nascent statist tradition was reinforced over time by Denmark's habit of losing wars. Pressure from Sweden in the mid-seventeenth century led to the loss of Skaane, Halland, Blekinge, Bohuslen, Herjedalen, and Gotland, and the introduction of a new absolutist state in 1660. While many absolutist states were but puny leviathans, Denmark came to resemble Prussia in being a genuinely bureaucratic absolutist state with real reach into its society. State penetration was enhanced by the fact that Danish absolutism was mild as it involved much consultation and compromise between the crown and elites.[3]

A reduction in the size of the state led not only to an increase in state capacity but also to the third legacy, that of the resolution of the national question. The language of the Oldenburg court was German, as was a large part of its administration. But by the late eighteenth century, resentment was developing toward Germans, in large part because they occupied so many elite positions and occasionally ruled in rather arbitrary ways. Various reforms kept these tensions in check for a while, but they came to a head thanks to the geopolitical disasters of the Napoleonic Wars, which ended with the Danish state's bankruptcy in 1813 and with the loss of Norway a year later. The proportion of Germans in the remaining territories increased from 20 to 35 percent, and their salience became more obvious given first cultural and then political unification in the German heartland. Thus began the slow and final dismembering of the Danish state.[4] In response to elite demands, as early as 1834 the monarchy established consultative assemblies in Roskilde, Viborg, and elsewhere. In 1849 a liberal-democratic constitution was introduced finalizing the shift away from absolutism. Henceforth Denmark would be governed by the people rather than by the crown. But the king's initial plan to establish a more democratic constitution triggered a civil war between Danish and German speakers, during which there was direct military intervention by Prussia. Different political options were debated at this time, including a federal solution that sought to give cultural autonomy to the Germans in

3 Østergaard 2006.
4 Jensen and Hall 2014.

Schleswig and Holstein. Another solution, proposed by the national liberals, sought ethnic homogeneity by redrawing borders, in particular by letting go some of Schleswig and all of Holstein. The aggressive nationalizing drive of the national liberals produced renewed military conflict in 1863 in which Denmark was completely defeated by Prussia a year later. Schleswig and Holstein were lost and with it much of the German-speaking population. As a result, the Danish state became something of a rump—a big small state in that it had a legacy of considerable state capacity but now ruling over a smaller territory occupied almost wholly by Danes.[5]

After 1864 Denmark was no longer deeply divided nationally; just as importantly, national sentiments had become more widely shared.[6] But in another sense the German problem was far from solved. Danish sovereignty was maintained in 1864 only because Britain and Russia objected to an expansion of Germany. Denmark's sense of vulnerability increased and remained extremely high thereafter—if not fearing Germany, then fearing the Soviet Union. Such vulnerable feelings led to social action. Peter Munch, an academic historian turned politician, argued that external threats to the small Danish state would always be present to such an extent that sovereignty might be lost eventually. Hence, an "internal front" should be opened to create an identity so strong that the nation would survive even if its state did not. The Danes achieved this by layering on top of their ethnic and religious homogeneity a popular, democratic, and egalitarian culture, which reinforced their sense of national solidarity.

This layering constitutes the fourth legacy underpinning Denmark's capacity for coordination and adaptability. To begin with, the political elite was discredited by the defeat of 1864. In response, the pastor, scholar, and Victorian sage N.F.S. Grundtvig and his supporters began at that time to define Danish national identity. The Grundtvigian movement cut across social classes and stressed the importance of individual freedom, classical liberalism, voluntarism, free association, and popular education. Among other things, the Grundtvigians built an alternative educational system for the masses alongside that which the state had already established during the period of absolutist rule. This system of alternative folk schools, which the state eventually helped to finance, emphasized the teaching of Danish history, poetry, and literature more than the traditional educational system and, thus, served as a key mechanism for the dissemination of the Grundtvigian cultural perspective and the development of a shared national identity. What it meant to be

---

5 Østergaard 2006.

6 The soldiers who fought in 1848–49 were peasant conscripts, most of whom had little idea of why they were fighting. Letters sent home by soldiers in 1864 show much greater awareness, indeed enthusiastic commitment to the national cause—as one might expect, given that participation in war is a prime mover of increases in national sentiment.

Danish changed. This was especially so, at least initially, among the large class of small farmers that had emerged after land reforms during the late eighteenth century and that provided the first clientele for the Grundtvigian program.[7] It also involved cultivating with the state's support voluntary associations in civil society ranging from agricultural cooperatives to health insurance associations to sports clubs, and, after the 1930s, to highly centralized labor unions and business associations. Agricultural cooperatives were especially important. One thousand and six had been established by 1900, allowing Denmark to produce high-quality butter that soon ousted Irish butter from the large English market. A brilliant study has noted that the origins of these cooperatives owed much to the fact that the country was so homogeneous: the route to wealth lay in cooperation, in contrast to Ireland where it lay in Catholics seeking to gain land from Protestant English landlords.[8] The whole process was symbiotic: the expansion of state capacities facilitated the organization of civil society while the associations supported the expansion of state capacities.[9] But the process was not automatic nor was it easy: the constitution of 1866 allowed the old regime to hold onto power until 1901, when the principle of majority rule in the parliament (Folketing) finally took root.

As important were the more overt politics of social democracy. Grundtvig's emphasis on the popular served as a bridge between the idea of the nation as ethnic and the idea of the nation as demos, and his viewpoint became mainstream when his legacy was embraced by the social democrats early in the twentieth century. Danish nationalism in 1864 shared its character with that of Germany: both stressed blood and language. But Danish nationalism did not take the German route of self-identification in purely ethnic terms.[10] After 1864 moderates from the left and right began to work more closely together and eventually passed a number of bills that reinforced political stability by establishing institutions that would reduce inequality and, thus, further unite the people of the nation.[11] This process was a contentious one, with the established church having long opposed the world that the left wished to create. The adoption of proportional representation was crucial, at once a product of and a reinforcement to compromise. The new electoral law passed in 1920 introduced multi-member constituencies together with proportional allocation of seats in the parliament. Modifications were made during the 1940s and 1950s that further increased the proportionality of the system.[12]

7 Korsgaard 2006.
8 O'Rourke 2006.
9 Kaspersen 2006, 2013, chap. 2; Korsgaard 2006.
10 Korsgaard 2004; Yahil 1991.
11 Kaspersen 2006.
12 Gallagher and Mitchell 2005.

The distribution of seats in parliament forced the parties to compromise to get legislation passed, thereby creating a political culture of consensus. The vulnerabilities of the interwar period explain this key development. Equally important was a fundamental ideological shift within the Social Democratic Party (SDP). In 1923 the party veered away from its Marxist roots toward a more popular position, serving farmers as well as the working class. The shift essentially guaranteed that the party was never likely to enjoy a clear majority in parliament. But it did lead to a stable governing coalition from 1929 to 1943 with the Social Liberal Party—whose role time and again in cementing consensual, centrist politics cannot be exaggerated.[13] In 1933 the Social Democrats, led by Thorvald Stauning, forged an alliance between farmers and industrial workers, which institutionalized popular democratic politics and social democracy for generations to come.[14] This did much to cement the nation in the hearts of the people in such a way that it survived Nazi occupation and behaved with great honor in helping much of its Jewish population to escape the Holocaust.[15] But it also formalized a politics of reciprocal consent among the social partners and between them and the state that was rooted in a sense of common culture and purpose.

A final layer was added after the Second World War by means of welfare state–building. Hal Koch in particular argued that democracy could be real only if the people had the material capacity to participate in the polity.[16] The demos became socialized. In fact, the development of fledgling welfare programs had begun in the late eighteenth century when the monarchy and its agents, influenced by Lutheran Pietism, first established, at least for a time, a comprehensive set of welfare benefits for the Danish people, first in Copenhagen and then in the countryside.[17] Postwar welfare state–building was extensive and was intended in part to further unify the Danish people.[18] It is very important to realize that the maximal point of consensus owed much to the Cold War, to the presence of a strong sense of vulnerability that made Danes wish to pull together. The lessening of those fears began to lead to a small crack in the social fabric as early as the 1970s, in the form of the radical populist politics of Mogens Glistrup. The crack became a chasm, as we shall see, once migration posed problems for what had been a hugely homogeneous country.

In sum, prolonged perceptions of vulnerability allowed the state to develop thicker and thicker institutions, including various inclusive systems of

13 Østergaard 2006, pp. 74–75.
14 Esping-Andersen 1984.
15 Korsgaard 2006.
16 Koch 1952.
17 Sørensen 1998a.
18 Kaspersen 2006.

consultation, proportional representation, and public welfare. This engendered in turn a popular social democratic culture that united the people as a nation and, therefore, imbued the state with considerable legitimacy, because most people believed it to be consensus oriented, trustworthy, and geared toward the national interest.

Thick Institutions at Work

Denmark is now habitually described as a coordinated market economy where economic activity is governed not just by market mechanisms but also by extensive public and private institutional arrangements.[19] Centralized peak associations represent most of the society's unions and businesses. For decades virtually all important policy decisions related to the labor market have been made collectively through corporatist deliberations involving the unions and business associations and occasionally the state. Hence, Denmark has become a negotiated economy in which all participants embrace the notion that they are part of a vulnerable community of fate that must act in concert and with an eye toward consensus–making for the good of the nation.[20] Because it is a small country where elites know each other and negotiate agreements again and again, inclusiveness breeds trust and legitimacy:

> I think what is really important is this whole idea of being a small, open economy. I think this is where the scene is set for that consensus approach that everybody is aware that we're exposed to what comes from the outside. We're a small country. We cannot set the agenda. I think that's very important ... We need to discipline ourselves.[21]

As a result, these negotiations openly stress the need to maintain or improve Danish competitiveness in the international economy.[22] This is why, for example, the Confederation of Danish Employers (DA) and the Danish Confederation of Trade Unions (LO) often meet together with various ministries in joint lobbying efforts for their common interests. Indeed, the top personnel of DA and LO have been meeting regularly for decades and deliberations between the two organizations at all levels often take place on a daily basis!

Negotiation and consensus are reinforced by the nature of the party system. For more than a century the main political parties were linked tightly to labor market associations. The SDP was established by unions and operated as their political wing. Similarly, the Liberal Party (Venstre) and Social Liberal

---

19 Hall and Soskice 2001; Soskice 2007. But see Campbell and Pedersen (2007).
20 Pedersen 2006.
21 Interview with senior official, FSA.
22 Interview with Mogens Lykketoft, Parliament.

Party (Radikale Venstre) were closely affiliated with agricultural interests while the Conservative Party (Konservative) represented business interests. Although there were significant ideological and programmatic differences between parties on the left and right, the electoral system, as noted, encouraged compromise and consensus. As one interviewee put it to us, "There's this pull towards the center if you want to stay in the government"—an observation reinforced by the fact that Denmark is a small country where all the key players know each other well.[23] Since 1925 only rarely has a party formed a government without at least one coalition partner. The rules of parliamentary procedure ensure that the opposition parties are routinely consulted in policymaking matters. When we asked a long-time Danish politician whether his country's particular system of proportional representation typically resulted in coalition governments and as a result consensus, his response was clear: "I think so, yes." He added as well that the more parties there are in the coalition, the greater will be the tendency for consensus, which is reinforced by the taken-for-granted—that is, legitimate—belief that people need to pull together in order to cope with international pressures.[24]

The organization of government further facilitates inclusiveness and consensus making. Legislative rules in Denmark are such that the executive branch is not overwhelmingly dominant over the legislative branch, which means that the two must work together to get things done. Moreover, both branches have relied for decades on independent advisory commissions. For instance, since the early 1960s the Danish Economic Council (DØR) has advised both branches on economic policy. DØR is tripartite in composition with representatives from DA, LO, other business and labor organizations, and the Danish National Bank (DNB), as well as with several independent experts including four economists—the so-called Wise Men—who chair the council.[25]

Familiarity is a further key to negotiation and consensus-making in Denmark, something else that is linked to the country's small size. We were told on several occasions that the decision-makers know each other, drink beer together, and are generally on friendly terms. According to one official with whom we spoke, "Coming back to being a small country, I know all the permanent secretaries in the relevant ministries. I have gone to university with these guys. I have been with them as colleagues for years.... We knew each other, so that's one of the advantages of being a small country."[26] An inter-

23 Interview with Henrik Bjerre-Nielsen, FS.
24 Interview with Mogens Lykketoft, Parliament.
25 Hardiman 2012, pp. 217–20.
26 Interview with senior official, DNB.

viewee explained that this tends to breed trust among decision-makers and among their staffs "in quite a different way than in many other democracies." He went on to say, "We have been—we've always been talking to each other running around in the same area, same people coming back. You can't cheat them because they will come back next year."[27] Friendships often develop: "something which is very striking about the Danish political system is that people are actually friends across party lines. Often you would find that your closest friends are from another party." [28]

Denmark relies heavily on expert economic analysis in policymaking, something that often bolsters consensus-making. There are several reasons for this, which require some attention because expert-based consensus-making was very important during the financial crisis. First, the economics departments at the University of Copenhagen and Arhus University have well-established graduate programs in quantitative economics. The fact that virtually all the state bureaucrats and civil servants working on economic policy graduate from one of these departments, know each other, think more or less alike, and often begin their careers in the Ministry of Finance before moving around occupationally reinforces the possibilities for consensus whatever is happening in the political realm. When the economists are in agreement, as they often are in what has been called a brotherhood of economists, it becomes hard for the politicians to disagree.[29]

Second, political parties further enabled expertise and consensus in the wake of stagflation and fiscal crisis in the 1970s, which precipitated serious balance of payments problems and stoked the national debt. They began to set aside ideological arguments in favor of those based more on pragmatic, sound economic analysis. A turning point in this regard was in 1982 when Prime Minister Anker Jørgensen and the Social Democratic coalition government realized that they had run out of ideas for resolving these problems. Facing an uncertain parliamentary situation, the government resigned without an election and handed power to Poul Schlüter's Conservative Party.[30] An economic advisor to the LO at the time explained that "in those days ... there was much more conflict ... regarding economic policy," due to ideological differences, particularly the social democrats' adherence to an ideology of class struggle.[31] The left believed in fiscal stimulus via public spending,

27 Interview with Mogens Lykketoft, Parliament. The World Economic Forum (2013) ranked Denmark fifteen, Ireland fiftieth, and Switzerland eleventh in the level of public trust in politicians. See also (Hardiman 2012, p. 224).

28 Interview with Henrik Bach Mortensen, DA.

29 Interviews with Henrik Bach Mortensen, DA; senior official, DNB; senior official, DBA.

30 Interviews with senior official, DNB; Henrik Bjerre-Nielsen, FS.

31 Interview with Henrik Bjerre-Nielsen, FS.

currency devaluation, incomes policy, and labor market regulation. Schlüter eventually changed the agenda by convincing most people that this approach was unsustainable given the balance of payments problem at which point leaders embraced a more restrained approach to fiscal policy that involved tighter incomes policy, higher taxes, and less public spending. He also pegged the currency to the deutschemark. Finally, in 1987 the LO and the government signed an agreement whereby the unions accepted wage moderation while the government supported labor market pension schemes.[32] In effect, Schlüter inaugurated a paradigm shift whereby Danish economic policy-making, which had previously been ideological and inward-looking, became more expert oriented and outward-looking in the sense that it was increasingly sensitive to Denmark's position in the international economy.

Key to all this was Denmark's perception of itself as a small, exposed, and therefore vulnerable nation-state that had to survive within an increasingly competitive international economy. The Executive Director of DA told us that by 1987 not only the social democrats but also the unions "accepted international competitiveness as the key variable." The unions in particular realized that they had to act responsibly in economic policy and that unlimited wage increases eventually jeopardized jobs. He told us as well that now all of this is "accepted by everybody!"[33] Mogens Lykketoft, a seasoned social democratic politician, agreed. When we asked him whether concerns about Denmark's international competitiveness are consciously articulated these days during policy negotiations, he was clear: "That's articulated, yes, yes, yes!" This paradigm shift was one reason why there was consensus in decision-making during the financial crisis. According to Lykketoft:

> The major change was in the early eighties. I think this was a defining moment ... and in that sense I would say that the whole—at least the way politicians dealt with the crisis in 2008 was sort of more an outcome of that approach that was taken in the early eighties; that we need to agree and let's not do politics on this. Let's just get it done.

Nevertheless, the new paradigm still contained an important element from the old one, namely acceptance of the idea that society has to look after those who are the worst off. For instance, a senior official at the Danish Bankers Association (DBA) told us that "the Danes treasure—they really treasure—the Scandinavian welfare model, and they understand that we can't jeopardize this sort of a model.... The welfare model is everything." He added that this belief held across all political parties. A high-ranking member of the Lib-

---

32 Interview with senior official, DNB.
33 Interview with Henrik Bach Mortensen, DA.

eral Party told us off the record that "we're all social democrats in one way or another in Denmark," a sentiment echoed nearly verbatim by our DBA contact. This sort of neo-Keynesianism, which blends a generous welfare state with more restrained fiscal policy, dominates economic policymaking today. In the end, the paradigm shift involved both the left and the right moving toward the center. During the 1980s and 1990s the social democrats and unions became more accommodating on the issue of wage restraint. During the 2000s, the center-right coalition under the leadership of the Liberal Party's Anders Fogh Rasmussen became more accommodating by being less antagonistic toward the unions and moderating their hardcore neoliberalism.[34]

A third reason why economic policymaking has become especially expert and consensus-oriented is that it was depoliticized considerably as a system of automatic stabilizers, such as unemployment insurance and active labor market policies, was gradually negotiated and implemented following the stagflation crisis. In this regard consensus on economic policy was institutionalized—automatic stabilizers were accepted and taken for granted by everyone as a legitimate means of adjusting Keynesian fiscal policy without much further political involvement.[35] Furthermore, automatic stabilizers were an institutionalized mechanism that guaranteed resilience in macroeconomic management. According to a senior official from the DNB, "Our automatic stabilizers are among the strongest, if not the strongest, among OECD countries."[36] He added that "the automatic stabilizers mirror the fundamentals of the system: welfare state, high-level expenditures, high level of taxation and with very broad support in the Danish society." Consensus occurs at two levels in Denmark. One involves people sitting at a table and negotiating compromises. But another involves the institutionalization of those compromises in such institutions as automatic stabilizers, which then become taken for granted as a normal and acceptable part of the Danish political economy even when politicians may have difficulty in reaching consensus on other matters.[37]

A fourth factor facilitating expert-oriented consensus is the transformation of a long-standing system of advisory commissions developed during the 1970s. Historically these were tripartite in composition, including representatives from labor, business, and the state. They provided recommendations on an extraordinary range of policy issues. However, since the mid-1980s this

34 Interview with Henrik Bach Mortensen, DA. In 1987 chairmanship of the SDP went from a former union boss, Anker Jørgensen, to an academic, Svend Auken, reflecting the party's ideological shift.

35 Interviews with senior official, DNB; Henrik Bach Mortensen, DA.

36 See also Lindvall (2012, p. 241).

37 Interview with Henrik Bach Mortensen, DA.

system has been largely replaced by ad hoc commissions composed more of experts on the particular issue at hand. Commissions have been convened to advise on welfare reform, tax reform, labor market reform, and other issues. Often their recommendations constitute the basis for legislative proposals to which parliament consents.[38]

Finally, the country's capacity for expert consensus-oriented policy-making was enhanced by the development of a massive infrastructure for economic analysis that is available to virtually all analysts in Denmark. Since the late 1970s the Ministry of Finance took an increasingly active role in eco-nomic policymaking and toward this end it launched initiatives to develop a number of sophisticated economic forecasting models. Bolstering this effort, Statistics Denmark, a state agency established in 1850, began building a huge database for micro-economic analysis. The state's development and institu-tionalization of these tools is another artifact of Denmark's small size. After all, developing such tools is very expensive and the state is the only organiza-tion with the resources for doing so. As one economist told us, "We are such a small country. And it takes some resources to actually build a serious eco-nomic model and maintain it."[39] But the broader point is that the common use of these models and data help people agree on causes and consequences and thus reach consensus on how to handle things.[40]

Overall, then, Denmark in the early 2000s had a political economy blessed with very thick institutions that were expert-oriented and inclusive and that facilitated negotiation, consensus-making, and social partnership. These in-stitutions included corporatist bargaining, frequently forming ad hoc com-missions, and creating a political system based on proportional representa-tion that allowed for the maintenance of a handful of political parties. For these reasons, as one former political advisor commented, the state con-formed to a "real Weberian ideal-type model" but also because it had very few political appointees and a large number of permanent staff in the minis-tries compared to other countries.[41] Its organizational capacities were also well institutionalized, perhaps most notably in its extensive system of auto-matic stabilizers. All of this augmented the trust and political legitimacy that was already rooted deeply in a strong and unified national identity fortified by the Danes' knowledge that they live in a small and vulnerable country, and therefore must pull together. Here again we see the paradox of vulnerability. Of course, people will pursue their own interests, but the elite strive to serve the national interest. With the financial crisis in mind, one interviewee noted,

38 Campbell and Pedersen 2014, chap. 5; Pedersen 2006.
39 Interview with Peter Birch Sørensen, former Chair, DØR.
40 Campbell and Pedersen 2014, chap. 5.
41 Interview with Søren Toft, former Chief Secretary of the Liberal Party political-economic secretariat (PØ).

"I think for some reason whenever there's a crisis in Denmark it hits every-body; whenever there's an opportunity in the economy everybody bene-fits.... And that's been the case this time."[42]

Origins of the Crisis

Denmark seemed to be well set at the beginning of the twenty-first century. By 2007 unemployment dropped to about 3.8 percent, inflation was 1.7 per-cent annually, national debt had declined to 34.6 percent of GDP, and the government ran a budget surplus of 5.0 percent of GDP. Long-term interest rates were also down and the current account balance remained positive. GDP growth, however, had slowed somewhat.

The right-wing government fueled this economic expansion during the early 2000s with neoliberal fiscal policy that included tax cuts and credit lib-eralization. Here the issue of national identity rose to the fore, and in wholly negative ways. Unlike previous governments in the 1980s and 1990s, which always consulted the opposition in order to achieve consensus, the govern-ments of Prime Ministers Anders Fogh Rasmussen (2001–9) and Lars Løkke Rasmussen (2009–11) not only were based on a coalition of their Liberal Party (Venstre) and the Conservative Party but also had the tacit parliamen-tary backing of the Danish People's Party (Dansk Folkeparti)—a new party founded in 1995 in the spirit of Mogens Glistrup, whose chief concern was rising immigration, initially from the Middle East but later from Eastern Eu-rope, which it viewed as a threat to Danish national identity and a burden on the welfare state.[43] Indeed, Anders Fogh Rasmussen's election in 2001 was historic because it was the first time since 1929 that it became possible to form a government without the support of the center, and to pass legislation without making compromises with the center or left-wing parties. Accord-ing to a member of the Social Democratic opposition, Mogens Lykketoft, during these years this was a "practical majority" that did not require much consultation with anyone—a very unusual thing in Danish politics. Within the coalition there was a division of labor: the People's Party focused on wel-fare policy, especially for the elderly, and on immigration issues, relinquish-ing virtually everything having to do with economic policy to the Liberals and Conservatives. Lykketoft explained, "What the Danish People's Party did was to say, okay, basically you [Liberal-Conservative government] run the economic policy if we get some concessions on immigration, things like

42 Interview with senior official, DBA.

43 Interview with Henrik Bach Mortensen, DA. According to Bach Mortensen, consensus-seeking in the 1980s and 1990s stemmed in part from the fact that governments had to appeal to shifting majorities in order to maintain parliamentary support. Remember that these were mi-nority governments.

that." This division of labor was cemented by the excellent personal chemistry between Anders Fogh Rasmussen and the People's Party's leader, Pia Kjærsgaard.[44]

In short, thanks to the increased political salience of immigration and the general issue of nationalism in which it was shrouded, the Liberals had a free hand in economic matters during the early 2000s, allowing them to pursue a variety of expansionary reforms more or less unilaterally.[45] But the Social Democrats were also culpable. Since they handed over power to Schlüter and the Conservatives in 1982, the party began drifting toward the center. As a result, during the 1990s there was more and more continuity in economic policy regardless of whether it was handled by a center-right or center-left government. Similarly, the Social Democrats raised few objections to most of Anders Fogh Rasmussen's economic policies.[46]

The good times were fueled by a booming real estate market thanks to reforms under both Social Democratic and Liberal-Conservative governments designed to reinvigorate a sluggish housing market and thereby encourage people to buy real estate as a means to accumulate wealth.[47] The boom was also driven by an increasingly loose monetary policy consequent on the Danish krone being pegged to the euro. During the 1990s mortgage and equity loans to homeowners became easier to obtain, rent controls on new private rental property were removed, and mortgage repayment schedules were extended from twenty to thirty years. A Social Democratic government introduced adjustable rate mortgages to help jumpstart a sluggish economy, and then Anders Fogh Rasmussen's government introduced interest-only loans to please the bankers and mortgage lenders. The traditional fixed interest rate mortgage regime was compromised. By the end of 2008 about 90 percent of all new loans had flexible interest rates.[48] Rasmussen's government also froze property taxes so that even if the assessed value of a property rose, the tax on it did not.[49] Over all, then, real estate prices rose sharply creating a

44 Interview with Søren Toft, former Chief Secretary, Liberal Party PØ.

45 Interviews with Mogens, Lykketoft, Parliament; senior official, FSA; Peter Straarup, former CEO, Danske Bank; Peter Schütze, former CEO, Nordea and former Chair, DBA; Henrik Bach Mortensen, DA. Lykketoft explained that Rasmussen was not a big believer in consensus in the first place and so was more than willing to take advantage of the situation.

46 Interviews with senior official, DNB; senior official, DBA.

47 Mortensen and Seabrooke 2009.

48 In contrast to the United States, where many of these were subprime loans, in Denmark they still tended to go to the financially sound middle class so that when the bubble burst it caused people to modify their consumption rather than lose their homes through foreclosure, as often happened in America.

49 Interview with Søren Toft, former Chief Secretary, Liberal Party PØ.

serious bubble in the housing market.[50] Between 2000 and 2007, prices grew by 85 percent for single-family houses and 105 percent for owner-occupied flats.[51]

The availability of international capital from Europe and the United States lay behind the real estate boom. In particular, the smaller and medium-sized banks could make big commercial real estate deals thanks to their access to foreign capital. As it turned out, about a dozen did just that, acting, according to one interview, like "crazy entrepreneurs."[52] The share of the Danish mortgage market held by foreign investors nearly doubled during the boom with foreigners holding about 20 percent of the total volume. By 2007 Danish banks had borrowed the equivalent of DKK 624 billion (€82 billion) of foreign capital, thus creating an enormous deposit deficit of 40 percent of GDP on their collective balance sheet.[53] By the time the international financial crisis hit, the Danish residential property market had become one of the most overvalued in Europe.[54] What all this reflected was a fundamental change in the banking sector's business model. Traditionally, Danish banks took in deposits and then loaned them out as mortgages. But increasingly they had borrowed cheap money in international capital markets so as to increase lending.[55] Banks worldwide were coming under increased pressure from institutional investors and others to increase their returns. Lucrative but more speculative banking was the result. Virtually nobody foresaw an international liquidity crisis coming; what in hindsight seem to have been high-risk investment strategies appeared at the time to be fine.

Few people worried about the real estate boom and those who did were generally ignored. The political parties and media remained largely silent. The National Bank and the Danish Economic Council (DØR) raised a few concerns, but did so rather quietly. Representatives from the National Bank raised the issue over lunch with the government and in a few public interviews.[56] The Financial Supervisory Authority (FSA), which regulated the banking industry, tried to raise a red flag too. According to its director at that time, as early as 2006 the FSA "warned them all [the banks] that ... there was a bubble in real estate and they should take [it] into account when they were making, you know, their individual solvency requirements." That year the FSA

---

50 Interviews with Søren Toft, former Chief Secretary, Liberal Party PØ; Peter Straarup, former CEO, Danske Bank.

51 Ministry of Business and Growth 2013, p. 6.

52 Interview with Peter Schütze, former CEO, Nordea Bank, and former Chair, DBA.

53 Carstensen 2013.

54 Carstensen 2013; Goul Andersen 2011; Mortensen and Seabrooke 2009.

55 Interviews with senior official, DNB; Henrik Bjerre-Nielsen, FS.

56 Interviews with senior official, DNB; Peter Birch Sørensen, former Chair, DØR.

even tried to invite relevant ministers and parliamentarians to a conference regarding financial crises, but none agreed to attend.[57] There were also some people in the banking community, including analysts at the DBA, who suspected that things were getting out of hand but had trouble convincing others. After all, "it is very difficult for a CEO in a bank to go to his board and say, 'Now we stop. Now we don't want to take any more risk, even though the future looks very bright.' It's really difficult to just be more conservative."[58] One of the few warnings came from Mogens Lykketoft, who wanted to introduce a tax on profits accruing from the sale of property as had been done in Sweden. When the Liberal Party heard of this, they orchestrated a media blitz that killed the idea before it could be introduced in the parliament.

There were several additional reasons why these warnings from experts went unheeded. In order to appeal to voters Anders Fogh Rasmussen was trying to rebrand his political party and get away from his reputation for wanting to roll back state spending. Furthermore, the national government could not control the spending of local governments. Moreover, the persistence of the boom for several years led much of the Danish elite to succumb to groupthink, to the assumption that the trend could go on forever.[59] People seemed to believe that they could "walk on water."[60] The prime minister went so far as to suggest that the few professional economists who worried about the boom and criticized him for pumping up the economy should rewrite their textbooks![61] In short, groupthink came to dominate Denmark's close knit brotherhood of economists. Moreover, due to Denmark's nation-state–building history, economic expertise was firmly embedded in a set of political institutions oriented to consensus-making. So although expertise was plentiful in Denmark, it tended to be relatively myopic in some economic policy matters.[62] For these reasons the potential for groupthink was not specific to banking and finance alone. But the aura of optimism was broad based, leaving its imprint on politicians, banks, government authorities, credit institutions, businesses, and ordinary households.[63]

Things began to sour badly in late 2007 with a sudden drop in real estate prices that was among the sharpest in the industrialized world and even worse

---

57 Interview with Henrik Bjerre-Nielsen, FS. Still, according to Peter Schütze, the FSA implemented new International Financial Reporting Standards, which unfortunately let banks reduce their capital reserves.

58 Interview with senior official, DBA.

59 Interviews with Peter Birch Sørensen, former Chair, DØR; Søren Toft, former Chief Secretary, Liberal Party PØ.

60 Interview with Peter Schütze, former CEO, Nordea, and former Chair, DBA.

61 Interview with Peter Birch Sørensen, former Chair, DØR.

62 Campbell and Pedersen 2014, pp. 197–99, 330.

63 Ministry of Business and Growth 2013, p. 5.

than in Ireland.[64] As prices fell, some small and medium-size banks began having trouble raising capital. This was due especially to their aggressive lending policies and heavy exposure in the commercial real estate sector. Bank Trelleborg became insolvent thanks to its high-risk lending to real estate developers. Similarly, in 2008 just prior to the collapse of Lehman Brothers, Roskilde Bank, Denmark's eighth largest, went bankrupt. When Lehman Brothers collapsed and the international financial crisis hit in 2008, the international capital markets froze, liquidity disappeared, the banking sector suffered a systemic financial crisis, and the Danish economy tanked as GDP dropped by 4.1 percent between 2008 and 2010.[65]

Danish banks ran into severe liquidity problems.[66] As one observer put it, "They had huge problems of refinancing their needs."[67] This was especially true for the dozen or so small and medium-sized banks that had been borrowing heavily in the international capital markets.[68] Moreover, Danske Bank, Denmark's largest, was so deeply invested in the Irish and Baltic banking sectors that investors did not know if its balance sheet was sound. In particular, Danske Bank had bought an Irish bank and set itself up as a branch in Ireland. Because it was foreign-owned, the Irish branch was not covered by the Irish government's bank guarantee when it was issued in the autumn of 2008 to save its own banking system. So Danske Bank's Irish branch "went, if you like, overnight, from being the best credit in Ireland to being the worst credit in Ireland, because all the other banks were guaranteed." As a result Danes worried about a possible run on the Irish branch that might take down Danske Bank.[69] Making matters even worse, in troubled times money tends to move out of small-country currencies to bigger countries with stronger currencies; Denmark, which maintained its own currency having not joined the Eurozone, faced a potential exchange rate problem.[70] Denmark's vulnerability could not have been more obvious.

Part of the trouble, at least in the smaller banks, stemmed from the fact that their governing boards were required to approve large credit deals. But

64 OECD 2009a, p. 18.

65 Ministry of Business and Growth 2013; Mortensen and Seabrooke 2009; Woll 2014.

66 Carstensen 2013.

67 Interview with senior official, DNB.

68 Interview with Peter Schütze, former CEO, Nordea Bank, and former Chair, DBA.

69 Interviews with Peter Straarup, former CEO, Danske Bank; senior official, DNB. Danske Bank also invested in retail banks in Sweden, Finland, Norway, and the United Kingdom (Woll 2014). But, according to Straarup, its exposure to bad loans was a small percentage of its portfolio: "Compared to the size of the bank it was not extraordinary." Still, Danske Bank's deposit deficit by 2008 had reached DKK 350 billion (€46.6 billion)—more than half of it stemming from its foreign units. Its total deficit was more than half of the deposit deficit of the entire Danish banking sector (Ministry of Business and Growth 2013, p. 11).

70 Interview with senior official, DNB.

the boards lacked the necessary expertise. In 2008 there were 138 financial institutions operating in Denmark—a very large number for such a small country and a number so large that it was impossible to recruit enough experts for all of their boards.[71] One banker explained that "the board members are local people normally, school teacher, whatever, local lawyer, probably good people. [But] what the hell do they know about credit granting?" This system had been in place for decades and had not been a problem because loans were made to local people whom board members knew. But as the deals got bigger, this was less and less the case. Riskier and more foolish lending resulted, especially in commercial real estate.[72] For example, some small banks from Jutland went to Copenhagen and with their boards' approval extended loans to developers that had already been turned down by Nordea Bank, one of the largest.[73]

The number of banks in Denmark caused another problem. Denmark abides by the Basel Accords, which are standards and guidelines issued by the Basel Committee on Banking Supervision for banks around the world. Because Denmark has so many small banks lacking sufficient expertise on their boards, the FSA spent an inordinate amount of time writing detailed regulations and guidelines on bank management so that they would be in line with Basel recommendations. According to one leading banker, by spending so much time doing this, the FSA paid less attention than it should have to ensuring that the banks were not engaging in excessively risky practices. For instance, the FSA could have demanded that banks maintain larger capital reserves.[74]

There was tremendous uncertainty when the 2008 crisis hit. People were scared. Things were happening very fast and there was little available information for making sense of things—especially during fall 2008 and early 2009.[75] Peter Straarup, the former CEO of Danske Bank, explained, "You have to re-

---

71 That most Danish banks are small stems from national vulnerability. According to Peter Schütze, since the 1864 military defeat the notion that everyone must look out for each other as a nation meant that policy makers would keep the smaller local banks running despite the inefficiencies involved. At the outbreak of the crisis only five had operating capital of over DKK 50 billion (€6.6 billion), and only twelve more had over DKK 10 billion (€1.3 billion) (Woll 2014, p. 142).

72 Interview with Peter Schütze, former CEO, Nordea Bank, and former Chair, DBA.

73 Interview with Kent Petersen, FSU. As a former member of two Danish bank boards, he acknowledged that boards sometimes extended credit when they should not have. Our DBA contact explained that the small banks that defaulted had made deals through personal connections with the same set of commercial real estate developers—a manifestation of a small country where "everybody knows everybody."

74 Interview with Peter Schütze, former CEO, Nordea, and former Chair, DBA; Ministry of Business and Growth 2013, p. 8.

75 Interview with Peter Straarup, former CEO, Danske Bank.

member this happened in a very heated period of time ... [in] a very turbulent environment." A senior National Bank official agreed, noting that there was a very strong "sense of urgency that something needs to be done now; otherwise it will go totally bad."[76] With this in mind, Straarup warned us of the dangers of analyzing the situation in hindsight: "Now, if you look at things, you always have to remember that you need to try to put yourself in the shoes you wore at this point in time from where you are now. I know I'm stating an obvious fact, but we did not know whether in the first quarter of 2009 we all were on our way to hell!" We now know, however, that the Danish crisis was indeed very serious, particularly judging from the fact that the aggregate write-downs in the Danish banking sector were large by international standards.[77]

The best way to highlight what has been said is to note that the institutional terrain of any country is lumpy. Some parts are thicker than others. Although Danish institutions were comparatively thick over all, the thinner spots contributed to the crisis. Some banks lacked the expertise required for prudent investment decision-making; warnings about an overheated real estate market were ignored; and most of the political elite succumbed to groupthink assuming that the booming real estate market would last forever, a view that certainly contributed to banking deregulation. Moreover, the regulatory authority's compulsion with enforcing international banking standards on so many small banks distracted them from broader risk management problems. But Denmark's vulnerability as a small, exposed nation-state was also involved insofar as it was dependent on international capital markets. According to a government commission, "Denmark is a small, open economy which is tightly integrated, economically and financially, with the rest of the world economy.... Denmark could not have avoided being hit by the international financial crisis."[78] It turned out, however, that Danish institutions were thick enough to cope with the financial crisis when it hit.

Crisis Response: The Six Bank Packages

Denmark's response to the crisis was state-led but in the early stages largely financed privately. Nationalization of banks was not in the cards, but imposing haircuts, recapitalizing and consolidating banks, and financing much of this through private associations was accepted. All of this was laid out in six Bank Packages.[79]

---

76 Interview with senior official, DNB.
77 Ministry of Business and Growth 2013, p. 9.
78 Ministry of Business and Growth 2013, p. 5.
79 Bjerre-Nielsen and Lang 2011; Danske Bank 2012; Woll 2014.

The Stability Package (Bank Package I) ran from October 2008 through September 2010 and was designed to rescue the entire banking system. Due to the rapidity and severity with which the international financial crisis was unfolding, it was set up in just one weekend. It involved an unlimited state guarantee for depositors and senior unsecured debt to banks belonging to the Private Contingency Association (PCA), an industry group to which virtually all banks belonged. This involved a potential commitment of 2.5 times GDP, so something on the order of DKK 4.8 trillion (€643 billion).[80] It was financed with DKK 25 billion (€3.3. billion) from the PCA with pledges from the banks for an additional DKK 10 billion (€1.3 billion) if necessary. If these funds ran out, then the state guarantee would kick in. Furthermore, the government and PCA established the Financial Stability Company (FS), a public company that managed the dismantling of financial institutions that had become insolvent.[81] This was an industry-financed scheme where the state would become involved only after losses exceeded DKK 35 billion (€4.6 billion).[82] It was designed to resolve what was perceived as a liquidity problem for the banks that could lead to a run on them that would jeopardize the stability of the currency.[83]

The Credit Package (Bank Package II), established in February 2009, was a recapitalization scheme focused on individual banks suffering liquidity problems rather than on the banking system as a whole. Banks could apply individually to the state for capital injections. In effect, this was an extension of Bank Package I, which would eventually expire.[84] The program was funded up to DKK 100 billion (€13.2 billion) and permitted the state to provide up to DKK 180 billion (€23.6 billion) in loan guarantees to the financial sector, for which participating banks paid a hefty fee to the state. The Ministry of Economic and Business Affairs administered these programs but the PCA shared

---

80 Kluth and Lynggaard 2012.

81 Bjerre-Nielsen and Lang 2011, p. 2.

82 In the end 132 out of 138 banks applied for the government guarantee and thus assumed obligations to contribute to the PCA. As of September 30, 2010, when the Stability Package expired, FS had lost about DKK 12 billion (€1.6 billion) but covered this loss with funds drawn from the PCA and associated pledges and guarantees. As a result, the government generated a profit from this bank package of DKK 13 billion (€1.7 billion) (Bjerre-Nielsen and Lang 2011, p. 4).

83 Interview with senior official, DNB.

84 The package had two parts. In one part a bank could apply to the state and pay for a guarantee of bonds that it would sell to private investors to increase its liquidity. The guarantee lasted until mid-2014. In the other part a bank could sell "hybrid core capital" to the state. This was a bond sold to the state for cash with a fixed interest payment and a three-year redemption obligation. If the bank did not redeem on time, the bond converted to stock and the state became a shareholder. Interviews with Peter Birch Sørensen, former Chair, DØR; Peter Straarup, former CEO, Danske Bank (see also OECD 2009a, pp. 37–39; Østrup 2010, pp. 84–85).

the costs.[85] Fifty banks and mortgage lenders applied for assistance by the closing date.

The first two bank packages were designed to solve the crisis but the Resolution Package (Bank Package III), introduced in October 2010, was about saving taxpayer money.[86] The idea was to replace the initial state guarantee in the first bank package, which was scheduled to end in September 2010. Now distressed banks would be closed over the weekend, FS would take charge, all unsecured and uninsured creditors would be subjected to haircuts, and depositors with deposits over DKK 750,000 (€98,700) would be exposed to losses. The state's Guarantee Fund for Depositors and Investors would cover deposits up to DKK 750,000 per depositor. Denmark was the first country to impose haircuts on senior creditors.[87] This package sought to avoid moral hazard problems that might arise from earlier bank packages.[88]

The Consolidation Package (Bank Package IV) of September 2011 entailed two new ways to consolidate smaller banks into larger ones if necessary. One was for a healthy bank to take over all the assets of an insolvent or distressed bank. The state would provide compensation—a dowry—to the healthy bank for whatever toxic assets the distressed bank may have had. The other was for a healthy bank to take on only the good assets of a distressed bank and for the toxic assets to be transferred to the FS, which would then receive a dowry for those assets from the state. In both cases the Guarantee Fund paid the dowry. Haircuts could be imposed on those holding debt in the distressed bank. All told, FS took over or dismantled twelve banks by the summer of 2012, including the fifth and sixth largest. This contributed to further consolidation.[89]

The Development Package (Bank Package V) began in March 2012 and had two objectives. It afforded all banks the possibility of transferring commercial real estate to the FS on a case-by-case basis, but it was really intended to rescue one large investment bank—FIH Erhvervsbank A/S—which was a prominent lender to the business community. The package was also designed to strengthen growth and exports by improving access to credit particularly for small and medium-sized enterprises, especially farmers, by enabling banks to free up funds and provide new lending to them. The state granted guarantees and loans to businesses for these purposes.

Finally, the Systemically Important Financial Institutions Package (Bank Package VI), passed in 2013, was intended to facilitate the identification of banks that were too big to fail and thus for which Bank Package III was not

85 Woll 2014, pp. 42, 150.

86 Interview with senior official, FSA.

87 Amagerbanken and Fjordbank Mors went bankrupt in 2011, and haircuts were imposed on senior creditors of 16 percent and 14 percent, respectively.

88 Interview with senior official, DNB. See also Bjerre-Nielsen and Lang (2011).

89 Ministry of Business and Growth 2013, p. 4; Woll 2014, p. 162.

really appropriate. The package did two things: it established a committee to identify banks that were systemically important and it provided more stringent capitalization requirements for them. In short, Bank Package VI created a special regulatory framework for these too-big-to-fail banks.

There was an explicit institutional division of labor in this process. The FSA determined which banks were in trouble. The Ministry and the National Bank decided which banks would receive assistance. FS figured out how to unwind the troubled banks once FSA had identified them. The fact that the six bank packages involved learning and adjustment is testimony to the thickness and resilience of Danish institutional structure. Out of the turmoil many small and medium-sized banks survived. So did bigger ones, including Nordea, Jyske, Sydbank and Danske Bank. But about twenty small and medium-sized ones disappeared because of their exposure in the commercial real estate market.[90] But the more important point is that this division of labor exemplified the deep organizational capacity available for crisis management.

Crisis Response: The Process

The character of the process by which the crisis was managed rested on cognitive assumptions deeply rooted in the history detailed earlier as well as in the institutional portfolio whose development we have traced. Four such assumptions deserve special highlighting, as they are all present in the account that follows. The first is the very general awareness of the vulnerability of the nation-state, graphically captured by one interviewee who reminded us of the disaster of 1864. The second taken-for-granted way of looking at the world is that of the desire for consensus, seen in the concern to consult all interested parties so as to reach compromise. The third element is of equally long standing, namely the realization that Denmark is and must be aware of market forces. The consequence here was the imposition of haircuts, the insistence, in other words, that market principles be obeyed. The final cognitive element was, however, of more recent provenance. The trauma of the downturn of the 1970s destroyed ideological divisions, encouraging a turn to empirical data, and above all to data handled by economists. This is the background to the great trust that, we will now see, was shown to these experts in the management of the crisis.

INSTITUTIONAL PREPARATION FOR THE CRISIS

Despite the fact that warnings of a housing bubble were unheeded, the Danes were not completely unprepared when the crisis hit in 2008. Institution-building specific to the financial services sector had taken place just prior to

90 Interview with Peter Schütze, former CEO, Nordea, and former Chair, DBA.

the 2008 crisis. To begin with, both the Guarantee Fund for Depositors and Investors and the PCA were in place providing key organizational capacities for financing the bank packages. The PCA came into existence in 2007 partly in response to a Nordic financial crisis in the late 1980s and early 1990s. Its purpose was to help distressed banks.[91] Furthermore, in 2007 the FSA, which had become concerned with the situation, joined forces with the Financial Stability Committee (not to be confused with the Financial Stability Company), where representatives from each of these three organizations discussed how to deal with a bank in the event that it developed liquidity or solvency problems. As a result, when the 2008 crisis hit they had a rudimentary plan on the shelf to which they could refer quickly. Part of their thinking was that in the event of a bank failure there should be a transparent system in place if government money was involved, something we shall see was sorely lacking during the Irish financial crisis.[92] They had also run some simulations of what would happen in the event of a big Nordic bank running into trouble and what they might do about it. This was all done rather quietly with no other participants involved.[93] Such closed bureaucratic backroom planning was not common and some we interviewed had not heard about it. Nevertheless, as part of Denmark's legacy of thick institutions, all this reflected the rising importance and institutionalization of experts and professional economists in helping to manage Danish economic policy. Their willingness to learn from past experience improved their organizational capacity for crisis management, thereby allowing for a remarkable degree of institutional resilience.

Nevertheless, it is now clear that some important lessons from the previous crisis were not taken to heart. For instance, characteristics of many of the small banks that failed in the wake of the 2008 crisis were largely identical to those of distressed banks during the earlier Nordic crisis, such as exhibiting high growth in lending and a high exposure in commercial real estate. An ad hoc government commission analyzing the 2008 crisis was "at a loss to understand why the lessons learned from the previous crisis had apparently been forgotten in the run-up to this crisis, especially by certain financial institutions, but partly also by the authorities."[94] Yet the fact that such a commission was established in the first place and that it noted as well as endorsed the bank packages and many regulatory changes made in response to the 2008

---

91 Due to the Nordic crisis, Denmark established the state's Guarantee Fund for Depositors and Investors (Garantifonden for Indskydere og Investsorer) in 1994 to help distressed financial institutions cover their liabilities and, if necessary, their dismantling. Eventually this was deemed contrary to EU rules so the industry set up the PCA (Det Private Berekskab), which was funded by participating banks (Woll 2014).

92 Interview with Henrik Bjerre-Nielsen, FS.

93 Interviews with senior official, FSA; senior official, DNB. This exercise was not designed to look at systemic bank failures but rather a single bank failure.

94 Ministry of Business and Growth 2013, p. 11.

crisis suggests that institutionalized learning is in fact a very important organizational capacity of the Danish political economy. Indeed, the commission
was surprised that policymakers and others had not learned enough the last
time around, as if such learning was taken for granted in Denmark. It wanted
to make sure that this did not happen again.

Another lesson from the 1990s influenced the way in which Denmark
managed the 2008 financial crisis. The decision to impose haircuts on bank
creditors and avoid the state shouldering the financial responsibility for rescuing the troubled banks was rooted in the legacy of the earlier Nordic banking crisis—particularly bearing in mind the way Swedes handled it through
state guarantees, forcing troubled banks to write down losses, transferring
toxic assets to asset management firms, and occasionally by nationalization.
Taking a page from the Swedish playbook, Denmark had passed legislation
that forced shareholders to face the real possibility of bankruptcy by preventing them from blocking the transfer of distressed bank assets to another firm.
The idea behind this was simple: "The interest of financial stability requires
that shareholders ... will just have to be wiped out if that's necessary."[95] So
when the 2008 crisis hit, "everybody just said this is how it should be: if you
supply risk capital to private firms, you should be losing money if the bank
goes into trouble ... this was not a sort of point of debate.... This was the accepted norm."[96] This was especially clear in the Liberal-Conservative government's decision to impose haircuts rather than nationalization. Indeed, the
head of FS said that its view was that Denmark "should have a system where
there should as a principle be no state money, no government money involved in saving Danish banks.... If the state is involved in Danish banking, it
is as an emergency measure. So get out of it as soon as you can ... the consistent principle is that shareholders or the investors should pay in line with the
principles of bankruptcy. First the shareholders, then the subordinated capital, then the depositors who are unsecured." By 2008 these views—deeply
rooted in respect for market principles—were taken for granted as legitimate
by virtually everyone and, as a result, helped set the stage for the haircuts and
privately funded bailouts imposed by the bank packages.[97]

Prior to Lehman's collapse, Roskilde Bank had, as noted, run into serious
trouble. The state provided aid to boost Roskilde's liquidity but by late August 2008 it was apparent that the rescue had not succeeded. The DNB took
it over with the help of a group of Danish financial companies for a purchase
price of about DKK 37.3 billion (€5 billion). It was soon liquidated and most
of its branches were sold off to Nordea, Spar Nord Bank, and Arbejdernes

95 Interview with Henrik Bjerre-Nielsen, FS.
96 Interview with senior official, FSA.
97 Interview with Henrik Bjerre-Nielsen, FS.

Landsbank. The European Commission approved the initial capital injection and subsequent dismantling of the bank despite the fact that it could have been seen as a violation of EU policies regarding unfair state aid to a private company. The concern was that letting Roskilde go bankrupt could bring down the entire Danish banking sector.[98] According to a senior official at FSA, the Roskilde bailout was the model used when Bank Package I was crafted. In this sense, he said that Roskilde "was a warm up to Bank Package I," and another example of institutional learning.

Finally, the National Bank and FSA had plenty of information about the condition of the banks to help guide crisis management when it was necessary. They were the only ones with access to all the banks' portfolios. The FSA, for example, would "come very frequently" to go through the bank's books to make sure that asset quality was what it should be.[99] The DBA did not have such information because it was proprietary. According to Peter Schütze, then DBA chairman, "The problem for the Banker's Association is that we do not have any numbers for the banks per definition. We are an organization for the bankers and not FSA.... We are not the Central Bank." However, the Association still had a "pretty good impression" of which banks were in trouble, because it met its members regularly and shared information.[100] The point is that the regulatory authorities had this crucial organizational capacity—access to the relevant information with which to manage the crisis once it hit—even if they did not utilize that capacity to avert the crisis in the first place.[101] The state's capacity in this regard was clear during negotiations about the bank packages. People tended to defer to the National Bank and FSA because their information was better than anyone else's.[102]

NEGOTIATION, CONSENSUS, AND THE ROLE OF EXPERTS

When the crisis hit, the DNB, the Ministry of Finance, the Ministry of Economic and Business Affairs, and the DBA were the main decision-makers putting together the first bank package, which guaranteed deposits in all the banks and required the banks to pay for it by contributing to the PCA.[103] Because the guarantee might involve substantial state funding, the Ministry of Finance balked initially but then acquiesced. Once they all agreed, the

---

98 European Commission 2008.

99 Interview with Peter Straarup, former CEO, Danske Bank.

100 Interview with senior official, DBA.

101 According to Peter Schütze, former CEO, Nordea, and former Chair, DBA, in hindsight the fact that the regulators had this information suggests that they dropped the ball in the run-up to the crisis.

102 Interview with senior official, DBA.

103 Interview with Peter Schütze, former CEO, Nordea, and former Chair, DBA.

government took over and informed the political parties.[104] Decision-making was based partly on the earlier planning and experience that has already been described. This was done fast—as noted, over the course of a weekend—and with little negotiation. In contrast, the issue of liquidity injections and the other bank packages involved more discussion. The FSA and FS were also involved.[105] All the political parties, except two on the far left, the Socialist People's Party and the Red-Green Alliance, quickly agreed to this for three main reasons: the crisis was severe, it unfolded very fast, and it involved complex technical issues.[106] We take each in turn.

Everybody knew that Denmark was a small and especially vulnerable country with little room to maneuver. This is why Anders Fogh Rasmussen wanted to include the Social Democrats in the conversation about crisis management. But he also did so because so much state money was at stake.[107] Furthermore, everyone worried that in a small country like Denmark when things go bad, capital can exit very quickly and undermine the local currency. They needed to shore up the banking system to prevent a run on the krone.[108] This is why the National Bank raised interest rates as the krone came under pressure right after the Lehman Brothers collapse.[109] However, a senior National Bank official told us that there was little room for maneuvering because the krone was pegged to the euro.[110] Much more was needed. According to our National Bank contact, politicians feared a collapse of the banking system and wanted to be able to tell their parties and constituents that they had done something to avoid catastrophe. Hence, they all eventually pulled together.

Secondly, there was no time to devise and debate more nuanced responses in the immediate wake of the Lehman failure as liquidity problems loomed large, especially for Danske Bank. More important, the options available were limited because the Danish banking system had a large number of banks and the banking sector was segmented into a variety of types of banks, including savings and loan associations, unlisted banks, and some foreign-owned banks. So what might help one type of bank might not help another. For instance, demanding hybrid core capital—corporate bonds that could later be

104 Interview with senior official, DNB.

105 Interview with senior official, FSA.

106 Interview with senior official, FS. Both parties objected to Bank Package I, but only the Unity List insisted on opposing the remaining packages. The Socialist People's Party had aspirations of joining a new government someday and so was more conciliatory (interview with Henrik Bjerre-Nielsen, FS).

107 Interview with Mogens Lykketoft, Parliament.

108 Interview with senior official, DNB.

109 Kluth and Lynggaard 2012.

110 He explained that the DNB had roughly 2 percent leeway on either side of the euro in which it could adjust the krone's exchange rate. See also Ministry of Business and Groth (2013, p. 6).

converted into stock—from them all could only have been done if they were all joint stock companies. This is one reason why in the first bank package it was agreed that the government would simply issue a blanket guarantee to depositors of all the banks.[111]

Finally, everybody realized that the issues were so technical that they required experts and professionals who knew what they were doing. Politicians lacked such expertise and did not want to get too involved; they abdicated authority to the experts. According to one of Anders Fogh Rasmussen's advisors, "It was, in a way, a highly technical area and very few people understood what the crisis actually was about and what had to be done."[112] Another interviewee involved in the negotiations told us, "I think you have to give the politicians some credit here. They know this is serious stuff. They also know its technical stuff. So you don't want to disagree with the FSA and the Central Bank on whether or not you want to do it this way."[113] So the National Bank, the Ministry, and the DBA with the assistance of the FSA and FS put it all together. They reached consensus rather easily because, according to a senior FSA official, Denmark is a small country where most of the people involved knew each other, having worked together previously in a variety of professional settings.[114] Once they were done they presented the package to the political parties and banks; it was accepted easily. People trusted the experts and viewed the process as legitimate.

In fact, all the bank packages were formulated without much formal input from anyone else, including the labor unions or business peak associations, except the DBA.[115] The political parties were formally involved only late in the process when they were asked to approve the packages in the parliament, as was necessary because the state was responsible for guarantees, capital infusions, and new regulatory authority.[116] That said, there was plenty of informal backchannel communication with the parties, particularly after Bank

---

111 Interview with senior official, FSA.

112 Interview with Søren Toft, former Chief Secretary, Liberal Party PØ.

113 Interview with senior official, FSA.

114 The FSU confirmed this: "The result of Danish bank recovery package negotiations was broad political agreement that not only bears witness to sensible political craftsmanship but also emphasizes the social importance of the sector" (Finansforbundet 2009, p. 8).

115 We were told in one interview that DI, the top association representing Danish industries, was "very involved," probably behind the scenes through its contacts with the Ministry of Economic and Business Affairs. The DA was not involved because its portfolio involved only labor market policy (interview with Henrik Bach Mortensen, DA). We also learned that Anders Fogh Rasmussen, the prime minister, lunched weekly with the head of DI. Hence, DI was undoubtedly kept informed and had backchannel input (interview with Søren Toft, former Chief Secretary, Liberal Party PØ).

116 Interviews with senior official, FSA; senior official, DNB; Peter Straarup, former CEO, Danske Bank; and Peter Schütze, former CEO, Nordea, and former Chair, DBA.

Package I. Furthermore, the prime minister had many meetings about the bank packages with his own economic staff, the relevant ministries, and representatives from the business community, notably the Confederation of Danish Industry (DI). He also pushed for consensus among the political parties.[117] All of this was very much taken for granted as part of Denmark's long history of consensual politics. Finally, the DNB exemplified corporatism: its board of directors included people from business, labor unions, consumer organizations, parliament, and various government ministries who, according to one off-the-record source, were at least kept informed by the DNB about how it was reacting to the crisis and about the positions it was taking during negotiations over the six bank packages. While decision-making was rather closed formally, it was much more inclusive in informal ways.

Economic experts played a crucial role in crafting the bank packages. Except for the weekend during which Bank Package I was negotiated when decisions were made very fast, the DBA had a team of five economists modeling the likely impact of various bank package scenarios as they were being developed. They were in close touch with their representatives at the negotiating table. The same was true for the DNB and the Ministry of Economic and Business Affairs. The analyses produced by these three sets of economists tended to be rather similar. Where there were differences they stemmed largely from different assumptions underpinning the models. So there was considerable agreement among the expert analysts that was conveyed to people doing the negotiating. This is not surprising. After all, the analysts all used the same basic econometric models, relied on data from Statistics Denmark, and received similar university training. Moreover, there was plenty of informal communication among experts across these organizations. A senior economist at the DBA told us, "I know those doing the work over there [at the National Bank] … and we meet from time to time, and we probably discuss, because we studied [at] the same places, we probably work together in some way." He added that they are "buddies" and have beers together "very often" all of which is, again, not uncommon in a small country like Denmark. He was also in close contact with his counterparts at the LO, where he had former colleagues. Finally, people tended to defer to the DNB during bank package negotiations not only because it had the best information on the condition of the banks but also because it had an excellent reputation for expert analysis and a larger analytic team than anyone else, perhaps four times bigger than DBA's team.[118] Again, expertise facilitated trust and legitimacy.

Nevertheless, the DNB was involved formally only in the beginning of discussions over the various bank packages. According to a senior DNB official,

117 Interview with Søren Toft, former Chief Secretary, Liberal Party PØ.
118 Interview with senior official, DBA.

at issue was the bank's independence: "We, so to speak, in some cases made the initiative, suggested what to do, and then the Ministry [of Economic and Business Affairs] took over and we withdrew because we wouldn't like to be at the negotiating table with the political parties ... due to our independence." Nevertheless, the bank remained informally in touch with everyone because its leaders knew all the key actors—thanks again to this being a small country.[119]

A senior official from FSA summarized the expert-oriented process of negotiating all the bank packages following Bank Package I. The principals involved in the negotiations produced—with the help of Rothschild, the British-based investment bank—papers describing various rescue models. "So we would come up with one paper describing some options, then there'd be questions ... over weeks papers back and forth and political meetings ... talking to the politicians, what did they want, coming up with models ... going back to the banks saying, 'can this work?'" When asked whether this sort of cooperation was typical, he exclaimed that it was: "We're a small country ... I've read from a distance and heard about the UK experience, which apparently was not that good in terms of getting people to work together. I think in that respect ... I would say [we have] a strong tradition for the ministries, the Central Bank and us ... working very good together in solving these issues. We know each other quite well and it's very informal and in that sense very operational." Then he referred to the fiscal and debt crises of the early 1980s when ideology began to take a back seat to pragmatic policymaking, which in his view surely helped the various bank packages to be assembled and passed quickly within a very consensus-oriented process.[120] Compromise and consensus were also necessary because the banks had not violated any regulations. According to a banker who participated in the deliberations, "It had to be voluntary. You cannot, under most countries' constitutions, certainly not this one, suddenly tell somebody you have to dilute your shares, unless you're in breach of some regulation. So it was a voluntary scheme."[121] The banks went along with it because they recognized the severity of the situation, accepting that these steps were necessary for the financial services community and the country. The chairman of the DBA told us that despite their reservations about haircuts, the association's members fell into line with most of the rest without much difficulty.[122]

Agreement on all the bank package issues was particularly noteworthy because it occurred under five different governments—three Liberal-Conservative governments headed by Anders Fogh Rasmussen; one Liberal-Conservative

---

119 Interview with senior official, DNB.
120 Interview with Peter Schütze, former CEO, Nordea, and former Chair, DBA.
121 Interview with Peter Straarup, former CEO, Danske Bank.
122 Interview with Peter Schütze, former CEO, Nordea, and former Chair, DBA.

government headed by Lars Løkke Rasmussen; and one Social Democratic-Social Liberal-Socialist government led by Helle Thorning-Schmidt. But it was also noteworthy because negotiations on the early packages occurred under the auspices of Anders Fogh Rasmussen's center-right government, which had tended to shy away from much negotiation and compromise until then. Why the change? As noted earlier, everybody recognized that the unprecedented severity of the situation was very dangerous for Denmark. According to Peter Schütze, who was CEO of Nordea as well as head of the DBA when the bank packages were negotiated, the political elite have been aware of Denmark's position as a small, vulnerable country in which people have to work together in order to survive ever since the 1864 defeat by Prussia. In his words, "You have to understand that Denmark, since we lost the war in 1864, ... there was this [attitude]—what you have lost to the outside you have to win inside." He said that this historical lesson was something he and others understood fully when they negotiated the bank packages.[123]

A comment about corporatist influences is important. The DBA was a key player representing the interests of its members in typical corporatist fashion. Like other industries in this country, banking has a long history of solidaristic collective action. Furthermore, the DBA generally does not need to cajole its members to gain their support; the banks tend to support the association's viewpoints. Throughout the negotiations over the bank packages the DBA was in close touch with its members and after intense discussions was able to garner their support for its ideas.[124] However, the Financial Sector Employees Union (FSU) was denied representation at the negotiating table despite several attempts to obtain it. But this is likely due to the fact that in contrast to the DBA the FSU lacked relevant technical expertise in these matters. Indeed, the FSU president told us that when the crisis hit, his organization tried to hire more economic advisors, "to try to get more influence on ... the situation about the crisis." But he also said that although he resented not being invited to the table, if he had been there he would have been in agreement with much of what was decided, although he personally favored the state taking shares in the banks.

This is not to say that everyone agreed automatically on every issue. The Ministry of Finance raised concerns about the initial guarantee and the Social Democrats and DNB wanted the government to take shares in the failing banks as the Swedes had done in the 1990s—and which had made their gov-

---

123 Interviews with Peter Schütze, former CEO, Nordea, and former Chair, DBA; Mogens Lykketoft, Parliament.

124 Interviews with senior official, DBA; Peter Schütze, former CEO, Nordea, and former Chair, DBA. See also Kluth and Lynggaard (2012). Peter Straarup was also involved formally in the negotiations as a deputy of the DBA but also had informal authority as CEO of Danske Bank.

ernment a handsome profit.[125] But in the end the guarantee was made, and haircuts rather than partial nationalization were imposed. People wanted to minimize the risks of moral hazard that might crop up if the government provided too much relief to the banks. Moreover, people wanted to ensure that tax payers did not foot the bill for bailouts.[126] Mogens Lykketoft explained that the opposition to nationalization was vehement and "characterized as 'North Korean economic policy' by the conservatives and the Minister of Economic and Business Affairs." The DBA opposed nationalization too. Those who negotiated the bank packages knew that taking shares in Nordea was impossible because it was Swedish owned. Finally, the government did not want to take on responsibility for running banks in which it would have a stake.[127]

Additionally, Danske Bank objected during negotiations over the first bank package to being asked to contribute a larger share to the general bailout fund than others. It wanted to pay only in proportion to its Danish operations. The other banks wanted it to pay in proportion to both its Danish and foreign operations. But the head of the DBA did not let his members leave their meeting until everyone agreed to the deal. Danske Bank agreed to pay the larger share. There was also disagreement over Bank Package III, the Resolution Package, which involved the imposition of haircuts. Some banks objected because this was not an issue of solving the crisis, as was the case with the first two packages, but rather of saving the tax payers some money. Some banks as well as the head of the DBA were willing to accept the package.[128] In the end everyone acquiesced because, as one individual close to the deliberations noted, "They were just run over basically by the politicians."[129]

The effects of vulnerability, nationalism, and resilience were apparent throughout the crisis management process. This was especially clear in one more important example. The DNB was short on funds for the recapitalization scheme and for defending the currency. Arbejdsmarkedets Tillaegspension (ATP), Denmark's largest pension fund with assets in 2008 of around DKK 436 billion (€57.3 billion), stepped up very quietly in late 2008 and 2009 to provide much needed liquidity to Danish banks when the international money markets froze. It provided a total of DKK 240 billion (€31.6 billion).

125 Interview with Peter Birch Sørensen, former Chair, DØR.

126 Interviews with senior officials, FSA and DNB; Peter Straarup, former CEO, Danske Bank.

127 Interview with senior official, DNB. According to Peter Schütze, former Nordea CEO, had Nordea not signed the agreements it would not have contributed to the PCA bailout fund—a rather large contribution relative to that paid by other banks. Hence, everyone knew that they could not impose measures so harsh as to alienate Nordea, or for that matter other banks.

128 Interview with Peter Schütze, former CEO, Nordea, and former Chair, DBA.

129 Interview with senior official, FSA.

This included DKK 40 billion (€5.3 billion) to cash-starved Danish banks (backed by a state guarantee) and the purchase of special thirty-year government bonds for DKK 50 billion (€6.6 billion). A bit later it provided another DKK 2.5 billion (€328 million) to become a part owner of the troubled bank, FIH Erhversbank A/S. Henrik Gade Jepsen, ATP's fund director, reported that all of this was a good business investment insofar as Danish interest rates were rising at the time more than they were abroad. But, according to Jepsen, ATP also provided funding because it "did not have any interest in seeing it [the banking sector] fall over."[130] Organizations with the capacity to do so stepped up to help resolve the national crisis.[131] It is also another example of Danish corporatism insofar as ATP was initially created by various labor market organizations and its board of directors includes representatives from both the DA and various labor unions.

INTERNATIONAL EFFECTS

International constraints were only a small part of the story of Danish crisis management. Although Denmark is not a member of the Eurozone it has now belonged to the European Union for decades. It was difficult for Denmark to defend against a run on its currency through conventional monetary policy, as noted, because the krone was pegged to the euro. As a result, it had to find other ways to convince the international capital markets that the financial system would not collapse. It did so not only by issuing the bank packages but also by raising interest rates and engaging in swap agreements with the European Central Bank (ECB) and U.S. Federal Reserve. Swap agreements with the Fed alone totaled $20 billion in September 2008; the DNB did not have enough money on hand to defend the krone and shore up liquidity without help.[132] Furthermore, beginning with the Roskilde Bank episode, the initial bank guarantees required European Commission (EC) approval insofar as they could be interpreted to be state subsidies to private firms, which are often prohibited by the EU. The EC could have viewed partial nationalization in the same light. However, it was by no means clear that the commission would have prohibited any of this. Lastly, the EU often requires that in the event that a bank becomes insolvent and exhausts its equity capital and other subordinated liabilities, haircuts should be imposed as in Bank Package III. Yet the chairman of the DBA at the time told us that this was not a knee-jerk reaction to EU rules. Politicians did not want the taxpayers to pay for bailouts—a well-institutionalized sentiment since the 1990s Nordic banking crisis. "The

---

130 Berg 2015.
131 Interview with Peter Birch Sørensen, former Chair, DØR.
132 Goldberg et al. 2010.

requirement from the EU that you have a resolution scheme ran, I suppose, concurrent with a desire among Danish politicians that the banks should pay for their own risk." After all, this bank package was passed with an over-whelming majority in parliament. Nevertheless, it is hard to argue that EU influence had much effect in this regard since the Danish norm preceded the crisis by more than a decade.[133] Similarly, new international regulatory mea-sures adopted by the EU have influenced some regulatory tightening in Den-mark, such as new liquidity and capital adequacy requirements. But this should not obscure the fact that "a wide political majority has also imple-mented a number of specific Danish rules."[134]

Although international rules and protocols may have limited the range of options that Danes considered as they struggled with the financial crisis, these things did not determine final decisions. In fact, many of these con-straints were apparently open for negotiation. Hence, domestic politics, in-stitutions, and national legacies were the crucial determinants in the end. As a small nation-state Denmark may have had to cope with international con-straints but it was not a slave to them.

Conclusion

Denmark's institutions were not perfect; some thin spots had contributed to the onset of the crisis in the first place. The most important factor was the emergence of the national question in negative guise. The Danish People's Party's close cooperation with the Liberal-Conservative government gave Anders Fogh Rasmussen an effective majority that he used to pump up the economy, and the housing market in particular, thereby contributing to the crisis in the first place. His was not the only government that helped to do this. But the emergence of nativist sentiments disrupted the consensus-oriented politics hitherto characteristic of Danish society.

Nevertheless, Denmark's resilient response to the crisis was rooted in thick institutions built up over many decades. Decision-making was inclusive. Reflecting long-standing corporatist traditions, the DBA represented the in-dustry as it deliberated with the DNB and Ministry of Economic and Busi-ness Affairs among others. Informal backchannel communications also peri-odically facilitated input from the political parties and others. Furthermore, reflecting the decades long shift toward expert-oriented policymaking, nego-tiations were dominated by experts in economics and finance. The political parties willingly abdicated the opportunity for formal input other than pro-viding parliamentary approval of the bank packages, because they recognized

---

133 Interview with Peter Straarup, former CEO, Danske Bank.
134 Ministry of Business and Growth 2013, p. 17.

that this was a time of extreme national urgency best left to the experts whom they trusted to work in the national interest. Indeed, throughout the negotiations, concerns about Denmark's vulnerability as a small, exposed state and the national economic interest, as opposed to the interests of individual banks, investors, or political parties, was paramount. Everyone realized that they were part of a vulnerable national community of fate whose future depended on solidarity, consensus, and collective action—concerns steeped in lessons learned as far back as the 1864 defeat by Prussia: "Being a small society, we have to look out for each other."[135] There was no question about the legitimacy of the crisis management process. Finally, policymaking was enhanced by a variety of institutionalized organizational capacities, such as blueprints for crisis management derived from lessons learned during the earlier Nordic banking crisis; the availability of funds from the PCA and ATP; a clear division of responsibilities between the FSA and the Ministry of Economics and Business Affairs and the DNB; and the regulatory authority's access to information regarding the banks' portfolios. In short, the Danish case fits our ideal-typical model of the paradox of vulnerability (figure 1.1) very closely.

We should note briefly that resilience was also evident in efforts to thicken the state's organizational capacities for expert regulation of the financial services industry, such as at the FSA. The FSA can now run bank stress tests; post the names of banks that do not comply with its directives or standards on the Internet to shame them into compliance; increase solvency ratios; remove a bank CEO; and even pull a bank's license if necessary. The FSA has also set up a credit register to which all financial institutions must report their major customers and certain detailed information about them, a move that makes it easier for the FSA to spot trouble brewing. Before the crisis, the FSA could advise banks to reduce their exposure in the real estate market, but now it can tell them that they *must* reduce it. In turn, the banks are increasingly inclined to comply with its edicts. Moreover, FSA set up a Macro Prudential Council to come up with recommendations for "leaning against the wind" the next time there is a housing bubble or other serious problem brewing in the banking sector. The idea is to give the government better advice—and to be able to do so in a more forceful manner even if it runs counter to prevailing public and political sentiments, something that did not happen during the housing bubble that led up to the financial crisis.[136] A senior official at the FSA told us that beefing up the agency's organizational capacities

---

135 Interview with Kent Petersen, FSU.

136 Interviews with senior official, FSA; Peter Schütze, former CEO, Nordea, and former Chair, DBA; Peter Straarup, former CEO, Danske Bank. See also Ministry of Business and Growth (2013).

was something that most people supported during the crisis and continue to support now that it has passed, even though a new government came to power in 2011. He said, "The parties [have] been agreeing on every financial change in the regulation[s] ever since.... The change of government hasn't basically meant anything because they have all agreed all along the way on these initiatives." Such agreement, he explained, stems partly from the fact that this is how Danes operate—they seek consensus—but, again, it is also partly due to the technical nature of the issues involved. Expertise, consensus, trust, and legitimacy continue to go hand in hand.

Not all banks were thrilled with these new regulatory tools, but in the moment they had little choice. As Peter Straarup, Danske Bank's former CEO, explained, "You know you lose authority when you have issues, and I suppose in hindsight the banks have to accept the fact that this has been a situation where they gradually have lost authority in the legislative process, because losses have been material."[137] Even something as seemingly mild as a public rebuke from the FSA was something a bank did not want, because it could create perceptions among investors and depositors that perhaps the bank was not being run properly or was in trouble. But Straarup confessed that shaming like this worked and added that having a regulatory scolding published on the Internet was quite unusual. "There's no other country in the world that publicizes the letters from the regulators. And then when I meet colleagues abroad and tell them this they shake their heads." This is another testament to the thickness of Danish regulatory institutions.

Beyond these regulatory adjustments, we were told in several interviews that no other institutions had changed much as a result of the crisis.[138] The innovative mortgage financing instruments, including adjustable rate mortgages and interest-only mortgages, are still available. The property tax freeze is still in place, so the assessed values of many properties are way out of line with the taxes people pay on them. Whether this leads to a new housing bubble remains to be seen.[139] Still, the absence of a more draconian regulatory overhaul makes sense insofar as these Danish institutions were already quite thick when the crisis hit. Nevertheless, Denmark clearly has the capacity to learn from its experience and take steps in the national interest to ensure that such a crisis will not happen again. Revealing in this regard is the fact that although the banking industry is somewhat disgruntled with some of these changes, it has apparently not launched a frontal assault on them as has occurred, for example, in the United States, where the financial services industry

---

137 Interview with Peter Straarup, former CEO, Danske Bank.

138 Interviews with Peter Birch Sørensen, former Chair, DØR; Søren Toft, former Chief Secretary, Liberal Party PØ.

139 Interview with Peter Birch Sørensen, former Chair, DØR.

has spent millions of dollars fighting tooth and nail against most regulatory reforms since the crisis hit.[140]

At this point we need to step a little outside the management of the financial crisis to say something about the Danish political economy in general. Perhaps we have given the impression, by and large, that all is for the best in this best of all possible social worlds. That is not so, as we have tried to emphasize quite as much. Crisis may loom because there is "something rotten in the state of Denmark." We end this conclusion where it began, with the Danish People's Party. The homogeneity of the country is so intense, so deep that it has the greatest difficulty in accepting immigrants from outside, especially if they are Muslim. The People's Party is social democratic in a fundamental way, but nationalist too insofar as it seeks to limit benefits to immigrants as well as some Danes. Here we have national socialism—or, less contentiously, "welfare chauvinism." Nonetheless, the party's rise has continued, with it becoming the second largest in the election of 2015. Despite its triumph it refused to take part in the government, preferring instead to support the minority conservative government of the Danish Liberal Party, led by Lars Løkke Rasmussen. From this position it has continued to press for tighter border controls, restrictions on immigration, and Eurosceptic policies. It has also succeeded in shifting budgetary resources away from higher education toward programs for the elderly, the People's Party's core constituency. This may in the long run undermine Danish resilience and economic competitiveness by compromising the occupational upskilling and human capital formation that has for decades facilitated Danish flexibility in the face of global economic challenges. So the reemergence of the national question—based not on ethnic divisions among Danes but on class resentment toward immigrants— puts the Danish model at risk.

140 Ziegler and Wooley 2016.

3

Ireland

We're still a very young state, still learning how to
manage the shop while the parents are away.

At first sight the Irish case does not seem to fit the ideal-typical model presented in chapter one. For Denmark and Ireland are both small and culturally homogeneous in terms of religion, language, and ethnicity, yet the former managed the financial crisis much better than its Celtic counterpart. Upon closer inspection, however, our theory turns out to explain the Irish case rather well. The story is complex, as noted in the opening chapter, so a brief preview is in order.

Both state and nation in Denmark felt, and continue to feel, vulnerable—thereby being driven to respond to the creative construction of their institutional portfolio. The situation in Ireland, however, has been very different. The island as a whole was subject to vicious colonial subjugation. Nonetheless, the British state had insufficient strength to move beyond destruction to creation, above all lacking the will and soon the desire to forcibly convert Catholics to their own hegemonic creed. In these circumstances autonomous institutional construction was impossible. But the drive for Catholic Emancipation laid the foundation for an Irish nationalist movement. Westminster's inability to agree on Home Rule together with its vicious repression of the Easter Rising of 1916 led to a war of independence between 1919 and 1921.

The newly independent country had no state tradition of its own on which to build, and so uncritically took much from the former ruler, mimicking rather than adapting institutions to its own needs. State-building was accordingly new, slightly defective, and limited. The national question added further weakness. The partition of the island that followed independence had led to civil war. The fact that the two sides that had fought in the civil war had in common both Catholicism and participation in the secessionist conflict meant that there was sufficient cultural homogeneity to consolidate democracy in the interwar period, a substantial achievement. But nationalist divisions lingered in ways that often compromised national solidarity and stifled institutional development. In this regard we must recall Ernest Renan's claim that the strength of a nation depends on its capacity to forget, thereby to create new narratives of social unity. Few Danes remember their possession of an empire or the civil war of 1848–1849, though the loss of territory to Germany in 1864 remains a live topic—and the subject of a blockbuster television series in 2014. But in Ireland nationalist memories and myths of all sorts—the massacres of Drogheda and Wexford, the battle of the Boyne, the Great Famine, the revolutionary Easter Rising of 1916, the war of independence, the partition of the island, civil war, and "The Troubles" in the north—are far from dead. So nation-building too is still incomplete.[1] A crucial consequence for our argument is the way in which residual nationalist animosities allowed Fianna Fáil to become a near-hegemonic political party, able to prosper on the basis of patronage and clientelism.

The fact that the former metropole had no intention of reconquering the newly independent country limited Ireland's level of geopolitical vulnerability. It is this measure of shelter for the newly independent country that, as noted, explains why it was able to drift for so long, to indulge Éamon de Valera's ideological fantasy of rural life backed by linguistic renewal and Catholic domination during his many years in power. The resulting thinness of Ireland's institutional portfolio is absolutely in line with the expectations of our theory: slight vulnerability, weak institutions. But there is a complexity here. Once it became obvious that de Valera's dream was hampering Ireland's situation—that is, once Ireland's vulnerability as an independent nation-state became frighteningly obvious—then national solidarity kicked in; an ideology of social partnership and a development model came to the fore in the late twentieth century. These perceptions of vulnerability did then lead to a modicum of institutional thickening, again, and to our delight, supporting our general view in, so to speak, a positive manner. Compared to Denmark, however, this was still a case of late and limited institutional development.

The Celtic Tiger that resulted was nonetheless based on thin political institutional foundations. Fianna Fáil's clientelist practices helped fuel a massive real estate bubble. Disaster followed once the financial crisis struck. A small, insulated handful of policymakers with virtually no input from experts or anyone else and with little advance preparation offered a huge state-funded

1 Malešević 2014.

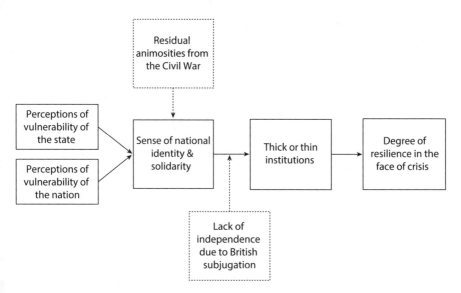

FIGURE 3.1. The Irish Case

guarantee to keep the banks alive—a move that ended in a severe state fiscal crisis. The sort of organizational capacities seen in Denmark were largely absent in Ireland—banking regulation, in particular, was quite weak. Europe and the IMF helped eventually by providing a bailout but only after forcing Ireland to adopt a harsh fiscal austerity program. Policymaking legitimacy and people's trust in Irish decision-makers were already low compared to Denmark, but austerity made things worse. In short, the guarantee and the bailout were both indicative of Ireland's thin institutions as well as its exposure to the outside world. But beneath the political sky, development in the economy has not ceased, allowing notable recovery from the crisis. Whether this can be continued is a question to which we turn in the conclusion.

Let us highlight the claims being made. The Irish case conforms to our ideal-typical model when we bear in mind that Ireland's lack of independence as a free nation-state as a result of prolonged British subjugation stunted institutional development, as did the measure of shelter that the metropole then provided. Equally, for a long time residual nationalist animosities stemming from the civil war undermined a strong sense of national identity and solidarity, which also hampered institutional thickening. These considerations can be seen in figure 3.1, indicated with dotted lines. However, once vulnerability was real and felt, then its paradoxical effect came to the fore: institutional construction began, with predictably positive results—seen in the Celtic Tiger and in some very recent developments that we consider in the conclusion.

From Colony to Nation-State

It is useful to expand for a moment the contrast of Ireland's situation with that of Denmark, which was once classified as a "big small state."[2] The territorial downsizing by 1864 left the core of the country with the central bureaucratic apparatus of a much larger entity. Moreover, Denmark possessed its own aristocracy. Ireland's colonial subjection within the British Empire was altogether different. Its aristocracy was imposed from abroad with Irish nationalism then coming from below, attempting, with success, to expel the foreign ruling class. But Ireland's situation differed from that of the great composite monarchies of the European continent, such as the Habsburgs. The units of a composite monarchy had their own rights, their provincial liberties to which the ruler had to accede. Ireland was different because it was a colony of a great power.[3] First, the control of Irish development was directed wholly from outside, with the country thereby being robbed of possibilities for autonomous political and economic development. Second, there was the complete unwillingness until very late of the British to make concessions to the native population. Third, the British elements, almost all Protestant, felt themselves to be wholly superior to the native Catholic peasantry. This situation resembled British rule in East Africa more than it did that in the Dominions of Canada or Australia.

Ireland had long been vulnerable to conquest by outsiders. The English crown was terrified for centuries by the threat of an emergent kingdom, not least as it might then ally with France. But the initial history of England's invasions was ineffective. Hence the Tudors and Stuarts launched campaigns to establish genuine control. Henry VIII claimed to be King of Ireland in 1541, and bloody wars followed, particularly under Elizabeth I. A key feature of these last years and of those of her successor, James I, was the founding of plantations, populated by English and Scottish Protestants. Irish Catholic landowners were displaced, with all Catholics soon suffering from Penal Laws that discriminated against all faiths other than the established Anglican Church of Ireland. In 1613 Protestants began to dominate the Irish parliament. But in 1641 Catholics rebelled, and created a Catholic Confederacy between 1642 and 1649. The rest of the seventeenth century proved to be the bloodiest period of Irish history. Oliver Cromwell reestablished Protestant rule between 1649 and 1653. If the highlight of that process in terms of historical memory was the massacres at Drogheda and Wexford, what mattered more was both the loss of perhaps a quarter of the population and the further dispossession of Irish landholders. Nonetheless, the wealthier Irish Catholics in effect rebelled once again, choosing to support the Catholic James II when

2 Østergaard 2006.
3 O'Leary forthcoming.

the English parliament replaced him with Queen Mary and William of Orange. His defeat at the battle of the Boyne in 1690 finally secured the Protestant Ascendancy.[4]

The eighteenth century was initially comparatively peaceful. In political terms 85 percent of the population was excluded from political life given that there was insufficient will to convert the Catholic majority to Protestantism. Economic life was run in the interests of absentee British landlords, uninterested in economic improvement. But severe famines resulted and tensions developed that eventually destroyed this system. By the end of the eighteenth century the resident aristocracy had become dissatisfied with the relations with England, especially given the absence of free trade between the two islands. For this short period, this local aristocracy gained an identity of its own directed in part against their metropole, albeit with the religious division between British aristocracy and Irish people remaining crucial. The official leader of such resentment was Henry Grattan, who sought both economic and political reform. The failure to achieve substantial improvement led to the emergence of the revolutionary resistance of the United Irishmen, consisting largely of Protestant dissenters who suffered as much as Catholics from the Penal Laws but who nonetheless called for Catholic Emancipation. The revolutionaries admired the French Revolution, they hoped for French assistance. But their revolt in 1798 was badly organized and it was all but over before a small French contingent landed. The rising led to the abolition of the Irish parliament in 1801 and to full incorporation into the parliament at Westminster.

Hopes were high not least among the Anglo-Irish aristocracy that this would lead to genuine reform. But Catholic Emancipation was denied again and again. As is so often the case, failure of reform by the state led to the emergence of a social movement that fought against it. The "Great Liberator," Daniel O'Connell, created a massive movement seeking Catholic Emancipation, eventually achieved thirty years after the incorporation of Ireland. But Catholics still lacked voting rights, while they remained under the control of English landlords. The latter condition played a significant part in the Great Famine, the single greatest demographic catastrophe of modern Europe. The famine and mass emigration reduced the population by half. In consequence, conflict revolved around the desire to gain land, with the Irish advancing their agricultural interests in court, on an individual basis, to regain land from British landlords. In contrast, the Danes, lacking a colonial legacy of land dispossession, advanced their interests collectively, as noted, by forming agricultural co-ops with state assistance to improve agricultural production techniques—a move that enabled them to take over the English butter market at the expense

---

4 Much of the following history can be found in Bartlett (2010).

of Irish producers.[5] Further, the eventual creation of a smallholding peasant class was designed to appease nationalist tensions rather than to improve agricultural development.

However, the focus of action moved away from the land wars toward the possibility of greater political autonomy by the turn of the century. The extension of the franchise in 1867 and 1884 was the base on which Charles Stewart Parnell sought Home Rule—Irish self-government within the British realm. Irish MPs at times held the balance of power in Westminster. Home Rule bills were accordingly passed by Gladstone's administrations in 1886 and 1892, and by Asquith's in 1912. But all failed, thereby illustrating the intransigence and lack of imagination of the metropole. For most people Home Rule would for many years have satisfied the desire for greater autonomy, with the country moving slowly to something like Dominion status. In this context some Irish voices were becoming more tolerant and inclusive—an early sign that anti-British nationalism was weakening in some quarters. For example, Arthur Griffith, one of the founders of Sinn Fein and a critic of Parnellism, argued for a system of proportional representation that would give strong representation and hence reassurance to Protestants. But influential sections of the British elite would have nothing to do with Home Rule and were viscerally opposed to Protestants being ruled by Catholics; they were diehard imperialists, who would not contemplate anything that would dilute imperial power.[6] Two points are important. First, had Home Rule passed, the Irish might have started building their own political institutions. At least that is what is suggested by Canadian and Australian history, where engagement in institution-building of self-governing dominions clearly mitigated the sort of patronage and clientelism that came to characterize twentieth-century Ireland. Repeated moves by the British to block the development of more inclusive political institutions were to blame. Second, the issue of Home Rule exacerbated nationalist tensions, which soon turned bloody.

The formation in 1912 of the Ulster Volunteer Force, a Protestant-based unionist militia opposed to Irish self-government, created a Catholic reaction. The outbreak of the First World War put everything on hold, but the Easter Rising of 1916, led by revolutionaries who wanted full separation from Britain, set everything in motion again. In December 1918 Sinn Fein won three-quarters of all seats in Ireland in the general election, largely because of generalized disgust at the brutality with which the rising was put down. Twenty-seven of these MPs assembled in Dublin in January 1919 to form a thirty-two-county Irish Republic in the first parliament (Dáil), which unilaterally declared sovereignty of the whole island. War for independence fol-

5 O'Rourke 2006.
6 Lieven 2000.

lowed between 1919 and 1921, a vicious conflict marked by assassinations on the Irish side and great brutality on the part of Lloyd George's paramilitary Black and Tans. In the midst of war, the government of the United Kingdom partitioned Ireland and set up elections for the two entities. It thus created Northern Ireland before negotiating with Sinn Fein, and further insisted on the following settlement: Ireland as a whole had the right to secede from the Union, provided Northern Ireland had the right to secede from Ireland, subject to a boundary commission if it did so; Ireland, however, did not have the right to secede from the Commonwealth/Empire or the Crown; and Britain insisted on supervising the constitution of the Irish Free State. A negotiating team led by Arthur Griffith and including Michael Collins reluctantly accepted these treaty terms. This led to the six northern counties opting out of the Free State, with the results of the boundary commission being accepted in 1926. The immediate consequence was that of a short civil war from June 1922 to May 1923 among those who had fought for independence, pitting those who accepted the partition that resulted from the Treaty against the anti-Treatyites. Nationalism, which had previously unified the Irish against the British, had turned divisive, pitting Irish against Irish.

It is extremely hard to recover from civil war, still more so to secure liberal democracy. The achievements of the Irish Free State are therefore very remarkable. One prominent characteristic of the new regime, headed by W. T. Cosgrave, was conservatism, designed to consolidate and preserve the newly independent state. There was no state tradition of its own to inherit, of course, in contrast to Scotland, whose incorporation into Great Britain in 1707 had not led to the destruction of many native institutions, making the move to increased powers at the end of the twentieth century far easier. Hence Ireland adopted many British institutions, including for a period the use of the British pound. Economic policy was markedly cautious. Perhaps the greatest innovation was the 1923 adoption of a proportional representation voting system indebted to Griffith's ideas—the single transferable vote in multi-member constituencies. This was designed less to include Protestants, of whom there were few in this increasingly culturally homogeneous country, than to dilute the vote of Sinn Fein, the revolutionary party that had lost the civil war. But it was also a matter of principle, a concern for social justice. The great idiosyncrasy of Irish politics is that this particular form of proportional representation system did not lead, as is typical everywhere else, including in Denmark and Switzerland, to the emergence of a handful of parties and to consensus-oriented coalition governments.[7] To the contrary, Irish politics has long been structured by the rivalry between two main political parties, Fine Gael and Fianna Fáil, the descendants of those who voted respectively

---

7 Gallagher and Mitchell 2005.

for and against the Treaty. More particularly, Fianna Fáil, founded in 1926 by Éamon de Valera, Seán Lemass, and others, enjoyed hegemonic dominance for decades. From 1932 through 2010 Fianna Fáil came in first in every national election and, as a result, formed either majority or minority governments in all but five of those twenty-four elections. The party's success rested on the claim to be the one and only national party—an appeal often coupled with favors delivered through clientelist networks that won votes from both small farmers and the urban working class![8] As one politician told us, "Fianna Fáil maintained the allegiance of the people by beating the tribal drum."[9] In other words, the party dominated politics in part by keeping alive memories of the old civil war nationalist divisions, thereby undermining the institutional possibility for the sort of inclusive coalition governments and consensus-making found in Danish electoral politics.[10]

The slow reintegration into the political system of Fianna Fáil led to the consolidation of liberal democracy. The process was complex, involving a split between that party and its republican left, and with de Valera choosing to accept for a short period the oath to the Crown. Fianna Fáil formed the government in 1932, thereby allowing for the whole population to democratically exercise its political voice. The last vestiges of colonialism were removed in 1937 with the passing of a new constitution for Ireland made without British supervision or impediment. This culminated a process of repealing the Treaty's provisions, confirmed by the withdrawal of the British naval presence and the recovery of the Treaty Ports in 1938. At the same time, de Valera fought an economic war against Britain from 1932 to 1938 refusing to pay a land annuity agreed to in 1922, with Ireland thereby suffering from the imposition of British tariffs against Irish exports. In effect de Valera won these battles. He exploited the Crown's weakness in 1936–1937, while Britain anyway followed a policy of appeasement given the greater threat posed by Nazi Germany. Complete independence from Britain was seen thereafter both in Irish neutrality during the Second World War and in withdrawal from the Commonwealth in 1949. No longer sheltered by the former metropole, Ireland finally had to learn to stand on its own two feet, as a fully exposed and vulnerable nation-state.

One might expect that this new-found vulnerability would have finally solidified Ireland's national identity. De Valera tried to accomplish this. He had maintained links to the Commonwealth in 1937 in the hopes that it might allow for reunification of the island, not least as the Constitution had re-

---

8 Finn 2011; interview with Cormac O'Grada, University College Dublin.

9 Interview with Pat Rabbitte, Minister of Communications, Energy and Natural Resources.

10 Arguably, Fianna Fáil's dominance was softened by Ireland's particular form of proportional representation. Moreover, the electorate twice prevented the party from switching to a single-member district system that would have strengthened Fianna Fáil even more.

claimed the North *de jure* on the grounds that the Treaty was "coerced." That this did not happen meant that there remained a fracture at the heart of the nation-state—illustrated by the fact that the most important committee in the Cabinet was concerned with internal national security, especially given the horrific violence that emerged in the North after 1969.[11] This, of course, was indicative of a legitimacy deficit in the new state.

What can we say about vulnerability and national identity at this point? Remembering and expanding the earlier comparison with Finland will help. Finland was another small, homogeneous, agrarian periphery of a great empire, first that of the Tsars and then of the Soviets, and one that had also suffered from civil war.[12] It is hard to get over civil wars, as noted, because the remaining scars can run deep. But the Finns managed this because the country was extremely exposed and vulnerable, threatened by both Nazi Germany and the Soviet Union. Civil war differences had to be put aside if it was to survive. Further, survival did not just mean quashing all reference to the civil war; equally important was the need to modernize the economy and state. As we have seen, the Danes also perceived great exposure and vulnerability following the 1864 defeat to Prussia and again during the Nazi occupation—and so achieved national unity relatively early, and with it institutional thickening. The bigger the perceived threat, the greater the possibility for both. This is the paradox of vulnerability.

The Irish situation was different. There was little likelihood of a British reinvasion, and so survival was not threatened once independence had been won. As a result, perceptions of exposure and geopolitical vulnerability were not so grave in the interwar years as to mandate significant state-building. Hence, patronage and clientelism prevailed, reinforced by Ireland's peculiar system of proportional representation; little attention was paid to developing much organizational capacity in the state other than for internal security purposes; political legitimacy was elusive; and, as we shall see, expertise was in short supply thanks to modes of education rooted in British legacies of the past and recruitment based more on tradition than merit. Irish politics continued to emit sound and fury based on the civil war divide, even though under the surface lay the considerable cultural homogeneity that had benefited political cohesion. However, the lack of international pressure meant that success in the political field did not need to be matched by progress in the economic field. De Valera's vision of the new nation-state was of one populated by people satisfied with frugal comfort living in cozy homesteads among joyous fields and villages—"the life that God desires men should live."[13] This

11 Interview with Ruairi Quinn, Minister of Education and Skills.
12 Kissane 2007.
13 Garvin 2004, p. 45.

was a backward looking dream for the nation: rural, Catholic, and with state policies designed to revive the Irish language. It stood in total opposition to the culture of Britain—a defense against the more modern, English-speaking world. It did not require much institutional development. Neither the Danes nor the Finns were culturally insecure, not least because they had their own languages. In addition, de Valera's economic war with Britain as well as his import substitution policies that ran for fifteen years after the Second World War hobbled economic development. So Ireland remained poor.[14] The Danes and Finns could never have accepted such a policy; the Irish, at once geopolitically safer but culturally more insecure, found it attractive.

Institutions, Legacies, and the National Question

After the Second World War a sense of crisis finally emerged. European countries that had suffered great destruction during the war suddenly shot ahead, leaving Ireland in their wake. Crucially, the country was unable to look after its own people: mass emigration took place, with exit thereby making the voice for change within all the weaker. A famous editorial in *The Irish Times* forty years after the Easter Rising noted, "If the present trend disclosed continues unchecked ... Ireland will die—not in the remote unpredictable future, but quite soon."[15] Perhaps most galling of all was the comparison with Northern Ireland: in 1926 the Free State had a population of 2.97 million, which dropped to 2.88 million by 1966; the North had a population of 1.25 million that rose to 1.48 million. There were elements here familiar to modern commentators of a failed state.[16] In short, the shelter provided by Britain immediately following independence had proved to be a dead end, resulting in rather squalid conditions. A sudden but visceral sense of vulnerability demanded action. The paradox of vulnerability began to have effect.

Seán Lemass played a central role in the change that followed. He had been opposed to the Treaty, and had thereafter been the principal creator and theorist of the protectionist economy created by Fianna Fáil. But he did not consider modernization to be Anglicization, and was sensitive to the weakness of the country in the postwar years, as his 1950 declaration in the parliament makes very clear:

> We have the prospect that the whole economic situation here may deteriorate after 1952. That is our zero hour. If we are going to do anything to strengthen the national economy, to repair the gaps in our industrial orga-

14 Interview with Cormac O'Grada, University College Dublin.
15 Bew and Patterson 1982, chap. 3; Bew 2007, p. 476.
16 Bew 2007, p. 490.

nization, to get into a position in which we can balance our international trade, we have to do it, if we can, before 1952.[17]

Lemass was not able to control the economic agenda until becoming prime minister from 1959 to 1966. One crucial change involved a more modern approach to nation-building. The education system was eventually transformed: Gaelic became less important as did religious education, with technical training gaining some prominence. Great stress was placed on entry into Europe, although the country's escape from Britain's shadow into this wider arena was delayed until 1973. Large amounts of money from European structural funds then allowed for a vast improvement of infrastructure, above all in roads. Another part of Lemass's plan involved a dramatic shift in economic policy. Protectionist policies were removed and free trade embraced. This went hand in hand with a determined effort to attract foreign direct investment from European companies and, later, once Ireland joined Europe, from the United States. The Industrial Development Agency (IDA), founded in 1949, proved to be an effective facilitator. Ireland was escaping from its past, assuming a new approach that looked at once to Boston and to Brussels.

Despite all this, the Irish economy continued to limp along from the 1960s to the 1980s.[18] Crippling government debt (117 percent of GDP by 1987), soaring budget deficits, sluggish growth, inflation, high levels of taxation, and labor unrest finally made people realize how dire the situation was and how exposed and vulnerable they were. A period of social partnership and corporatism ensued—facilitated by the analytic work of the National Economic and Social Council (NESC), a kind of social partnership think-tank created in 1973 and provided with greater political support after 1987 by Charles Haughey's third Fianna Fáil administration. This was a response to the ineptitude and failures of the Irish state; the social partners could no longer ignore the situation.[19] The NESC provided a forum where a shared understanding of policy issues could be developed. The NESC involved the government, unions, and employers, and later a "social" pillar largely comprising various nongovernmental organizations. It was based, according to one official, on the Scandinavian model "that we consciously took off the shelf ... [replacing] the Anglo-Saxon model of government that we'd inherited."[20] Beginning in 1987 corporatist negotiations led to wage moderation in exchange for tax cuts and various industrial development strategies.[21] NESC issued triennial reports and established a crucial talking shop. Importantly, the lowering of tax rates

17 Garvin 2004, p. 218.
18 Kirby 2010a, chap. 1; Girvin 2010.
19 Correspondence with Rory O'Donnell, NESC.
20 Interview with Ruairi Quinn, Minister of Education and Skills.
21 Interview with Tony Donohoe, IBEC.

made Ireland more competitive, allowing the unions to buy into the deal, while agreement led to a fundamental change in industrial relations—away from British-style strikes and confrontation to a new situation marked by industrial peace.[22] Finally, and also in an effort to attract foreign investment, the state promoted and often financed research and development, better management practices, and the growth of a network of centers, associations, and other institutional supports for business, usually at the local level.[23] At last institutions were starting to become more inclusive and organizational capacities were beginning to thicken.

However, corporatism was less developed in Ireland than in Denmark. It was newer and less centralized.[24] It was also less encompassing. Property developers had their own organization, the Construction Industry Federation, and so were not part of the Irish Business and Employers Confederation (IBEC), the top employer association negotiating within the NESC framework. Nor was the Irish Banking Federation an IBEC member, although the big banks were members on an individual basis. In short, the builders and bankers were not enmeshed in the institutional arrangements of social partnership, relying instead on bilateral, clientelist relations with government. In contrast to its Danish counterpart, IBEC did not collect wage data and did not have as much direct influence on the parliament in terms of shaping legislation. Nor did the unions. As noted by one IBEC official, "The embeddedness of the social partners in the institutions is much greater [in Denmark]."[25] In the end, the social partnership framework was discredited "because instead of tripartite bargaining and reaching a consensus to move forward, which involved a certain amount of pain and gain for everybody, it ended up as buying off the public sector ... public sector pay went through the roof, including politicians'. Everybody was bought off."[26] As a result, the system's legitimacy was undermined.[27] But the broader point is that social partnership institutions in civil society were rather thin, particularly compared to those of Denmark. At one point Bertie Ahern, the Prime Minister, invited Robert Putnam, a world renowned authority on civic associations, to advise on ways to bolster civil society and social solidarity.[28] Some found this laughable inso-

22 Interviews with John Fitzgerald, ESRI; Rory O' Donnell, NESC. Also bringing unions to the table was awareness of how Mrs. Thatcher assaulted unions in Britain (interview with Pat Rabbitte, Minister of Communications, Energy and Natural Resources).

23 Ó Riain 2004, chap. 1, 2014, chap. 2; interview with Cormac O'Grada, University College Dublin.

24 Barnes and Wren 2012; Ó Riain 2004.

25 Interview with Tony Donohoe, IBEC.

26 Interview with Ruairi Quinn, Minister of Education and Skills. See also Barnes and Wren (2012, p. 301).

27 Correspondence with Rory O'Donnell, NESC.

28 Interview with Tony Donohoe, IBEC.

far as the problem was less the organization of civil society and much more the dysfunctional politics and inferior organizational capacities of the state over which Ahern presided.[29]

But the Irish economy was hybrid, possessing an important second leg. The development of an educated, English-speaking workforce within the European Union, various state-sponsored development projects, and favorable taxes on multinational enterprises eventually made Ireland the preferred destination for high-technology and pharmaceutical investment from the United States. The multinational element had great access to the state. A prominent labor leader explained that "the premier institution in this state is the IDA [Industrial Development Agency]" representing the multinational sector, with further access to the state coming from the Irish-American Chamber of Commerce and the financial services sector. He added, "They're the people who had real killer power—and it's not public at all."[30] The banking system also exemplified Irish economic dualism in the early 2000s. There were many foreign financial institutions operating in investment banking and fund management. These offshore firms accounted for roughly half of the Irish financial sector. Such a low-tax policy was only possible in the EU, of which Ireland is a member, because there was little recognition at the start as to what was happening. "Had France or Germany tried to reduce their corporation profits tax rate to 12½ percent the ramifications would have been huge. But they were inclined ... to say 'It's Ireland; it's a small country; who cares?'"[31]

Three points need to be made about this element of the political economy. First, the presence of the multinationals did a great deal to ensure that regulation of the economy was limited. The state's organizational capacities in this regard remained thin.[32] Secondly, there is much debate about the bargains struck between the state and the multinationals. There is a crucial difference between the multinationals who actually produce goods in Ireland and the shell companies used merely to transfer profits elsewhere. The former add perhaps 5 percent to Irish GDP, whereas the latter add nothing—except for the considerable amount of employment given to legal experts. Some have wondered whether the multinationals would stay were the transferring of profits ever to stop—an issue that remains live, given recent American and European concerns over the matter. Finally, the multinationals, especially in information technology, pharmaceuticals, and health, trained a generation of Irish citizens who became capable of setting up spin-offs of their own, not

29 Correspondence with Rory O'Donnell, NESC.
30 Interview with David Begg, Irish Confederation of Trade Unions (ICTU).
31 Interview with Cormac O'Grada, University College Dublin.
32 Ó Riain 2014.

least as the large firms sought to outsource various activities. This exemplar of small nation-state innovation and flexibility has had, we shall see, growing importance over time.

The consequence of these developments was that the high levels of indebtedness of the late 1980s were gradually lowered. Economic growth was strong through the 1990s and early 2000s, only temporarily interrupted by the dotcom bubble collapse of 2001–2. Emigration ceased, and there was an inflow of labor—both of Irish citizens who had emigrated and later of workers from other European Union countries, above all from Poland. Some of this was due to catch-up with the rest of the continent, but the particular form of the political economy mattered. The Celtic Tiger was born.

But these economic innovations took place within a country affected by three British legacies that had been adopted when the Irish state was founded and that contributed to the general thinness of Irish institutions. First, liberalism in economic affairs was prominent, the presumption being that the state should keep its distance from the private sector. This philosophy was reflected in the Irish banking sector's light regulatory touch.[33] A dozen onshore banks, six of them Irish, dominated the sector, including virtually all retail banking, with the real heavyweights, such as the Anglo Irish Bank and Bank of Ireland, enjoying privileged personal access to the public authorities, thanks in part to Ireland's system of political patronage and clientelism. Further, the Irish Banking Federation played a less prominent role in Ireland than did its counterpart in Denmark.[34] In some respects, then, Ireland resembled the political economies of many other peripheral countries.[35] Judicial activism in economic affairs was also distinctively liberal in character.[36] We learned in one interview that there is a cultural side to this paucity of regulation as well, which is particularly pronounced compared to Denmark's oversight of economic activity and goes straight to the issue of national identity: "From what I can see of Denmark, Sweden, they do put their idea of building a society up there as a political goal whereas here it tends to be individualistic.... Help out your own clan or whatever but not this idea of everybody moving towards a societal sort of ideal."[37] Liberalism, then, fettered the development of both national solidarity and the state's organizational capacities.

Second, the political system was based on that prevalent in Westminster. The ruling party has enormous power. Parliamentary rules are such that the party in power rarely needs to consult the opposition; the executive branch

---

33   Woll 2014, p. 141.
34   Woll 2014, p. 143.
35   Ó Riain 2014.
36   Interview with David Begg, ICTU.
37   Interview with Jamie Smyth, *The Financial Times*.

dominates the legislature. The party whipping system in the parliament is extraordinarily harsh: failure to toe the party line can lead not just to forfeiting your committee seat but even to expulsion.[38] Further, the Irish cabinet is weak; real power is held by a very small, tight group of people around the Prime Minister and the Minister of Finance. There is no committee structure to create consensus. Compared to the Danish political system there are relatively few checks and balances. Reliance on independent advisory boards is less developed than in Denmark, as indicated, for example, by the fact that Ireland has nothing comparable to the Danish Economic Council (DØR).[39] Further, Ireland's single transferable vote form of proportional representation created incentives to vote for someone who will look out for the local interests. Unlike Denmark's proportional representation system where citizens must vote on a list of candidates drawn up by their party, the Irish system enables citizens to vote across party lines, and so to elect independent candidates.[40] Indeed, one former MP told us that he had quit politics entirely when he realized that holding a seat in the parliament meant that he had to constantly kowtow to the wishes of his local constituents rather than attend to more important national matters. When people had problems, such as a broken streetlight, they would call him rather than the appropriate administrative agency. In this sense one interviewee told us that Denmark was the "mirror image" of Ireland.[41] This was not a world that was based on institutionalized inclusivity and continual consultation but rather its opposite.

This brings us to the third British legacy in Ireland—the institutional thinness of the state itself, particularly marked with respect to the use of experts.[42] As one person told us, Ireland has an "institutional capacity problem" in the sense that there is a "constitutional infrastructure that's created a political administrative system that just is not proactive; is not thinking; is not alert, alive to dangers."[43] This has limited the provision and utilization of economic expertise by policymakers.[44] The new Irish state inherited the administrative apparatus established under British rule wherein the civil service tended to hire generalists.[45] John Fitzgerald, an economist, noted, "They didn't believe they needed economics expertise. The philosophy is British ... that you should be able to do anything ... it's been a problem in the Irish

---

38 While we were in Dublin, members of parliament were threatened with expulsion from their party if they voted against an abortion bill currently under consideration.

39 Hardiman 2012, pp. 217–20.

40 O'Toole 2010, chap. 2.

41 Interview with David Begg, ICTU.

42 Ó Riain 2014, chaps. 4, 5.

43 Interview with Dan O'Brien, *The Irish Times*.

44 Christensen 2013; Donovan and Murphy 2013, p. 88; Hardiman 2010.

45 Interview with Philip Lane, Trinity College Dublin. See also Christensen (2015, chap. 4).

public service." For instance, he said that the Department of Finance had no macroeconomic model of its own, farming out this crucial matter to the Economic and Social Research Institute (ESRI). As late as 2010 only 7 percent of the officials at the Department had formal economics training at the master's level or higher—far less than comparable departments in other countries— and only two had PhDs![46] A recent government inquiry into the crisis confirmed that sufficient expertise in financial stability and prudential regulation was seriously lacking in the Board of the Central Bank of Ireland.[47] Moreover, the 1963 Official Secrets Act—another throwback to Britain—constrained policymakers and others in the state from conferring with outside experts.[48] Nor was recruitment to administrative leadership positions meritocratic. For example, the Governor of the Central Bank came from within the civil service because the position was seen as a normal promotion for the Secretary General of the Department of Finance, with the Board of Governors not including economists.[49] In addition, parties typically appoint one of their own to key positions, including that of the Financial Regulator, not through some sort of conspiracy but because "it's just the way things were" and everybody knew it.[50] The proportional representation system also contributed to the lack of expertise in government. "Because of the very unusual electoral system ... you end up having a bunch of quite decent people ... but in terms of capacity, the individual caliber of individuals ... [t]hey have no sort of intellectual formation in terms of public policy issues."[51] The lack of sufficient expertise was also due partly to Ireland's educational system. The Irish system had been modeled on that of nineteenth-century Britain favoring general rather than technical education. This was reinforced by the Catholic Church, which controlled much of the educational system, especially in the countryside, and concentrated on teaching humanities and religion at the expense of natural and social science to cultivate future generations of good Catholics. Finally, Irish families pushed their children to pursue high-status careers in medicine or law rather than in economics or other less prestigious fields if they scored highly on national tests.[52]

46 Christensen 2015, chap. 4.

47 Joint Committee of Inquiry 2016, chap. 4.

48 Interview with Philip Lane, Trinity College Dublin. See also Dorney (2013). The World Economic Forum (2013) ranked Ireland fiftieth in the world on the level of public trust in politicians—far below Denmark and Switzerland (see also Hardiman 2012, p. 224).

49 Interview with Philip Lane, Trinity College Dublin.

50 Interview with Pat Rabbitte, Minister of Communications, Energy and Natural Resources.

51 Interview with Dan O'Brien, *The Irish Times*.

52 Interview with Cormac O'Grada, University College Dublin. More recently there has been a growing emphasis on math and science, at least for boys, and regional technical colleges have come into existence.

Let us turn finally to the lingering national question. Violence continued in Northern Ireland (and England) both during the Second World War and in the 1950s. Matters became much worse once the struggle of the Catholics in Northern Ireland for civil rights resulted in "The Troubles" that led to the deaths of several thousand people and to direct rule from London. This only ended slowly, after the intergovernmental Easter Peace Accord of 1998. More important for our argument is the fact that the unresolved national question is the core reason for the prolonged success of Fianna Fáil; it "defined itself very early on not as a party but as a national movement."[53] The party had the character of a southern European populist affair: brokerage politics based on the localism privileged by the voting system all-too-easily morphed into patronage and clientelism. Of course, all small, homogeneous countries tend to breed interpersonal familiarity, and it is certainly true that "Ireland is a very homogeneous society in terms of religion, race and small-scale familiarity."[54] Yet Denmark avoided patronage and clientelism. One reason was that its system of proportional representation did not encourage political localism; party lists mattered more, and this allowed for greater expertise in the members of the parliament.[55] A second reason lay in the organization of civil society. Denmark's system of checks and balances, ad hoc commissions, and greater reliance on experts both inside and outside of the state inhibited the development of closed, insulated, and potentially corrupt decision-making.

We can highlight what is involved by distinguishing between two types of consensus. Consensus-making in Denmark is open, based on free discussion of ideas with a conclusion being reached after dissenting opinions have been examined and experts have been consulted. This is the inclusive sort of consensus in our model that is likely to bolster legitimacy. But the consensual nature of politics in Ireland is closed and closeted politically, less reliant on experts, and the product of a culture that is suspicious of people who speak out against the prevailing view: "It means that when you write critical things, say critical things if you are a politician, if you are a journalist, if you're an academic, if you're in any sphere of life, often you can get a very strong reaction either isolated, excluded or shouted down."[56] Moreover, "people within the system didn't want to put themselves in a position where they were shown up to have limited expertise."[57] It may be that Catholicism stifled intellectual development and encouraged obedience; certainly the grafting of a rigidly puritanical Catholic moral code onto a peasant society became one of the

53 Interviews with Rory O'Donnell, NESC; Pat Rabbitte, Minister of Communications, Energy and Natural Resources.
54 Interview with Rory O'Donnell, NESC.
55 Interview with Jamie Smyth, *The Financial Times.*
56 Interview with Jamie Smyth, *The Financial Times.*
57 Interview with Dan O'Brien, *The Irish Times.*

defining features of the new Irish state for decades.[58] Of course, the high level of class conflict that occurred from the 1960s was a major motivation for the creation of social partnerships. But once established nobody wanted to return to the bad old days; industrial peace was a big prize that few wanted to forsake by rocking the boat too much.[59] All of this meant that there was no "infrastructure of dissent." [60] Further, the fact that the two main center-right political parties, Fianna Fáil and Fine Gael, were so similar ideologically and sought broad-based electoral support further mitigated whatever propensity there might have been otherwise for debate and dissent.[61] One interviewee suggested that the absence of conflict has been a disadvantage insofar as "conflict will generate thinking and will generate ideas.... [W]e don't have a tradition of dissent. It is a very cohesive society. Irish people don't like confrontation."[62] Cultural homogeneity of this sort is dangerous because it can encourage a tremendous amount of groupthink. Small nation-states often open themselves to the world, but at times they can be claustrophilic.

Of course, perceptions of vulnerability and crisis occasionally came to the fore, especially in the late 1980s, but the daily business of politics often revolved around the pursuit of narrower interests. Several of our interviewees lamented the fact that patronage and clientelism often took precedence over meritocratic recruitment and more inclusive policymaking in the national interest. Expertise was in short supply in the civil service and elsewhere. The organizational capacities of the state, particularly in terms of business and banking regulation, remained underdeveloped. And legitimacy deficits continued thanks to nationalist divisions and the absence of an infrastructure of dissent. Certainly, there had been big advances in institution and nation-building since independence, and particularly during the 1980s and 1990s. But neither corporatist bargaining and social partnership nor the Celtic Tiger phenomenon lasted long. As one politician explained, "We're still a very young state, still learning how to manage the shop while the parents are away."[63] Such institutional thinness affected the way in which Ireland managed its financial crisis. It also bore responsibility for the onset of the crisis itself.

Origins of the Crisis

At the beginning of the new century the Celtic Tiger impressed the world. By 2007 unemployment was around 4.7 percent, inflation at 4.9 percent, long-term interest rates at around 4.3 percent, while government debt had

58 Finn 2014, p. 48.
59 Correspondence with Rory O'Donnell, NESC.
60 Interview with Dan O'Brien, *The Irish Times*.
61 Interviews with Jamie Smyth, *The Financial Times*; Dan O'Brien, *The Irish Times*.
62 Interview with Dan O'Brien, *The Irish Times*.
63 Interview with Ruairi Quinn, Minister of Education and Skills.

declined to about 28 percent of GDP. But there were signs of trouble. Between 2000 and 2007 the balance of payments, reflected in the current account, slipped into negative territory; the government's budget surplus evaporated; and annual economic growth cooled from a red-hot 10.6 percent to 5.0 percent. Ireland's extraordinary economic growth had led to a housing boom of unprecedented proportions. This was fueled between 2003 and 2008 by a 108 percent increase in the amount of mortgage lending and an astounding 337 percent increase in property and construction lending. Between 1995 and 2008 the average price of a house in Ireland rose from about €70,000 to €270,000.[64] The IMF concluded in 2009 that Ireland had been the most overheated of all the advanced economies.[65] Soon the housing bubble collapsed and brought the banking system to its knees. Four factors caused this collapse, all involving the underdeveloped nature of Ireland's institutions.

ECONOMIC POLICY

The long history of land dispossession and eviction at the hands of the British made the prospect of home ownership enticing.[66] Property development was especially attractive in nationalist terms when it meant taking over the former British aristocracy's mansions and townhouses.[67] As Alan Dukes, former Chairman of Anglo Irish Bank, told us, "There's always been kind of a love for property development here." The taken-for-granted assumption is that you get married, buy a house, have some kids, and trade up for a bigger house. The prospect of home ownership became reality thanks in part to a variety of mistaken economic policies. To begin with, the government manipulated fiscal policy in ways that overheated the economy. Charlie McCreevy, the Finance Minister in Bertie Ahern's government from 1997 to 2004, cut personal income taxes, slashed corporate taxes by half, and provided a slew of tax breaks to real estate developers and builders that stimulated speculative real estate development. These policies were supported by the entire construction sector that "has always had a very strong political influence, particularly in Fianna Fáil."[68] One result was the so-called ghost estates in the northern part of the Shannon River basin, houses that were built but not occupied. Another result was €330 million in public funds spent to subsidize hotel construction.[69]

64 Donovan and Murphy 2013, pp. 65, 67.

65 Kirby 2010a, p. 1.

66 Interview with George Lee, RTE.

67 Clarke and Hardiman 2012, p. 35; O'Toole 2010, pp. 100–102.

68 The pressure for tax incentives for property development were especially strong from the Construction Industry Federation during annual budget negotiations (Christensen 2015, chap. 4).

69 See also O'Toole (2010, pp. 86–90, 118).

McCreevy's Special Saving Incentives Account scheme, introduced in 2001, was particularly important. Infuriated at having been told by the EU to cool off the economy by spending less, he introduced a tax-free savings scheme in which the state contributed funds directly to individual savings accounts provided that they were not spent within five years. The government contributed €1 for every €4 the individual deposited. Large amounts of money accordingly accumulated and became available in 2006 at a moment when cooling the property market was desperately needed.[70] Whereas the state had depended initially on high income taxes and value added taxes, it came now to rely much more on stamp duties—that is, taxes on transactions and fees. As long as the property markets boomed, the state's fiscal health was assured, which created further incentives for policymakers to pump up these markets.

Clientelism and patronage played a huge role as well. The government encouraged "an atmosphere of insider intimacy in which cronyism thrived."[71] The links between Fianna Fáil and property developers and builders were close. Local developers received all sorts of zoning accommodations from the party's local politicians who depended on their support for reelection. Some local authorities were susceptible to bribes from developers and builders.[72] During Bertie Ahern's years as prime minister, envelopes of cash reputedly passed between developers and politicians in the Fianna Fáil tent at the Galway horse races. There were certainly large donations: in the ten years leading up to the crisis 40 percent of disclosed donations to the party came from builders and property developers.[73] "Fianna Fáil was making it pretty easy for property developers in all sorts of ways and there is a crony capitalism key to that."[74] The banks were eager supporters of all this because they stood to make millions in the mortgage markets. Such clientelism was mostly local: "I think there's plenty of funny business going on but that was kind of local … so that has explained why the building boom was so big and so extensive."[75] Still, the government's 2002 budget provided substantial interest relief on borrowing for residential properties and a reduction in stamp duty as a result of lobbying by developers and builders.[76] The fact that some quarters of the media had diagnosed huge abuses within Fianna Fáil under both Haughey and Ahern is indicative of institutional thinness insofar as the legitimacy of the system was drawn into question publicly.

70 Interview with George Lee, RTE.
71 McDonald and Sheridan 2008; O'Toole 2010, p. 26.
72 Chari and Bernhagen 2011; Clarke and Hardiman 2012, p. 34.
73 Finn 2011, pp. 20–21.
74 Interview with Cormac O'Grada, University College Dublin.
75 Interview with Philip Lane, Trinity College Dublin.
76 Donovan and Murphy 2013, pp. 64–65. It appears that such overt influence peddling involved the politicians, not the regulatory authorities (Honohan et al. 2010, pp. 16–17).

INTERNATIONAL BORROWING

Ireland's entry into the Eurozone in 1999 contributed to the boom because it drove down Irish interest rates.[77] The Eurozone is dominated by the German economy, whose low interest rates affect the currency as a whole. Peripheral countries in the Eurozone could borrow very large amounts of money at low rates. In the Irish case, borrowing rose to 40 percent of GDP, as noted, an enormous amount when considering that the Swedish banking crisis of the 1990s involved borrowing an amount only equivalent to 5 percent of GDP.[78] "When we got into the euro and interest rates came down to near German levels," one banker noted, "this [was] heaven!"[79] The availability of foreign investment essentially gave Irish banks carte blanche to borrow and lend freely. So, for example, when banking regulators criticized the Irish Nationwide Building Society for loose borrowing and lending, the effective response was emphatic and a clear indication of the thinness of the state's organizational capacity for regulating the banks:

> You can't stop us. We are in a single currency now. We can borrow internationally. We are not reliant on deposit bases for any of this money. If we don't lend it out our customers and our clients will get the money from overseas. The British Bank will come in, The Deutsche Bank will come in, and the Danish bank will come in and lend us the money.[80]

The gap between the Irish banks' lending and their retail deposits rose from €26 billion to €129 billion between 2002 and 2008, largely from short-term borrowing abroad.[81]

Making matters worse, according to Alan Dukes, Irish banks relaxed their lending standards, especially for residential and commercial real estate, and engaged in more aggressive lending products and practices in response to an ever more internationally competitive banking environment—a manifestation of Ireland's integration into the EU that one observer described as "competitive nationalism."[82] Consequently, housing prices skyrocketed. According to Dukes, "The biggest factor that was pushing up the prices [of houses] was the looseness of lending policy on the part of the banker." Of the total stock of bank loans outstanding to the private sector by March 2008, more than €3 out of every €5 were related to real estate and property development,

---

77 Honohan 2008; Regling and Watson 2010, p. 24.
78 Interview with Philip Lane, Trinity College Dublin.
79 Interview with Alan Dukes, former Chairman, Anglo Irish Bank.
80 Interview with George Lee, RTE.
81 Donovan and Murphy 2013, pp. 77–78.
82 Clarke and Hardiman 2012, p. 11; Joint Committee of Inquiry 2016, chap. 1; Kirby 2010a, pp. 36–37; Regling and Watson 2010, pp. 14–15.

a manifestation of Ireland's light regulatory touch.[83] Those banks with the biggest ties to the real estate sector were Anglo Irish Bank and Irish Nationwide Building Society, which together had about 75 percent of their loans tied up in real estate in 2006. Allied Irish Bank (AIB) had 32 percent and Bank of Ireland had 16 percent of their loans in real estate.[84] In short, because the banks and mortgage firms had made huge bets on the property sector, the real estate markets boomed.

As a result, the political economy became wildly unbalanced. Job growth after 1999 depended massively on construction—the fastest-increasing sector in terms of job growth during the early 2000s. Between 1999 and 2007 the number of people employed in building and construction doubled from 8.9 to 13.4 percent of total employment.[85] The state's finances also became unbalanced as stamp duty on property transactions brought in larger and larger amounts.[86] However, the monies gained were not saved but rather used to increase spending in the public sector, without much thought that the former can collapse quickly while the latter, once expanded, is very hard to cut.[87] This meant that a fall in housing prices would not just hurt the banks but the state too, thereby potentially triggering a fiscal crisis. The broader point is that while Ireland's entrance into the Eurozone created opportunities for growth, thanks to being under the protective wing of the euro, it also created the potential for great exposure and vulnerability as this small country became increasingly indebted to some of its bigger neighbors, notably Germany and France.[88]

GROUPTHINK AND HUBRIS

Warning signs were available, not least in the Irish Council on Social Housing's Bacon Report, in the collapse of Paribas in 2006 and Bear Stearns in 2007, in critical comments coming from the NESC and from Morgan Kelly, an economist at University College Dublin, and in an ESRI report to the Ministry of Finance.[89] But even then the warnings were often half-hearted. The Central Bank of Ireland's financial stability reports offered only "the very gentlest and most polite indications that maybe the property sector was getting out of control.... Never at any point did the financial regulators say to any

83 Barnes and Wren 2012; Kirby 2010a, p. 157.

84 Woll 2014, p. 144.

85 DKM Economic Consultants 2008, pp. 47–48.

86 Kirby 2010a, p. 63.

87 Interviews with Alan Dukes, former Chairman, Anglo Irish Bank; Ruairi Quinn, Minister of Education Skills; George Lee, RTE.

88 Armingeon and Baccaro 2012, p. 174.

89 Interviews with George Lee, RTE; John Fitzgerald, ESRI.

bank, 'You should now—you must now stop giving more than 100 percent [on mortgages]'.... They had all this information coming into them, obviously, [but] nobody putting it together to read what it meant for the fragility of the banks."[90] This was another indication of a lack of expertise, or at least a lack of respect for what little expertise there was on hand.

In any case, these warnings were ignored because groupthink and hubris were widespread. Something similar happened in Denmark, not least when Anders Fogh Rasmussen had suggested that Danish economists rewrite their textbooks. But in Ireland Prime Minister Bertie Ahern went further, famously recommending that doomsayers consider suicide! The Irish economy during the 2000s was booming, and in turn immigration was rising such that the demand for housing seemed as if it would go on forever.[91] As we learned in one interview, "there was a hubris where people were going on lecturing about how wonderful the Irish miracle was ... which was pretty stupid," because Ireland's success stemmed to a considerable extent from artificially low interest rates on foreign borrowing, structural funds from the EU, a booming international economy, and other factors largely beyond its control.[92] Yet the Irish assumed they had created the good times all by themselves. It was as if to assume that the cock crowing at dawn was responsible for the sunrise.[93] One journalist told us that between 2005 and 2007 "the very clear sense I got from people here was a sense of invulnerability. It can't go wrong. We have got this cracked. We know how to do it. Everything is okay.... There is no risk. And a lot of people ... particularly in government said that there is no downside; we don't have to fiscally prepare for a downside because it can't go wrong."[94]

Groupthink was not restricted to politicians; the public succumbed too. When the ESRI issued a warning about the housing bubble, it was not well received. "The information was there, but nobody wanted to hear it. It's not just the government who didn't want to hear it, it was the people of Ireland [who] didn't want to hear, and it's how you get a herd mentality." Escalating property values were in effect compensation for stagnating middle-class incomes, particularly in rural areas, which is another reason why politicians continued to feed the bubble.[95]

There were several additional reasons why groupthink was so pervasive beginning with the absence of the infrastructure of dissent mentioned earlier.

90 Interview with Alan Dukes, former Chairman, Anglo Irish Bank.

91 Interview with Alan Dukes, former Chairman, Anglo Irish Bank.

92 Interviews with John Fitzgerald, ESRI; Ruairi Quinn, Minister of Education and Skills. See also Kirby (2010a, chap 2) and Regling and Watson (2010, p. 22).

93 Interview with George Lee, RTE.

94 Interview with Dan O'Brien, *The Irish Times*.

95 Barnes and Wren 2012, pp. 309–310.

It was difficult for people to criticize the property bubble because there was a culture opposed to rocking the boat. This included most of the media, which failed to sound alarms.[96] One journalist noted,

> Ireland, it's a very small country, a very close and closeted political estab-
> lishment, a culture that doesn't ... it doesn't accept people who speak out
> against the consensus. And I think that's one of the main causes of the
> crisis here.[97]

For example, secret internal emails, now public, within the Department of Finance warned of a housing crash but were dismissed and systematically erased from draft answers to parliamentary questions.[98] Furthermore, David Begg, a Central Bank of Ireland board member, told us that he met with Prime Minister Brian Cowen in May 2008 warning him that the economy and property markets were overheating and urging him to cool things down. Cowen refused and nobody else would listen either because buying "was the thing to do. They wouldn't listen to any kind of ideas about cooling down." No wonder because, according to Begg, "there was a hue and cry from the people in the property markets who pushed back." In some cases the possibility for push back caused people to fear for their jobs if they spoke out.[99] One person who ran the national debt agency suspected that Anglo Irish Bank was in trouble following the collapse of Bear Stearns. Despite the fact that he was a "tough bastard ... not one of these wimpish bureaucrats" he very quietly began pulling the state's money out of Anglo Irish without alerting the government that he was doing so. The reason he handled it so circumspectly was that "if Anglo got hold of it or heard about it, they would use their political connections to stomp on him.... He didn't wave a red flag more widely because of the fear that the politically connected owners of the bank would then use their connections to come back at him."[100] Similarly, politicians and other state officials sought to limit dissent by withholding funds from those organizations in civil society that might rock the boat, particularly at the local level and through various social partnership discussions.[101]

The possibility of groupthink was exacerbated by the fact that Ireland was a very small country in the Eurozone, merely a "tiny dot." Nobody in the rest of Europe paid much attention to it.[102] This may have been one reason why neither the IMF nor the EU spotted the problems brewing in the housing

96 Interview with Dan O'Brien, *The Irish Times.*
97 Interview with Jamie Smyth, *The Financial Times.*
98 McConnell and Lyons 2012.
99 Interview with Dan O'Brien, *The Irish Times.*
100 Interview with Dan O'Brien, *The Irish Times.*
101 Honohan et al. 2010, chaps. 4–5; Kirby 2010a, pp. 176–79.
102 Interview with Rory O'Donnell, NESC.

market. Another was that Ireland was in compliance with the Stability and Growth Pact, which mandated that Eurozone members keep government deficits and debt within certain parameters.[103] But the fact that the government budget was in surplus was beside the point; the problem was in the housing market. This should have been obvious because the current account deficit was growing thanks in large part to increased bank borrowing on international capital markets. As a result, "The IMF and EU should have called us," said one ESRI member.[104] Finally, there was plenty of external reinforcement for groupthink. "There were people coming from abroad and wondering how the Irish had got it right. And there were books written about the success of the Irish economy and [Paul] Krugman and various other people [were] involved in saying how wonderful things were."[105] Jean-Claude Trichet, head of the European Central Bank (ECB), visited Dublin in 2007 pointing to the Irish economy as a model to be emulated.[106]

Of course, there was some groupthink in Denmark in the sense that most Danish politicians and economists were in agreement, as noted earlier, about how to run the economy and did not worry too much about a housing bubble. The difference, however, was that in Denmark it stemmed from the common training that most economists had and the national consensus-making institutions within which they and most politicians operated. The Danes did not resort to exclusive rule by economists; they accepted that technical expertise should be put into the service of consensus-making, a combination of democratic process and technocratic influence. For them it was not an either/or choice. But in Ireland groupthink stemmed from a widespread political culture averse to rocking the boat that was rooted in patronage and clientelism. There was no infrastructure of dissent in Ireland because those who might have dissented knew they would suffer push back from the beneficiaries of patronage or even lose their jobs. This was a taken-for-granted part of everyday life in Ireland. Furthermore, those in the Eurozone who might have spotted trouble did not because Ireland was only a "tiny dot." Finally, people very much wanted to believe that housing prices would continue to rise because it was a way to make up for stagnant wages, which were part and parcel of Ireland's history of economic underdevelopment. In short, although groupthink and hubris manifested in Ireland, as in Denmark, in sector-specific ways that affected the onset of the crisis it was a product of broader national conditions.

103 Interviews with David Begg, ICTU; John Fitzgerald, ESRI.
104 Interview with John Fitzgerald, ESRI.
105 Interview with Cormac O'Grada, University College Dublin.
106 Interview with David Begg, ICTU.

LACK OF EXPERTISE AND REGULATION

Many interviewees told us that the Ministry for Finance, the Financial Regulator (Irish Financial Services Regulatory Authority), and the Central Bank of Ireland lacked sufficient expertise to see what was brewing, particularly but not only at the senior level.[107] For example, the boards of both the Financial Regulator and Central Bank were drawn traditionally from the civil service and a wide variety of professions.[108] The head of the Financial Regulator had served elsewhere in the civil service since the age of seventeen.[109] One seasoned politician referred to the Minister of Finance in the years immediately preceding the crisis as "charming in many ways but not qualified for the job" because his expertise was as a lawyer not an economist. Worse still, he described the Governor of the Central Bank in those days as simply "a fool … who was out of his depth and who refused to recognize that."[110] Another interviewee confirmed this, off the record: the Governor "was simply out of his depth … and then probably found himself colluding in the Irish fashion with the bankers to keep the lid on things." The lack of expertise was also one reason why the regulatory authorities at the Central Bank "were scared of the banks. The banks ruled the regulators, not the other way around."[111] The problem boiled down to thin institutions—there was more of a "patronage culture" than a "talent-based culture" in the Irish public sector.[112]

The argument is not that there were no economists in these organizations, rather that they were not the right sort of economists—more particularly not those who specialized in the macro-prudential analysis needed to analyze how bank lending and borrowing might affect the stability of the financial system as a whole and the economy in general. Moreover, problems of inadequate expertise went deeper than the leadership of these organizations. The Financial Regulator lacked expertise in assessing systemic risk.[113] At the Central Bank whatever limited expertise there was resided in isolated silos at lower levels in the organization, and even there the expertise was typically

---

107 Interviews with John Fitzgerald, ESRI; Alan Dukes, former Chairman, Anglo Irish Bank; Cormac O'Grada, University College Dublin; Ruairi Quinn, Minister of Education and Skills; Pat Rabbitte, Minister of Communications, Energy and Natural Resources; Dan O'Brien, *The Irish Times*. See also Barnes and Wren (2012, pp. 299–300).

108 Honohan et al. 2010, chap. 3.

109 Interview with Philip Lane, Trinity College Dublin.

110 Interview with Ruairi Quinn, Minister of Education and Skills. As a Labor Party member, Quinn acknowledged that his view may have been biased.

111 Interview with John Fitzgerald, ESRI. See also Finn 2011, p. 11; Honohan et al. 2010, chaps. 4–5; O'Toole 2010, pp. 194–197.

112 Interview with Jamie Smyth, *The Financial Times*.

113 Honohan et al. 2010, p. 9, chap. 5.

more in accounting than in finance and macro-prudential analysis.[114] Part of the limited expertise at the Central Bank of Ireland was simply that it never had much to do. The currency was pegged initially to the British pound and then to the euro; so somebody else was managing interest rates and monetary policy. Compounding these problems, laws concerning secrecy meant that the Central Bank could not turn, as noted, to outside academic economists. Finally, experience was unnecessary insofar as the prevailing cognitive framework in both the Central Bank and Financial Regulator favored a light regulatory touch, inspired by the British assumption that firms have robust enough internal governance for effective self-regulation and voluntary compliance with legislation, codes, and rules.[115]

Overlap among the worlds of banking, politics, and public service also undermined effective regulation. Career mobility between the boards of the banks and the Central Bank was common. Indeed, at one point directors of both AIB and Bank of Ireland held simultaneous appointments on the Central Bank's board![116] The regulatory authorities knew that there was a system of networks and connections with powerful politicians at the center. Senior regulatory authorities sent clear signals to their staff that inhibited them from raising red flags about the banks' financial stability and the overheated housing market, again most likely due to lobbying objections from the banks.[117] This is another reason why the regulatory authorities deferred to the wishes of the banking community.[118] Hence, even the most intelligent and careful analysts never looked closely at the banks' asset books prior to the crisis.[119]

Given the state's limited expertise when presented with misleading or false information by the banks (notably by Anglo Irish, which we now know to have lied to the government), the regulators failed to spot the problems.[120] When it came to preparing their annual financial stability reports the Central Bank not only suffered analytical weakness but also enough groupthink to ignore warning signs that the banks and property markets were in trouble.[121] It issued reports from 2005 through 2007 where the evidence pointed one way, suggesting that the Irish real estate market was seriously overvalued, but the conclusions pointed the other way, saying that things were alright because

114 Interview with Alan Dukes, former Chairman, Anglo Irish Bank.

115 Chari and Bernhagen 2011; Clarke and Hardiman 2012, pp. 26, 30; Hardiman 2010, p. 75; Honohan et al. 2010, chaps. 4–5; Woll 2014, p. 141.

116 Clarke and Hardiman 2012, p. 31.

117 Honohan et al. 2010, chaps. 6–7.

118 O'Toole 2010, chap. 3.

119 Interview with John Fitzgerald, ESRI.

120 Norris 2013; Woll 2014, p. 154.

121 Donovan and Murphy 2013, chap. 5.

demand for housing had grown too—thanks to McCreevy's Special Saving Incentives Accounts. Why the contradiction? "You have to understand that we are a small country, a small population, a small number of policy people, a small number relatively of people who understand these debates. It becomes difficult to be marked out as the guy who is the nuisance, or the girl who is the nuisance." Even though a few mid-level bureaucrats warned that problems loomed, the real decision-makers were not the right type of people to rock the boat.[122] Fear and lack of confidence resulted from inadequate training and expertise.[123]

The banks lacked adequate expertise, too, especially in risk management, where older managers with expertise were encouraged to retire and were replaced with younger staff without such knowledge.[124] This was another reason why the banks borrowed short and lent long. As a result, when Lehman Brothers collapsed and short-term lending froze in international capital markets, Irish banks were immediately in crisis.[125] Moreover, the banks failed to realize that developers often had loans from one bank invested in property development schemes with other banks such that the whole thing was a systemic house of cards. The banks all passed the limits of prudential lending without realizing the dangers involved. Loan-to-equity ratios were badly skewed and loans were over-concentrated in the construction and real estate sectors.[126]

In sum, Irish institutions were thin and so bore considerable responsibility for the financial crisis. Insulated clientelist politics contributed to misguided economic policies, including favorable tax treatment, zoning variances, and state subsidies for developers that pumped up the real estate and construction industries beyond sustainable levels. Patronage and clientelism also led to speculative lending and shady deals involving bankers and developers. Trouble stemmed as well from Ireland's entry into the Eurozone, because membership meant that bankers and developers could borrow money on a breathtaking scale—something that compromised the state's organizational capacity to regulate banking and the real estate markets even when it wanted to do so. Institutional thinness was also evident in leadership at the Financial Regulator and Central Bank of Ireland, which were ill prepared for what was happening because they, like the banks, lacked sufficient expertise to spot trouble. Moreover, Ireland's thin institutions contributed to group-

---

122 Interview with George Lee, RTE.

123 Interview with Philip Lane, Trinity College Dublin. See also Clarke and Hardiman (2012).

124 Interview with John Fitzgerald, ESRI. See also Donovan and Murphy (2013, p. 70); Regling and Watson (2010).

125 Interview with David Begg, ICTU.

126 Interview with Alan Dukes, former Chairman, Anglo Irish Bank.

think, not to mention hubris, which also prevented people from either rec-
ognizing the warning signs of impending financial doom or being taken seriously if they did. A summary judgment came from one critic who compared
Ireland's "underdeveloped system of political governance and public morality" during the 1990s and early 2000s—long run by Fianna Fáil—to the corrupt
political machines of nineteenth-century America. His solution for Ireland?
"Undertake some quite old-fashioned exercises in nation-building."[127]

Crisis Response: The Guarantee and Troika Bailout

The collapse of Britain's Northern Rock bank and its Irish subsidiary in 2007
revived memories of what a run on a bank involved, with fears increasing as
news filtered out piece by piece of the trouble facing the Royal Bank of Scotland. Irish bank shares came under pressure throughout the summer of 2008.
But it was the American decision to let Lehman Brothers go bankrupt that
triggered the Irish crisis. Ireland's initial response to the crisis was even more
rapid than Denmark's. Crucially, the guarantee was to be paid for by the state
rather than privately with funds from the banking sector as was a big part of
the plan in Denmark. It involved two major parts—first a package of state
guarantees, capital injections, and efforts to clean up the banks' loan books;
second a bailout deal with the EU-ECB-IMF Troika. We take each in turn.

On September 15, 2008, Lehman Brothers filed for bankruptcy sending
money markets into a tail spin and freezing international credit markets.
Anglo Irish Bank revealed in private that it would default without government support, and both the Bank of Ireland and AIB admitted that they too
were in trouble. A decision was taken on the night of September 29 to issue
a complete guarantee to all Irish banks for a two-year period covering all
deposits, senior debt, and dated subordinated debt. This involved a potential
commitment of 3.5 times GDP, for a figure over €330 billion—the estimate of
all bank deposits and liabilities that night—which was easily the largest of any
country's state guarantees in late 2008.[128] Later that year the government
provided capital injections to the troubled banks. In January 2009 Anglo Irish
was nationalized. Finally, in April 2009 in order to remove toxic assets from
the banks' books the government established the National Asset Management
Agency (NAMA), charged with responsibility for purchasing all troubled
development-related loans above a certain value from the banks, repackaging
them, and, hopefully, selling them to investors later. Five banks participated:
Anglo Irish Bank, AIB, Bank of Ireland, Irish Nationwide Building Society,
and EBS Building Society. NAMA began taking over loans in 2010. The first

---

127 O'Toole 2010, pp. 216–17.
128 Carswell 2010; Honohan 2008, p. 5.

phase of transfer involved €71 billion in outstanding loans. Haircuts were not imposed on bondholders.[129] The banks had to pay a quarterly fee to receive the guarantee. Capital injections also came at a price, including share ownership. For instance, at AIB and Bank of Ireland the government bought 25 percent of the ordinary voting shares, gained a say in the appointment of directors, governance, and executive compensation, and received dividends of 8 percent.[130] By late 2010 three other Irish banks had been nationalized too.[131]

As the state spent more and more money on the banks, the banking crisis was transformed into a state fiscal catastrophe because the government bailout was "a crushing liability for one of the Eurozone's smallest economic units."[132] Thanks to the guarantee and state capital injections, the state's 2009 budget deficit jumped to 14.5 percent of GDP and 32 percent of GDP a year later. Government debt as a percentage of GDP more than tripled from 25 to 87 percent by the end of 2010.[133] Moreover, because the state guarantee expired in September 2010, private funders that had supplied some capital to help the ailing banks pulled out. In turn, the banks asked the Central Bank of Ireland for more liquidity, which they received. Making matters even worse, NAMA's purchases of toxic assets exceeded expectations by late 2010 and Anglo Irish's new management team decided it needed yet more capital injections. Finally, in summer 2010 Ireland's projected economic growth rate was revised downward suggesting that the state's fiscal crisis was even more severe than anybody had thought. This triggered the second part of the Irish response to the financial crisis.[134]

In November 2010 the government requested a bailout from the EU and IMF. After negotiations with the Troika, they arranged a deal worth €85 billion, roughly 54 percent of Ireland's GDP in 2010, some of which was provided domestically by Ireland's sovereign wealth fund and other public sources. The remaining €67.5 billion was provided evenly by the ECB, the IMF, the European Financial Stability Fund and loans from Britain, Sweden, and Denmark. Under the terms of the agreement €50 billion was for the Irish state so that it would not have to rely on the bond markets to fund its fiscal deficit or roll over existing debt during the next three years. Another €10 billion was for further capital injections for the troubled banks. The final €25 billion was contingency funding to be used in case additional capital injections were required. The deal also required that third-party assessments of the banks' loan

---

129 However, NAMA bought bad bank loans for only about half the value of the debt (Kirby 2010b).

130 Woll 2014, p. 146.

131 Kirby 2010b.

132 Finn 2014, p. 66. See also Lane (2011).

133 Trading Economics 2015.

134 Lane 2011.

books be conducted to better determine their quality. Structural reforms were mandated too, including improving the banks' capitalization ratios so as to reduce their level of risk, transferring additional risky loans to NAMA, further downsizing the banks, and winding down Anglo Irish Bank and Irish Nationwide Building Society. Again no haircuts were imposed on bondholders, many of whom were German and French.[135] Finally, Ireland was required to cut government spending by €15 billion by 2014, with almost half of the cuts coming in 2011. The idea was to get the government's budget deficit under the 3 percent limit required of Eurozone members—a task made all the more difficult by charging Ireland what some viewed to be punitively high interest rates on the loans.[136]

Crisis Response: The Process

Confusion and chaos permeated the atmosphere as policymakers struggled to resolve the situation. In the three weeks leading up to the fateful meeting on September 29, a dozen major financial institutions around the world had filed for bankruptcy, been rescued by the state, or absorbed by rivals while under stress. During the crucial meeting that night in Dublin the proceedings were interrupted to announce that the U.S. Congress had failed to pass the Troubled Asset Relief Plan, which sent financial markets tumbling.[137] So the reminder of Mario Draghi, current ECB president, is particularly germane in Ireland's case: "It is a very big mistake to look at past events with today's eyes. You should go back and consider what was the situation at the time."[138] Nonetheless, cooperation and coordination were absent, and institutions were thin, as Ireland tried to cope with the crisis.

As in Denmark the events in question in Ireland rested not only on a particular institutional portfolio but also on certain historically given cognitive frames. We have already seen that Ireland's experience with land expropriation by the British instilled in many people a deep desire for home ownership; this had helped generate the crisis in the first place. But taken-for-granted assumptions were also important for crisis management. First, the absence of well-developed corporatism meant that Irish decision-making was closed and insulated; only a tiny handful of Irish politicians, civil servants, and stakeholders were involved in the initial crisis management process. They all felt that this was appropriate. The opposite was true in Denmark, where it was assumed that the decision-making circle should be wider and more inclusive.

135 Cardiff 2016, pp. 180–81; interview with Philip Lane, Trinity College Dublin.

136 Armingeon and Baccaro 2012, p. 174; Cardiff 2016, pp. 183–84; European Commission 2013; Lane 2011, p. 20.

137 Cardiff 2016, pp. 35, 54.

138 Boland and Spiegel 2014.

Second, decision-makers assumed that they could handle the situation without extensive input from outside experts—a throwback to Ireland's proclivity for general rather than specialized education of its civil servants and politicians, a legacy of British rule we have already noted. Third, there were few objections to the decisions being made, a reflection of Ireland's Catholic heritage of accommodation and the general absence of an infrastructure of dissent. Finally, closed insulated decision-making devoid of much expertise or criticism was also a hallmark of Ireland's history of near-hegemonic party rule, patronage, and clientelism.

THE GUARANTEE

The decision of September 29 was taken behind closed doors. It is not entirely clear exactly what was said: there is no official record, no minutes were taken, drafts of proposals discussed are not available, and people's memories are now quite fuzzy.[139] As we were told in one interview, "We need an inquiry to figure out exactly what happened and who said what. And there is still a lot that is in the dark."[140] It was only in January 2016 that results of a public inquiry into the events were released. Prime Minister Brian Cowen, Finance Minister Brian Lenihan, Central Bank Governor John Hurley, Attorney General Paul Gallagher, and senior officials from the Department of Finance and the Financial Regulator were there. Top executives from AIB and the Bank of Ireland participated part of the time.[141] Lenihan had little economic experience and was terminally ill with cancer. AIB and Bank of Ireland told him earlier that day that if Anglo Irish Bank went down, they would too and that interbank lending would crumble. They called for either a blanket guarantee or the nationalization of Anglo Irish and perhaps Irish Nationwide Building Society.

That night the government officials met to discuss options, some of which had been provided by the banks and others by American financial institutions. The banks presented policymakers in the room with draft language for a bank guarantee, which served as a template for writing the crucial legislation later. The banks also convinced policymakers not to impose haircuts on bondholders in order to keep open the flow of funds. Whether the banks lobbied policymakers about this in a coordinated fashion is unclear, but it is hard to imagine that bank executives did not have informal conversations with policymakers about all of this. Nevertheless, until autumn 2010 the Irish authorities, including the Ministry of Finance, did not want to impose haircuts

---

139 Joint Committee of Inquiry 2016, chap. 7; interview with Pat Rabbitte, Minister of Communications, Energy and Natural Resources.

140 Interviews with Cormac O'Grada, University College Dublin; George Lee, RTE.

141 Boland 2015a; Cardiff 2016, chap. 2; Joint Committee of Inquiry 2016.

for fear of jeopardizing the credit rating of Irish banks and seriously damaging the government's ability to borrow.[142] But when the decision was finally made on September 29 to issue the guarantee, there seems to have been only one economist in the room—an environmental economist not versed in banking and finance, present only because the Green Party was part of the government. The Financial Regulator and head of the Central Bank apparently did not play important roles, presumably because they had been discredited by not having anticipated the crisis. People from the National Treasury Management Agency were standing by elsewhere waiting for hours. The unions were left out. The NESC was left out. The Irish Banking Federation was left out. Even the banks were left out when the key decisions were made. Nobody consulted outside experts except those from Merrill Lynch.[143] The Labour Party only found out about it the next morning when Lenihan phoned its leader to ask for the party's support. The remaining banks heard the news from the Financial Regulator.[144] So the decision was taken by a very small group of politicians in consultation with a few bankers rather than with experts on financial crisis or macro-prudential management.

Three things are clear about the events of that night. First, most people would agree that "the government made an awful mistake in the guarantee."[145] Second, according to one well-known economist, "They didn't think it through to a degree saying, well, what if this goes really badly? Who's going to pay for it? ... They didn't go down the decision tree." Proof of this is that the guarantee was based on the assumption that this was a liquidity crisis when it actually turned out to be a solvency crisis.[146] The Financial Regulator assured the public in early September 2008 that the Irish banks were among the best capitalized in Europe. But by December the government realized that they all needed recapitalization and that Anglo Irish Bank alone would require €1.5 billion. It turned out later that Anglo Irish needed €4 billion![147] Third, one economist told us that the institutions "were not up to it," that is, not up to solving the crisis.[148]

142 Cardiff 2016, pp. 30, 48–49, 56–57, 184–90; Joint Committee of Inquiry 2016, pp. 252–57.

143 Interviews with Rory O'Donnell, NESC; David Begg, ICTU; George Lee, RTE; Alan Dukes, former Chairman, Anglo Irish Bank. See also Woll (2014, pp. 151–52). Dukes said that the government briefly consulted Morgan Stanley, and that outside economists offered advice but that the government paid no attention.

144 Carswell 2010.

145 Interview with John Fitzgerald, ESRI.

146 Interview with George Lee, RTE. Some in the meeting of the 29th worried that some banks may have been insolvent but generally most did not (Joint Committee of Inquiry 2016, pp. 260–63, 268–69).

147 Interview with Alan Dukes, former Chairman, Anglo Irish Bank.

148 Interview with John Fitzgerald, ESRI.

A big part of the problem was that policymakers failed to consult the experts or anyone else who might have been able to shed light on the situation. "They wouldn't talk to anybody and I think it was the bunker mentality.... They had no internal expertise."[149] The one exception seems to have been Alan Gray, an economist at the Central Bank, whom Cowen phoned during a break in the meeting on September 29 to ask for advice about a possible guarantee. Representatives from the Treasury were not consulted, although apparently their views were represented by others at the meeting.[150] Given the lack of expertise on the supervisory boards of the Financial Regulator, Department of Finance, and the Central Bank, it is surprising that during discussions of the guarantee nobody consulted their European counterparts or the ECB before the decision was made.[151] According to Cowen, in testimony before the government's Joint Committee of Inquiry, Central Bank Governor Hurley had been in touch with ECB president Jean-Claude Trichet the weekend before but was told that "there was no euro-wide initiative in the offing and just as other countries had to take decisions on their banks, it was clear that we were on our own, we would have to deal with this at a national level."[152] Trichet himself confirmed to the Joint Committee that there had been "no contact between the Irish government and either me or the ECB.... We were not kept abreast of any development in Dublin by the Irish authorities."[153] The EU and ECB only found out about the guarantee the next morning, at which time they expressed concern about "the lack of international consultation prior to the Irish decision."[154] Trichet complained to Cowen that the ECB Governing Council disapproved of the blanket guarantee.[155] Part of the problem was that events were moving so fast that there was no time to consult with other countries or international authorities.[156] Furthermore, the laws on secrecy ensured that civil servants and politicians could not and did not consult freely with independent economists, most obviously Patrick Honohan, an internationally renowned Irish expert on financial crises at Trinity College Dublin.[157] In sharp contrast to Denmark, then, at the critical moment Ireland's institutions were particularly thin regarding expertise.

Just as bad, the banks did not have enough risk management and auditing expertise to understand their own situations. When Lenihan appointed Alan

149 Interview with John Fitzgerald, ESRI. See also Cardiff (2016, p. 9).
150 Joint Committee of Inquiry 2016, pp. 249–50, 255–57.
151 Woll 2014, p. 145.
152 Joint Committee of Inquiry 2016, p. 246.
153 Joint Committee of Inquiry 2016, p. 247.
154 Honohan et al. 2010, p. 126. See also Cardiff (2016, p. 61).
155 Joint Committee of Inquiry 2016, p. 276. See also Cardiff (2016, pp. 61, 121).
156 Cardiff 2016, p. 59.
157 Interview with Philip Lane, Trinity College Dublin.

Dukes as Chairman of Anglo Irish Bank in December 2008 after the guarantee had been given, everybody still thought the bank was solvent. However, an internal investigation soon showed that it was not; its situation was much worse than anybody had thought. But the government doubted the claim, suspecting that the bank was trying to pillage the state's coffers, and so the government launched its own investigation, realized eventually that the bank truly was insolvent, and, as a result, nationalized it.[158]

Groupthink and hubris played a role. Ireland's recent economic success—and especially the belief that this was its own doing and that there was no end in sight—blinded most people to the reality of the situation.[159] The problem was that because everyone had bought into this mindset, almost nobody knew what to do when the crisis hit. This is another reason why they mistook a solvency crisis for a liquidity crisis—people could not believe that the banks, which seemed to have fostered such growth, were in such terrible shape.[160] To its credit, then, the only party to oppose the guarantee was the Labour Party, who wanted to nationalize the banks and implement major regulatory reforms.[161]

The closed nature of the crisis deliberations between politicians and a few bankers was another manifestation of the institutional thinness that characterized Irish politics. In contrast to Denmark, the key Irish banks "had privileged personal and individualized ties with the public authorities, while banking association organizations and collective bargaining played a much more crucial role in Denmark."[162] Moreover, in Ireland corporatism was absent in the response process. As one minister told us, corporatism "was on the back burner" by the time the crisis hit.[163] This is another reason why the sort of inclusive formal and informal consultation with people and organizations that we saw in the Danish case was absent in Ireland when the guarantee decision was being made.[164] There were many complaints, not least in our interviews, about such highly insulated political arrangements. In this sense the thin nature of Irish institutions was reflected in a lack of legitimacy. Institutional thinness was also evident in the fact that at least one bank, Anglo Irish, successfully hid its liabilities from the regulatory authorities, who did not have good access to the banks' books—another example of the state's thin organizational capacities. At the September 29 meeting the Financial Regulator reported that all the banks were in compliance with their required capital

---

158 Interview with Alan Dukes, former Chairman, Anglo Irish Bank.
159 Interviews with Dan O'Brien, *The Irish Times*; Jamie Smyth, *The Financial Times*.
160 Interviews with George Lee, RTE; Rory O'Donnell, NESC.
161 Interview with Ruairi Quinn, Minister of Education and Skills.
162 Woll 2014, p. 143.
163 Interview with Ruairi Quinn, Minister of Education and Skills.
164 Donovan and Murphy 2013, p. 83.

ratios and capable of meeting their obligations but that liquidity was becoming a critical issue for them.[165] They were mistaken. In contrast, the regulatory authorities in Denmark had this crucial organizational capacity and, therefore, access to the relevant information with which to manage the crisis once it hit. Even the Danish Bankers Association had a "pretty good impression" of which banks were in trouble, because it met its members regularly and shared information.[166] There was nothing comparable in Ireland during these initial discussions.

Some have argued that Ireland had no choice but to issue a blanket guarantee given the severity of the crisis.[167] Matters are not so simple. Alternative courses of action were available and had been discussed secretly during the months prior to the initial decision to issue a guarantee. The possibility of bank nationalizations, haircuts, and other options were discussed at the meeting of September 29. Lenihan favored nationalizations but Brian Cowen opposed them.[168] Furthermore, it would have been possible for the Central Bank of Ireland to print more euros (allowed within the Eurozone unless blocked by a vote within the ECB) so as to deal with a crisis of liquidity, thereby to gain time in which to learn more about the banks' situations. Why this option was not pursued is unclear. Moreover, we heard several times in our interviews that haircuts of some sort could have been imposed on the bank bondholders.[169] Apparently, Lenihan was prepared to guarantee depositors but not bondholders, which would have somewhat eased the state's fiscal crisis. Again, however, Cowen convinced him otherwise, although it is not clear why.[170] On the one hand, Cowen was connected deeply to the developers and especially to high-ranking officials at Anglo Irish Bank, with whom he often met.[171] The banks did seek a broad guarantee for themselves.[172] Old-time clientelism may have been at work.[173] On the other hand, by then the politicians were pretty sure they would not get reelected so there was no incentive to play such games.[174] Besides, the situation was too dire for anyone to engage in favoritism or patronage. "I don't think that they were creating favor with the banks. I think they were just so desperate that they . . .

165 Joint Committee of Inquiry 2016, p. 244.

166 Interviews with Peter Schütze, former CEO, Nordea, and former Chair, DBA; senior official, DBA.

167 Barnes and Wren 2012.

168 Cardiff 2016, chaps. 1–2; Joint Committee of Inquiry 2016, pp. 250–51.

169 Interviews with Philip Lane, Trinity College Dublin; John Fitzgerald, ESRI.

170 Joint Committee of Inquiry 2016, p. 264.

171 Interview with Philip Lane, Trinity College Dublin. See also Barnes and Wren (2012, p. 305) and Woll (2014, p. 153).

172 Joint Committee of Inquiry 2016, p. 263.

173 Woll 2014, p. 146; Grossman and Woll 2012.

174 Interview with Philip Lane, Trinity College Dublin.

needed the advice of the banks, and the banks would tell them what they needed so they gave it to them."[175] Put differently, Ireland's vulnerability was so obvious in the moment that policymakers shelved whatever parochial interests there may have been and did what they believed was necessary to save the country. "It was all hands on deck now!"[176] Finally, the absence of haircuts as part of the guarantee also stemmed from concern over Ireland's national reputation and not jeopardizing foreign investment, the backbone of the Celtic Tiger. To renege on debts, even if they were incurred stupidly, would have been disastrous in this regard. [177]

The two years between the guarantee and the bailout saw an astonishing 14.5 percent decline in GDP. Unemployment soared from 4.5 to 13 percent and average house prices dropped by 28 percent.[178] Fitch downgraded Ireland's credit rating from AAA in early 2009 to A+ about two years later.[179] Just as serious was the continual dribbling in of bad news as the banks' liabilities increased while values on the property market declined. NAMA tried to stop the rot but an air of crisis persisted. Ireland's thin institutions hobbled whatever impetus there might have been toward a more resilient response. Cooperation and coordination were absent; key decisions were taken behind closed doors. For reasons having to do with the state's thin organizational capacities, accurate information about the real condition of the banks was absent, and so policymakers, short on expertise, did not know how bad the situation was; and outside experts at universities, the EU, the ECB, and other European countries who might have proposed alternative rescue plans were not consulted. Denmark was in much better shape in this regard, and accordingly more innovative. In terms of organizational capacities it is also worth remembering that the large Danish pension fund, ATP, helped finance the bank rescue effort in part because it did not want to see the banking sector collapse—another example of Danish national solidarity insofar as organizations with the means to do so moved quickly to help resolve the national crisis (and in doing so put themselves at financial risk).[180] Nothing like this happened in Ireland, where the state ultimately had to turn to the Troika for help.

What is especially puzzling is that Ireland handled the crisis so poorly despite the fact that there was some initial preparation on the state's part. In 2006 a Domestic Standing Group (DSG), including representatives from the Central Bank, the Financial Regulator, and the Department of Finance, was set up to update crisis management manuals in each organization, perform

175 Interview with George Lee, RTE.
176 Interview with Ruairi Quinn, Minister of Education and Skills.
177 Cardiff 2016, pp. 184–90; interview with Cormac O'Grada, University College Dublin.
178 Trading Economics 2015.
179 Country Economy 2015.
180 Interview with Peter Birch Sørensen, former Chair, DØR.

crisis simulations, and prepare for dealing with a bank crisis. This was similar to preparations taken in Denmark except that in Ireland it was done in response to EU protocol, whereas in Denmark the state did it of its own volition. Furthermore, Ireland updated its Black Book, a crisis management manual initially written in 2001 with guidelines instructing the Central Bank what to do during a crisis—a document that addressed specific issues in the Northern Rock case and outlined how to provide emergency liquidity assistance. As the international crisis began to unfold in early 2008 the Central Bank, Financial Regulator, Department of Finance, and the National Treasury Management Agency started to think about how to cope with a run on or collapse of a bank.[181] In early 2008 a Liquidity Group was also set up, directed by the Central Bank, to monitor liquidity flows. Finally, the DSG considered in mid-2008 two main crisis options if a bank ran into trouble: assisted private-sector acquisition and nationalization. As the situation deteriorated in 2008 policy discussions with all of this in mind ramped up.[182] So there was a modicum of crisis planning just prior to the events of September 2008. But to our knowledge, policymakers did not take any of this into consideration on September 29. Some learning had occurred, but the lessons never penetrated the inner circle where crucial decisions were made.

THE TROIKA BAILOUT

As the state gave more and more money to the banks things only got worse; the banks' solvency crisis morphed into a fiscal crisis of the state. In late 2009 the unions offered to negotiate a new social partnership deal to save money by having public-sector employees take unpaid holidays. Fianna Fáil refused, seeking instead to cope by means of two emergency budgets. The government also asked the unions to accept a pension levy—that is, additional contributions from current employees to the pension fund. The unions refused, and so the government moved unilaterally to do it anyway. Cooperation and consensus-making had broken down; this was the end of the social partnership model.[183] It was also indicative of growing distrust in how the government was handling things—a legitimacy deficit in the making over and above long-standing general concerns about patronage and clientelism. Moreover, it had become increasingly difficult for the government to borrow money. The yield on Ireland's ten-year government bond skyrocketed toward 9 percent by November 2010.[184]

---

181 Carswell 2010.
182 Cardiff 2016, chaps 1–2; Honohan et al. 2010, chap. 8.
183 Interviews with David Begg, ICTU; Rory O'Donnell, NESC.
184 *The Economist* 2010a, p. 85; Lane 2011, p. 18.

As the severity of the crisis grew, the political parties inched modestly toward cooperation. The former Fine Gael Prime Minister Garret Fitzgerald warned that it was "a critical moment" for Ireland, meaning that it was time for the political class to put country before political party.[185] In October 2010 the incumbent government, knowing that it would lose the next election, assumed a worse-case scenario for the economy and decided to pursue a very conservative budget strategy, including reducing the budget deficit to 3 percent by 2012. In effect this was a gift to the incoming government because the pain of austerity would have been inflicted before they took office so that its predecessor would be blamed. A participant at the meeting where this was decided explained that "there was de facto collaboration across the political system to find a solution" to the fiscal crisis.[186] Perceptions of extreme vulnerability had finally sparked political cooperation in the national interest. The paradox of vulnerability had begun to appear again. Unfortunately, it was too little too late.

The government was forced to ask the Troika for a bailout. According to letters between ECB president Trichet and Finance Minister Lenihan, Trichet threatened to cut off further ECB funding for Irish banks unless Lenihan requested the bailout and agreed to the Troika's terms—above all else the imposition of a severe austerity package.[187] By accepting the deal the Irish government lost to the Troika whatever room for maneuver it had left for managing its fiscal situation. Ireland's exposure and vulnerability to international forces was suddenly thrown into sharp relief as it had little choice but to do what the Troika demanded if it were to get help.[188] In that sense Ireland was weak and vulnerable. It was weak thanks to its limited state capacities for managing the crisis itself; and it was vulnerable to the Troika thanks to its membership in the Eurozone. When all was said and done, the pain was inflicted on property developers, those who lost shares in the banks that closed, people facing foreclosure, and the newly unemployed who were victims of the austerity package and recession. But in the absence of haircuts, the bondholders lost nothing. This, of course, was a different situation from that of Denmark, which was not a Eurozone member.

Some people we interviewed suggested that Ireland could have taken a tougher stand in negotiations with the Troika by threatening to default on its debts in the absence of a better deal. As one economist noted, "You can't help thinking that had they not made more noise like the Greeks did that they

185 *The Economist* 2010b, p. 72.
186 Interview with John Fitzgerald, ESRI.
187 Boland and Spiegel 2014. It is not entirely clear how much of a threat this really was because Trichet's letter came after the ECB and Irish authorities had been in talks for weeks where it was clear that Trichet's demands were about to be met anyway (Cardiff 2016, pp. 198–69).
188 Interview with Rory O'Donnell, NESC.

might have got a better deal."[189] Labour leader David Begg was one of those who believed that Ireland should have pushed back more aggressively, noting, as did a recent government inquiry, that by this time the IMF disagreed with the European view calling instead for bondholders to be punished. Furthermore, by then the Irish authorities had also come to favor haircuts because the economic situation had changed since 2008: the government had temporarily ceased borrowing on the bond markets and also saw haircuts as a way to help ease the weight of accumulating deficits and bank capitalization costs, which were becoming very hard to sustain. In fact, the Irish and IMF had concocted a plan whereby the IMF's managing director, Dominique Strauss-Kahn, would try to persuade the ECB and European Commission that large-scale haircuts were in order. He failed. The Irish government inquiry concluded that there would have been no Troika program if haircuts had been administered to senior bondholders.[190] According to Begg, the problem was with the ECB and EU.[191]

> The Troika are neoliberal ideologues. The people, the individuals who represent them here, they are just, you know, I have never met people in my life that I couldn't find some degree of common ground with. But you just cannot find it with the ECB and the EU people and the Troika. It's just not possible at all.

Why such European intransigence? By late 2010 the whole EU financial system was in crisis, with Ireland in particularly bad shape. Trichet's concern was with stabilizing the Eurozone system by preventing contagion effects from ripping through it. Accordingly, he would not countenance haircuts and began twisting arms in Dublin to that effect.

Trichet succeeded because Dublin had little bargaining power since it had become apparent that the situation was out of control, with information still incomplete as to the very considerable amount of bad housing loans.[192] "We had no choice. The Troika came in; they called the shots.... If you were going to get any money, you had to do this."[193] Pat Rabbitte, a Labour Party politician and cabinet member, insisted that because the ECB and other external saviors held all the cards, "we had no chance as a small country to change that." There is something to the view that the extent of bad loans made the situation in Ireland different from that in Denmark. But judgment in this area is difficult, not least because the assumptions involved in any set of figures are

189 Interview with Cormac O'Grada, University College Dublin.

190 Cardiff 2016, pp. 186–90; Joint Committee of Inquiry 2016, chaps. 10–11.

191 Others agree with Begg (e.g., Armingeon and Baccaro 2012, p. 174).

192 Interview with Philip Lane, Trinity College Dublin. Eventually, the European position on haircuts softened (Cardiff 2016, p. 202).

193 Interview with George Lee, RTE.

open to question. What, for example, are we to make of the fact that by 2011 the Danish government had actually made a slight net profit (€720 million) thanks in part to selling bank shares it had acquired and collecting fees for various guarantees, while the Irish government had suffered a significant net loss (€36 billion), and would suffer more in the ensuing years?[194] Danish success here certainly rested on its thick institutional portfolio, including its ability to force the banks to contribute and its insistence on haircuts, while the sheer size of the Irish problem clearly reflected the institutional thinness of its state. One can suggest counterfactuals. Had Irish institutions been present in Denmark there most certainly would not have been a relatively inexpensive resolution, while the presence of Danish institutions in Ireland might have meant that things turned out significantly better. Such counterfactuals are, of course, guesses, though these have plausibility. But our argument concerns the moment of crisis, life in the midst of the squall. Here we have a measure of certainty. The Danes worked out what to do, and were exceptionally nimble in their changing responses. The Irish were shell-shocked, incapable of mastering their fate.

Conclusion

Our ideal-typical model explains the onset of Ireland's financial crisis as well as the disastrous way it was handled. British subjugation stunted nation-building and state-building, and this, in combination with residual nationalist divisions, limited institutional development. Compared with those of Denmark, Ireland's institutions were exclusive rather than inclusive, lacked expertise, were viewed by many as being less trustworthy and legitimate, and never developed the robust organizational capacities necessary for effectively regulating the financial sector or coping with the crisis when it hit. This negative picture does not, as we have seen, tell the whole story: the paradox of vulnerability had led to the creation of some institutions, notably a fledgling form of corporatism, and the Celtic Tiger most certainly rested upon them. However, in the midst of the squall absences mattered more than innovative presences—although we will see in a moment that this may not be the whole story.

Further proof of Irish institutional thinness can be seen in the fact that the crisis precipitated substantial efforts to thicken some institutions. The Central Bank and Financial Regulator were separated in 2003. According to David Begg, this was a major policy error that weakened the state's institutional capacity for effective regulation. As a result, they were reorganized in October 2010. Among other things, the Central Bank assumed responsibilities

194 Woll 2014, chaps. 2 and 7.

for regulating financial institutions and markets with a new risk-based approach to supervision designed in part with macro-prudential concerns in mind.[195] A Fiscal Advisory Council, a Public Appointments Commission, and an Ombudsman were established. The state also created an Economic Management Council to help avert another crisis.[196] The level of expertise was also beefed up in the Central Bank, the Department of Finance, and the Financial Regulator. Steps were taken to open up the Department of Finance to outside economic expertise from both the public and private sectors. Patrick Honohan became Governor of the Central Bank in September 2009 and a new slate of Deputy Governors and board members was installed, many from foreign countries and more with greater economic expertise than their predecessors.[197] Philip Lane, a top economist from Trinity College, then replaced Honohan. The Central Bank and the Financial Regulator gained staff and larger budgets. According to one of the new Central Bank board members, the politicians have agreed to step out of the way and let the Central Bank and the Financial Regulator do their jobs without interference, because they wanted someone "to come in and fix the problem . . . the political system accepts that this is how it should be."[198] Moreover, people are less amenable to the light regulatory touch nowadays.[199] Efforts are also underway to reorient banking activity. NAMA proved to be rather successful in dealing with bad bank assets. Further, the government has talked with NESC, the development agencies and others about how to refocus the banking system more on promoting the growth of the domestic economy, particularly among small and medium-sized enterprises. The idea is to encourage the banks to shift back to traditional business banking rather than speculative, risky property development.

Yet some people are skeptical. Alan Dukes told us that, "most of them [new expert staff] have come from banks, and while they're not the people who made the most egregious mistakes in the banks, they're the ones who on the whole implemented what the bosses told them to do, and they won't have necessarily any great understanding of where the risks are." He also lamented that the government's technical capacity is "better now than it used to be, but it's still grossly deficient." Others agreed.[200] Another observer was bothered by the ongoing lack of public questioning: "What hasn't changed is the polit-

---

195 Central Bank of Ireland 2015.

196 Interview with Ruairi Quinn, Minister of Education and Skills. See also Donovan and Murphy (2013, chaps. 5 and 6).

197 Interview with Alan Dukes, former Chairman, Anglo Irish Bank; Cardiff 2016, p. 242.

198 Interview with John Fitzgerald, ESRI.

199 Interview with George Lee, RTE.

200 Interview with John Fitzgerald, ESRI.

ical culture.... When push comes to shove people will [still] close down."[201] He explained that three or four reports have been issued investigating the crisis but none of them went so far as to name the people responsible. It appears as well, according to the new Fiscal Advisory Council, that the government is poised to repeat some of the mistakes of fiscal profligacy that got it into trouble in the first place.[202]

Ireland's economy has recently staged a strong recovery despite the institutional problems we have described, and in November 2014 the government announced its intention to repay the IMF loans within months, several years earlier than planned. Ireland is now free from control by the Troika. Some of this is due to sheer luck. Ireland's main export markets, the United States and Britain, rebounded fairly quickly after the crisis; oil prices fell dramatically; the euro remained weak further boosting exports; and interest rates for bonds worldwide had fallen, making debt repayment rather easy. But other factors mattered as well. It is worth asking why, despite the depth and severity of the crisis, social cohesion did not breakdown. This may be because during the period of social partnership a dense network developed formally and informally among influential people, their social partner organizations, and the government that remained and still provided input into policymaking. Importantly there was nothing like the Danish reaction to immigrants, or to incoming labor from the EU. For one thing, Ireland had its own stabilizer in this matter, namely a tradition of leaving the country when times are difficult. For another, that very experience seems to have made the Irish more open-minded, more tolerant of difference. Both these points show the positive role played by national sentiment, determined to bear costs so as to succeed.[203] Perhaps, too, accepting the vicious austerity regime gained the respect of German Chancellor Angela Merkel, thereby allowing a measure of renegotiation. But austerity does not explain the recovery, not least when we remember that similar programs have done little to help Ireland's Southern European Troika-controlled counterparts. The best explanation for the recovery must involve attention being given to developments within the real economy.[204] Most of the new jobs created since the crisis were not within multinational firms but in various Irish spin-offs, some of them designed to service them. Crucially large amounts of investment came to such companies, both from the United States as the result of quantitative easing and—though at a higher price—from Irish banks for the simplest of reasons: the

201 Interview with Jamie Smyth, *The Financial Times.*
202 Boland 2015b.
203 We thank Tony Donohoe, IBEC, for this observation.
204 Brazys and Regan 2015; Hardiman et al. 2016.

presence of a cluster of high-powered, flexible human capital. These last considerations bring to mind the mixed character of the Irish case, its combination of weakness and success. The paradox of vulnerability played some part in the Celtic Tiger's success, and it seems to be at work here too in the way in which skills have been developed to ensure survival—with the determination to bear burdens so as to survive the clearest indicator of the social psychology so prevalent in small nation-states.

This adds complexity to the Irish case, but this latest development is by no means fully guaranteed. The political system still lacks the inclusive consensual mechanisms that we saw to be present in Denmark. One astonishing development has been the recovery of Fianna Fáil in the election of 2016, returning in one electoral cycle to be Ireland's second-largest party. Perhaps there is change here, in that Sinn Fein now stands to the left of the party: it is as hard yet to tell since the presence of Gerry Adams as Sinn Fein's leader creates great distrust, reminding the citizens of the Republic of the difficult situation to the north. As such, political consensus is still hard to come by, but also because certain political-institutional features, such as the committee system in the parliament, have not changed. Furthermore, the future will present severe challenges. Both the United States and the European Union are questioning the favorable tax regime offered to multinationals. Might the withdrawal of this regime diminish multinational involvement in the real economy? It is as yet far too early to tell, above all because of the massive spanner thrown into the works by Brexit. This might hurt Ireland significantly. But perhaps it might help it quite as much. Ireland has an educated workforce that speaks English, and it remains part of European Union and the Eurozone. One could imagine banks currently in London moving to Dublin. India is reputed to be likely to invest in Europe. Why not in Ireland?

4

Switzerland

This has a lot to do with the small country thing. . . .
We try to be resilient. . . . We have to adapt.

In a celebrated scene in Carol Reed's film version of Graham Greene's *The
Third Man*, the underworld figure Harry Lime, played by Orson Welles, makes
a comment about Switzerland. He contrasts the exciting period in northern
Renaissance Italy marked by poisonings, pillage, and the glories of Raphael,
Michelangelo, and Leonardo, with the comparatively boring five hundred
years of brotherly love in Switzerland, held—in fact, incorrectly—to have
produced the cuckoo clock. The scene is marvelous but misleading. Switzerland is far from boring. A good deal of violence has been present in Swiss
history, and the country is home to a complex, multi-layered society. Moreover, Switzerland appears on the surface to be a direct refutation of the claim
of our ideal-typical model about the success of small homogeneous nation-
states. After all, this is a mountainous country with four officially recognized
national languages (Swiss German, French, Italian, and Romansch) and two
main religions (Protestantism and Catholicism) and it is one of the richest
countries in the world. It also managed the 2008 financial crisis deftly. How
can this be?

In Ireland we found that cultural homogeneity did not lead inevitably to
national solidarity due to the effects of British domination on nation-state
development. In Switzerland religious and linguistic differences did not pre-
clude national solidarity because institutions afforded all groups a voice in
the political process. In particular, Switzerland has a highly developed form
of federal and consociational democracy. As a result, although Switzerland
is multicultural to a fault, it possesses a common national identity strong

enough to override these nominal cultural differences. The result was a set of thick institutions—expert-oriented, inclusive, and legitimate with well-developed organizational capacities—that laid the foundation for resilience in managing the 2008 financial crisis, which involved near disaster for Switzerland's two largest banks, UBS Financial Services and Credit Suisse. Crisis management was pragmatic and technocratic but due to the exceptional circumstances so closed and insulated that it was largely devoid of any political interference at all. As in Denmark, this was a clear reflection of everyone's confidence and trust in the experts in charge. In turn, the crucial decisions, including a massive bailout of UBS by the Swiss National Bank (SNB) and by the Confederation, were met with widespread consensus among politicians and much of the public.

As a result, Switzerland conforms to our ideal-typical model, but with two important modifications. First, the Swiss have long had great respect for their cultural diversity and have come to view themselves as members of a multi-ethnic nation-state. This respect is an integral part of Swiss national identity. This is because in Switzerland the perceptions of vulnerability were so strong as to overcome nominal cultural differences that might otherwise have undermined a strong sense of national identity and in turn muted institutional thickening. Second, this respect for cultural difference was reinforced time and again by the development of various institutions, notably federalism and consociationalism. As a result, the relationship between national identity and solidarity, on the one hand, and institutional development, on the other hand, evolved in a recursive process. These modifications to the ideal-typical model are illustrated in figure 4.1.

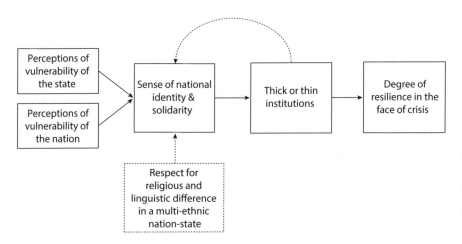

FIGURE 4.1. The Swiss Case

Vulnerability and the Creation of Switzerland

It is important not to read the present back into the past in the case of Switzerland. Contrary to late nineteenth-century nationalist mythology, the decisive formation of the Swiss nation-state is as recent a phenomenon as it was in much of the rest of continental Europe. But this is not to deny that certain path-dependent elements from the early modern period lend distinctiveness to the country that we know today.

Geography plays some part in Swiss distinctiveness. Three ecological zones can be distinguished: the high pastures marked by powerful communal egalitarianism; the settled agriculture of the plains; and the urban areas principally to the north, but with Geneva to the west and Lucerne to the south. This was a decentralized world of independent towns and bishoprics, often serving as the head of cantons, many of them exploiting their surrounding lands harshly, and with most blessed with the status of imperial freedom. There was competition among the cantons, but most of them looked outward given the fundamental fact that major trade routes between southern and northern Europe passed through the Alps. The desire to benefit from trade led to cooperative agreements between cantons whereby they swore oaths to limit violence so as to protect their markets. The practice of sworn agreement morphed slowly into genuine confederal accord by 1386 and was characterized by occasional meetings, habitually among the leading thirteen cantons, though with the associated status of eight more. The driving force here was resistance to external threats—perceived exposure and vulnerability was beginning to help people transcend their regional and cultural differences.[1] As one respondent explained to us, "we are interested as a small state in a system of collective security."[2]

Switzerland is a centripetal or "coming-together" federation—a confederal defensive alliance initially formed against the Habsburgs.[3] Once the Habsburgs securely led the Holy Roman Empire they were as tempted, as other European rulers had been, to homogenize their territories. If the desire to protect liberties drew the cantons together, success in so doing depended both on mountainous terrain and military prowess. Swiss pike men became the most effective military force of later medieval Europe, able to destroy feudal cavalry with great brutality. If their prowess foiled Habsburg attempts at domination at the battle of Sempach in 1386, they did much more to thwart Burgundy, the great cultural center of late medieval Europe, destroying it completely at Nancy in 1477. This in turn led to one confederate union seeking to expand into northern Italy. Defeat on that occasion led to retreat to the

---

1 Steinberg 1996, chap. 2.
2 Interview with Jacob Tanner, University of Zürich.
3 Swenden 2006, pp. 42–45.

central areas, albeit one that had as yet no certainty as to its borders. The result of these developments in the European polity was the emergence of a confederal area that other states felt it best to leave alone both because it was too dangerous to conquer and because it was likely that it would stand by a self-proclaimed and ever more firmly embraced desire to be neutral in international affairs. Thanks to this long history of coming together by the early seventeenth century, some cultural sense of "Swissness" had emerged, not least in tales told about William Tell—a mountaineer and crack shot with a crossbow who according to legend refused to bend to Habsburg authority, thereby triggering a rebellion that led to the formation of the Swiss Confederation. Recognition of this status came in 1648 at the Treaty of Westphalia: Switzerland was freed from the demands of the Holy Roman Empire, of which however it remained a member.

The Confederation had a material base. For one thing, the pike men brought great profits, returning from mercenary service for the European powers with significant monies. For another, geographical location led to a remarkable level of regional specialization. St. Gallen, for example, became famous for embroidery and Zürich for textiles while living standards were raised by transhumance—the seasonal movement of people and animals between summer and winter Alpine pastures. This is the classic world of proto-industrialization, that is, of industrial production within the countryside.[4] From this follows a central characteristic of Swiss history. Max Weber's claim that the discipline-prone members of autonomous cities were attracted to Protestantism seems true of Switzerland. Zwingli and Bullinger pioneered the Reformation in Zürich while Geneva was for a long period placed under the austere regime of Calvin. Large parts of this world were precociously literate. However, the Catholic valleys of the south central area were much less so, and this proved to be the seed from which civil war was later to sprout.

Even in these early times Switzerland was a country of "liberties." It is important to realize that these liberties are not at all what people have in mind today when they talk about political liberty. The former refer to autonomies and rights of particular groups or territories, which in this case eventually led to a more plural and tolerant state. But life within any such territory was by no means egalitarian or soft. Very much to the contrary, the towns were often hierarchical, even reactionary, and some of them faced constant challenges from the peasants of the lands that they dominated. In this regard Switzerland had as "ancient" a regime as did most of continental Europe in the eighteenth century, although a few cantons exhibited signs of proto-democracy. The emergence of the Switzerland that is familiar to us took place very much in reaction to changes associated with the French Revolution.

4 Kriedte et al. 1982.

Most immediately, the conservative, slightly stagnant but contentious old regime was destroyed by Napoleon in 1798. But the centralized Helvetic Republic that the French imposed on the Swiss lasted a mere five years. Diversity was sufficiently entrenched as to make the area hard to rule. The Act of Mediation of 1803 accordingly restored many cantonal privileges. This situation gained further support at the Congress of Vienna; the Great Powers accepted Switzerland's borders and endorsed its stance of neutrality.

But the carapace of order hid internal developments that led to four fundamental changes that gave rise to the modern Swiss nation-state. The first involved the establishment of a federal constitution. The northern cities, largely Protestant and mostly German-speaking, were attracted to republican ideals— the radicals viscerally so, the liberals with considerably less fervor. In the period after Vienna they sought to modernize and to develop, to reform all sorts of social practices in the name of reason and enlightenment. However, a counter movement developed, that of the conservative, rural Catholic cantons. They formed an association, the *Sonderbund*, which was illegal at the time. A civil war followed in 1847 lasting less than a month, won by the reformers at the cost of less than two hundred dead. Almost immediately, a fully federal constitution was created in 1848 with a government led by a seven-member Federal Council interestingly designed in part to protect the interests of the eight *Sonderbund* cantons.[5] As a result, and in sharp contrast to Ireland, national healing after the civil war was relatively rapid. The fact that the language issue was never politicized and did not coincide with religion helped the process of reconciliation quite as much:

> The new state elite came from all parts of the country, including the French- and Italian-speaking communities, the main criterion for recruitment being that they belonged to the liberal movement. In fact, most of them were Protestant.... It is telling that the parliament almost forgot to add a constitutional article that declared all three languages national and official.... The same logic of multilingualism was pursued in other fields: two of the seven federal councilors were (and still are) usually from the French-speaking or from the Italian-speaking Ticino, the Latin parts of the country.[6]

In the end, the constitution laid the foundation for federalism, which allowed the two sides to lay down their arms and in doing so granted full religious freedom. It guaranteed the protection of the Catholic minority. It further recognized French, German, and Italian as national languages receiving recognition as official working languages of the Swiss federal center but with the

5 Swenden 2006, p. 261.
6 Wimmer 2011, p. 31.

cantons being assured linguistic autonomy. The successful formula was that of multilingualism at the center but mono-lingualism by choice in most cantons.[7] Romansch was declared another national language in 1938. The establishment of federalism and with it protection for linguistic, religious, and regional difference was one of the most important changes leading to the modern Swiss nation-state. Institutional inclusiveness was thereby assured in politics.

A second crucial change underpinning the formation of the nation-state further reinforcing inclusiveness was that of the introduction of referenda procedures at the federal level. This important mechanism of direct democracy creates incentives for cooperation among political parties. After all, only through cooperation can the mobilization of veto power through referenda be avoided or overcome.[8] While it is true that Swiss politics was dominated by the Protestant ascendancy until 1891, the deeper truth of the new world was that it was an essentially liberal system, and so never wholly coercive. The radicals essentially monopolized power for the first forty years or so but the Catholic cantons maintained their liberties. In 1874 the constitution was completely revised. Three types of referenda were introduced that provide ample opportunities for citizens to propose constitutional changes and either approve or reject changes proposed by parliament. Since 1848 Switzerland has held 553 national referenda.[9] The introduction of referenda was the background condition that allowed for the full integration of the party that had been defeated in the civil war. The liberals and Catholics formed an alliance because both were conservative in character and therefore opposed to radicalism, especially as it moved in a socialist direction. This is one example of the myriad complexity of a world of cross-cutting alliances. Equally important is the position of the French-speaking cantons: little can be changed without some form of alliance with them, given their formidable blocking powers. As one respondent explained, "You can't do things against the local resistance." This is one reason why Swiss politics is often so conservative and incremental—it usually takes a long time to muster enough consensus to avoid blocking power.[10]

---

7 Steinberg 1996, chap. 2; Swenden 2006, p. 44.

8 Linder 2010, chap. 3.

9 "Mandatory referenda" are required when parliament proposes any constitutional change or international agreement (requiring a double majority of parliament and the electorate); "facultative referenda" are triggered when opponents of a law passed by parliament get 50,000 signatures on a petition for repeal (requiring a simple majority of the electorate); and "popular initiatives" happen when groups wanting to change the constitution get 100,000 signatures (requiring a double majority of cantons and the electorate) (Christoffersen et al. 2014, pp. 157–59; Swenden 2006, pp. 52–54).

10 Interview with Georg Kreis, University of Basel.

A third change facilitating the formation of the modern nation-state had a different character. The rise of nationalist sentiment at the end of the nineteenth century led the Swiss to ask themselves about their own identity. The most immediate answer was to stress the notion of Switzerland as a *Willensnation*, an identity based on political principle instead of ethnic solidarity—one that thereby reinforced Switzerland's already strong national identity. The fact that this notion was so widely shared made it a cultural fact in itself. But as in other countries the national identity was bolstered by a plethora of organic myths. By the late 1880s further stress was placed on the figure of William Tell, German-speaking perhaps but Catholic as well, to which was added the purported creation of Switzerland in a primal act of union in 1291 in the meadow at Rütli, where representatives from three communities supposedly swore an oath to help each other defend against anyone, most notably the Habsburgs, attempting to subject them to external authority. The year 1891 saw a massive celebration of that "first" founding, thereby adding cultural depth to political loyalty.[11]

The final change that facilitated Swiss nation-state building was that of the entry of the working class into the political system, a development that increased political inclusiveness. Conditions during the First World War caused great distress leading to militancy on the part of the unions and the social democrats and resulting in a General Strike in 1918. Their demands, joined with those of the Catholics and some regions, created a fundamental change in the political system, namely the installation of voting by means of a system of proportional representation designed to avoid conflict, protect the losers, and produce coalitions. The result is a system that is today perhaps the most complicated in the world.[12] This change ended the hegemony of the radical party. Adding representation of workers over time to that of Catholics ensured political balance—the creation of a polity bound to seek consensus instead of one in which a mere majority could dominate minorities. Up until then Switzerland's fledgling ideology of social partnership had stemmed from the strengthening of its national identity irrespective of class relations. The demise of class warfare strengthened it further, and led eventually to a long period of power sharing, beginning in 1959 among the four main political parties—Liberals, Catholics, Socialists and People's Party.[13] Further factors consolidated this expansion of national identity: the openness of Swiss democracy, which afforded socialists and communists a political voice; economic

11 Interview with Georg Kreis, University of Basel. See also Zimmer (2003).

12 Interview with Georg Kreis, University of Basel. In fact, proportional representation already existed in many cantons, and twice before 1918 initiatives to adopt it at the federal level failed. The rise of these political tensions finally pushed it through. See also Linder (2010, chap. 1) and Steinberg (1996, pp. 75–76, 260–65).

13 Linder 2010, chap. 4.

crisis during the 1930s; and the rise of fascism in Italy and Germany, which revealed to the Swiss proletariat that it had a homeland worth fighting for.[14] In 1937 the Metalworkers' and Watchmakers' Union signed a historic "peace agreement" with the Federation of Metal and Machine Industry Employers, soon emulated by other industries, which effectively ruled out the strike as a weapon in collective bargaining, thereby setting the stage for Swiss corporatism for decades to come.[15]

Nonetheless, the fact that Swiss politics privileges consociational practices, corporatism, and consensus should not for a moment hide the normality of basic national behavior. Crucially, the working class in power was keen to maintain its rights, and so thereafter sought immigration controls to ensure its domination of the labor market by regulating the number of foreign workers allowed into the country.[16] This meant that Switzerland had no official unemployment problem in the stagflation crisis of the 1970s for the most basic reason: the loss of hundreds of thousands of jobs did not show up statistically because of the huge number of guest workers forced to leave the country. The behavior of such a labor aristocracy meant that links to the Social Democratic Party (SP) were necessarily limited. Importantly, workers benefited from private welfare schemes with the universal ideals of the SP being upheld as much by intellectuals as by workers.

The claim being made is that Switzerland is a much more homogeneous society in practical political terms than one might expect given its nominally heterogeneous features, although it is a unique society in that holding the double identities of state and canton is so very marked. It is as well to highlight the two main factors that have made this possible. First is the distinction drawn in chapter 1 between nominal and politicized ethnicity—that is, between a latent identity and one that matters actively in political life. We have seen that linguistic, religious, and regional differences were accommodated institutionally so as to provide all with sufficient political voice. A thriving guild movement provided a further democratic impetus to social relations.[17] We have also seen that language was not politicized at the moment of state formation. The explanation for this resides in the presence of a rich civil society before the age of nationalism.[18] Shooting clubs, for instance, had members from different groups and felt it natural to hold their meetings at different places within the confederation. Equally, compulsory military service brought

---

14 However, the socialists were still excluded from the executive until 1944–1951, when Ernest Nobs because the first social-democratic Federal Councilor. We thank Wolf Linder for this insight.

15 Linder 2010, chap. 1; Steinberg 1996, pp. 60–61.

16 Christoffersen et al. 2014, chap. 9; Wimmer 2002, pp. 249–68.

17 Steinberg 1996, chap. 2.

18 Dardanelli 2015; Wimmer 2002, 2011, 2013.

different ethnic groups into close contact. The legacy of such connections is evident in modern times in the fact that political parties are not based on language, religion, or region, but rather encompass the whole territory of the state.[19] Indeed, depending on the issue in question, different political coalitions form and dissolve regardless of these cultural distinctions; this facilitates a particularly pragmatic approach to politics. One respondent was particularly clear on this point in terms of linguistic diversity:

> If you have national parties which cover the whole country, all the linguistic groups, then you can manage it [multi-ethnicity] because political parties still have an interest to integrate and to resolve the conflicts internally, and not playing in the public. This is completely different in Belgium, where you have two parties of every color. Then they play the linguistic card, and here it's never played.[20]

So there are a plethora of extraordinarily complex institutional factors that crystallize Swiss national identity despite cultural differences, and that were built deliberately to do just that. Indeed, the cellular, cross-cutting nature of Swiss politics, full of rights and blockages, is valued and is itself a key part of the Swiss identity. "The essence of Swiss identity," in the words of an historian of the Swiss, "is the preservation of even the smallest ethnic, linguistic and cultural units."[21]

The second factor that precipitated national unity despite much cultural heterogeneity was Switzerland's exposure and vulnerability to outside threats. Switzerland held together because it faced such great vulnerability; divisions had to be put aside for the alternative was always much worse. Geopolitics has threatened the Swiss in the form of the Holy Roman Empire, Napoleon, Austro-Hungary, and in more recent times because of the fear of the Nazis and later of the Soviets. One response to this has been neutrality. But that neutrality has been heavily armed. It is important to stress in this matter the building of the *reduit*, the inner mountainous defenses that the Swiss believed would allow for them to survive, together with what can only be termed the citizen militarization of society. Compulsory military service involved virtually the whole male population, giving Switzerland one of the largest armies in Europe. One consequence of this was a generalized mixing within society, among Italian, German, and French ethnicities and among different religions, as everyone had been required to serve in the military. Another was being exposed to a standardized training curriculum that socialized everyone to

19 Interview with Jacob Tanner, University of Zürich. Language nearly became politicized during the First World War especially by some German-speakers. This did not last long and actually helped reaffirm Swiss identity.

20 Interview with Wolf Linder, University of Bern.

21 Steinberg 1996, p. 97.

embrace a common national identity and work for the collective national interest.[22] Moreover, compulsory military service facilitated network building, particularly among the elites, that cut across nominal cultural differences.[23]

One respondent summarized the Swiss case like this: "I think this has a lot to do with the small country thing.... We try to be resilient.... We have to adapt." He added quickly that what makes the Swiss case exceptional "is really this heterogeneity, and then this institutional setup of consociationalism, of power sharing, of strong cantons, of oversized party governments ... this makes it a very consensus-driven system."[24] Put differently, due to its considerable exposure and vulnerability and in spite of its nominal cultural heterogeneity, Switzerland possesses thick and resilient institutions.

The Institutional Portfolio

What then is the nature of the modern Swiss social formation, both in itself and insofar as it affects economic life? The central contention here is simple: while homogeneity does not guarantee consensus, as the Irish case illustrates, nor does ethnic diversity necessarily prohibit it. Consensus was achieved in Switzerland as the result of a strikingly unique and very thick institutional portfolio. This can be explained by considering federalism and direct democracy, before turning to the structure of the economy.

We have seen that Swiss history has effectively been that of organized consociationalism, of bargains between the elites of different regions in the face of external threats. Since the adoption of the Swiss Federal Constitution in 1848, Switzerland has been an independent federal democracy with a very high degree of power sharing compared to other advanced countries. Citizens are subject to three legal jurisdictions—communal, cantonal, and federal—with a strong element of direct democracy that allows citizens to propose new laws and to challenge proposed legislation through referenda. As a result, "Swiss federalism spreads a denser net of political institutions over the body politic than any other system in Europe."[25] Because Swiss federalism was designed to accommodate cultural differences within the population it also increases the perception of legitimacy and feeling of trust in the political system.[26]

The practices of communes vary enormously, but they have vital general significance in that acceptance by a commune is a necessary step on the road to Swiss citizenship. Moreover, the cantons and federal government each reg-

---

22 Interview with Wolf Linder, University of Bern.
23 We thank Fabio Wasserfallen, University of Zürich, for this insight.
24 Interview with Fabio Wasserfallen, University of Zürich.
25 Steinberg 1996, p. 87.
26 Christoffersen et al. 2014, pp. 147–49; Swenden 2006, chap. 3.

ulate different aspects of a wide variety of policies, and the cantons are generally responsible for implementing federal laws and regulations. For more than a century, for instance, there have been a number of so-called canton conferences that facilitate cooperation among the cantons in financial, fiscal, educational, and health policy areas. Despite recent tendencies, this is still not a centralized political system, rather quite the opposite. As one respondent told us, "France is nonexistent in Switzerland!"[27]

The cantons enjoy more fiscal autonomy than regions in any other West European country, having, for instance, their own rates for income and property taxes. In particular, income taxation is primarily a cantonal rather than a federal responsibility.[28] Furthermore, almost all cantons use fiscal referenda—another manifestation of direct democracy—to approve expenditures for major projects above a certain spending limit. This is a key element of blocking power. One result is that if the government wants to spend more money on a project than the majority of voters want, then it tends to scale back its proposal in order to gain referendum approval. The danger, of course, is twofold. First, through referenda citizens might be inclined to approve greater spending while limiting taxes thus generating deficits in the long run. Second, under these conditions legislators advocating fiscal restraint run the risk of being voted out of office. The solution to this problem has been "debt brakes," discussed in further detail later in this chapter, created first by the cantons and adopted later at the federal level. The combination of fiscal referenda, debt brakes, and cantonal tax autonomy has enabled cantons to maintain fiscal stability. In this regard, federalism and direct democracy have been very successful in encouraging prudent fiscal behavior.[29] Importantly, tax competition within Switzerland is attenuated through cooperation in regional networks of finance ministers.[30]

What about institutions at the federal level? The parliament in Bern has two houses. The lower house, the National Council, has 200 seats divided among cantons, with elections for parties being based on proportional representation. The upper house, the Council of States, gives two seats to every canton, and a single seat to half cantons, with most elections here coming as the result of majority voting. The parliament is best described as a "militia parliament" for most members are part-timers. As a result, parliamentary administration has been historically weak, making members heavily dependent on the knowledge of experts and the pressures from interest associations.[31]

27 Interview with Andreas Huber, CCFM.

28 Interview with Andreas Huber, CCFM. See also Christoffersen et al. (2014, pp. 149–53) and Swenden (2006, pp. 121–24).

29 Christoffersen et al. 2014, chap. 6; Kirchgässner 2013.

30 Gilardi and Wasserfallen 2014.

31 Kriesi and Trechsel 2008, p. 69.

The use of expert commissions is widespread. The sense of an elite-driven technocratic politics is massively reenforced when one turns to the Federal Council, that is, to the apparatus that rules the country. The Council is made up of seven members elected by an Assembly of the two houses of the parliament. Very considerable care is taken here to balance linguistic, regional, religious, and, more recently, gender representation while respecting the proportions of the national vote. The postwar era is perhaps best characterized as a permanent "Grand Agreement" insofar as the Council has routinely included members of the four main political parties (Liberals, Christian Democrats, Social Democrats, and the Swiss People's Party, previously a centrist Protestant party but now a radical right nationalist party).[32] Each member of the Council heads a Ministry, but civil servants do most of the work. The ethos of the Council has been consensual and private, although the arrival of the populist People's Party in the Council has changed this somewhat.

Politics may be elite-driven and technocratic, but they are heavily constrained by the principles of direct democracy.[33] Unlike nearly all other European countries, review of federal legislation is a matter for the people (via referenda) not the Swiss Federal Court, which does, however, have the power of judicial review over cantonal law.[34] Furthermore, various forms of referenda help keep more extreme forms of legislation from being either proposed or enacted in the first place. So too does the fact that the Swiss vote at least four times a year on a variety of issues, including whatever referenda there may be.[35] But in the largest sense what matters about direct democracy is less the holding of referenda than the threat that they might be held, something which is always in the back of policymakers' minds. Proposed legislation is circulated through an extensive review process to relevant social and economic groups so that it can be vetted in varied venues before it is actually passed, precisely to avoid conflict in public and rejection by referenda. This is one of the most important means for ensuring consensus in policymaking. By the same token, the frequent use of expert commissions, as in Denmark, in the initial preparation of a bill is also intended partly to ensure consensus once it moves to parliamentary consideration and partly to avoid possible referenda problems later.[36] As Arend Lijphart famously observed, the political life of majoritarian systems like Britain is very different from consensual systems like Switzerland. The former are able to push through legislation dis-

32 Christoffersen et al. 2014, pp. 142, 161; Swenden 2006, p. 260.

33 Interview with Klaus Armingeon, University of Bern. See also Swenden (2006, pp. 260–63).

34 Swenden 2006, p. 88.

35 There are regularly four votes a year on national issues and additional votes at the cantonal and communal levels.

36 Christoffersen et al. 2014, pp. 161, 290; Steinberg 1996, pp. 102–13.

liked by most people in a country and all too prone to economic irresponsibility so as to gain electoral advantage.[37] Switzerland is totally different. There is something to the view that a system containing so many veto points would hamper legislation or slow policymaking to a crawl. But several of our interviewees insisted that this was not usually a problem. Here is one typical comment:

> I mean, we do have all these veto positions, which makes it difficult, but we have also techniques, some formal, some informal, to escape from deadlocks, and with the two chambers it really works.... [T]o be able to make compromises, to learn and to adapt and to reform and reshape projects, it was a necessity always in Switzerland because of the different languages of the different regions.[38]

So the workings of institutions facilitate learning and adaptability—that is, resilience—and are backed by the political culture, which includes a very high level of trust and legitimacy in those institutions, the people who run them, and the expert technocrats upon whom they rely.[39]

But an additional factor is at work, namely the debt brake rule that has ensured fiscal stability. The rule requires the federal government to maintain a balanced budget while allowing for cyclical developments. In other words, spending can exceed revenues to a degree during lean economic times but the gap must be reduced during more robust times. Their purpose is to limit deficits.[40] Like Denmark's automatic stabilizers, the debt brake is an important element in organizational capacity. The rule can best be seen as Keynesianism properly understood—deficit spending in times of economic recession with repayment of debts when surpluses are available, relying on an enlightened political elite to behave in a fiscally prudent manner. In Switzerland it seems that the citizenry values economic responsibility. There may be something culturally Swiss here, an essential conservatism present particularly in rural areas characterized by an embrace of classical economic liberalism. Yet it is more likely that this sense of responsibility results, as any reader of Tocqueville would expect, from ruling oneself at the local level and experiencing the consequences of one's own actions—an experience much more likely in a federal system such as Switzerland's than in majoritarian systems elsewhere. Put differently, the institutions of direct democracy have helped encourage economic responsibility in Switzerland. Indeed, thanks to the voter-approved debt brake, low levels of debt have characterized both cantonal and federal

37 Lijphart 1999.
38 Interview with Wolf Linder, University of Bern. See also Swenden (2006, pp. 221–24).
39 Christoffersen et al. 2014, pp. 136, 174–79.
40 For further details, see Kirchgässner (2013) and OECD (2009b, p. 32).

governments, and federal debt has declined in recent years despite the fiscal burdens of the financial crisis.[41]

Fiscal stability has been complemented by the Swiss National Bank's stabilizing monetary policy. Since its founding in 1907 the SNB has been an extension of Swiss federalism. Unlike most national banks, the SNB is not a state bank per se. Rather it has shareholders, mainly the cantons and other public bodies but also a few private shareholders. The government appoints its three directors—its Board of Governors—who meet monthly with an advisory board to discuss policy. The advisory board, the *Bankrat*, consists typically of people from business, law, academia, and politics. However, the directors are not obliged to follow the advisory board's recommendations. This system is an extension of the generally inclusive Swiss system of consultation with a wide group of interests.[42] That said, the SNB is ultimately independent and prohibited by the Swiss National Bank Act from responding to outside political pressure. It also provides organizational capacity for handling monetary policy because—unlike its Danish counterpart, which has long pegged the krone to the euro, or its Irish counterpart, which uses the euro—the SNB pegged the Swiss franc to the euro only from 2011 until 2015. The handling of monetary policy has been less constrained.

Corporatism matters as much as federalism and consociationalism. Business associations are well organized. For example, the peak association, *Economiesuisse*, is the umbrella association representing the Swiss economy and that includes one hundred trade associations. One of these is the Swiss Bankers Association (SBA), which has 360 institutional members (banks, auditing firms, securities dealers), represents the interests of its members in dealings with the authorities in Switzerland and abroad, and helps regulate the industry in consultation with the regulatory bodies. In addition there are eleven other associations representing various interests in the financial services industry.[43] While it is the case that labor is represented at key meeting places, the Swiss corporatist model is not social democratic in a Scandinavian sense. Rather the Swiss have what Peter Katzenstein called "liberal corporatism" fundamentally based on consultation and agreement between the layers of the state and business interests with labor being a weak partner in most negotiations, scarcely a surprise insofar as the left is much weaker in Switzerland than in Denmark.[44] The welfare system is less developed, partly because foreign labor has comprised nearly 20 percent of the work force since the early 1970s. Private schemes look after Swiss working-class members quite effec-

---

41 Kirschgässner 2013, p. 1.

42 Steinberg 1996, pp. 201–2; interview with Andreas Huber, CCFM. See also http://www.snb.ch/de/iabout/snb/bodies/id/snb_bodies_council.

43 Swiss Bankers Association 2010, pp. 28–29.

44 Katzenstein 1984; Christoffersen et al. 2014, pp. 143–46.

tively. Strikes are rare, and the interests of Swiss members of the working class are carefully taken care of. There is little industrial policy and instead a more straightforward appreciation of market forces—to which the highly educated Swiss labor force has been able to adapt. But there is one feature missing from the model of liberal corporatism drawn by Katzenstein. The Swiss economy is highly liberal in its external orientation and in its activities abroad, but it has been extremely protectionist domestically, notably in regard to agriculture.[45]

The classic point that we have made about countries lacking physical size and resource endowments is that of their need to participate in larger markets. Openness is required in order to allow the specialization that would be impossible inside a small and protected market. Switzerland is exemplary in this regard. First, the Swiss have created significant multinational companies, specializing in banking, watches, chocolate, chemicals, and drugs. In 2014 Switzerland ranked eighth in the world in terms of its share of Fortune Global 500 companies.[46] The country has more of these companies per capita than Germany, France, the United States, or Japan.[47] Second, Switzerland has provided a home for foreign companies due to its attractive tax regime. Third, the extent to which the Swiss economy depends upon the immigration of skilled labor is not sufficiently appreciated. Many of the multinationals based in Switzerland are now headed by foreigners, quite often American, while academics from Germany are heavily represented in the university system. Moreover, the Swiss have manipulated immigration policy like a safety valve to ease unemployment when it is high and recruit labor when it is low.[48]

Detailed consideration of a single sector, that of finance, can flesh out these generalizations—a sensible move in any case given that the crisis that affected Switzerland after 2008 derived from problems in banking. The Swiss financial sector is one of the largest in the world relative to the size of the overall economy.[49] Bluntly, "the financial sector is the cornerstone of the Swiss national economy," and its added value to the economy has risen steadily since 1990, primarily as a result of banking.[50] When the financial crisis hit in 2008, financial services, including banking but also insurance, brokerage, accounting, and credit cards, contributed nearly 12 percent to Swiss GDP—compared to about 5 percent in France, Germany, and the United States, and 9 percent in Britain.[51] Banking alone contributed 7.6 percent to GDP. Nearly

45 Interview with Klaus Armingeon, University of Bern.
46 Stats Monkey 2015.
47 Breiding 2013, p. 7.
48 Interviews with Klaus Armingeon, University of Bern; Jacob Tanner, University of Zürich.
49 Christoffersen et al. 2014, p. 124.
50 Federal Department of Finance 2010.
51 Breiding 2013, p. 126.

6 percent of all Swiss workers were employed in financial services—4.1 percent of them in banking.[52] Furthermore, the asset value of all Swiss banks combined by the end of 2008 was equivalent to nearly 600 percent of GDP, while UBS and Credit Suisse's assets by themselves were equivalent to 355 percent of GDP![53]

There were several reasons why Swiss banks became world leaders, especially in wealth management. First, Switzerland's small domestic market meant that its banks could grow only by tapping foreign markets and cross-border asset management.[54] Hence, much Swiss private banking was offshore: during the crisis it accounted for 26 percent ($2.2 trillion) of all the world's offshore privately managed assets—twice as much as its closest international competitors.[55] Second, Swiss banks managed their accounts with unprecedented discretion.[56] The federal 1934 Banking Secrecy Law ensured that the identity and account information of bank clients would be protected—something the vast majority of citizens believed in ever since.[57] Third, the SNB had kept inflation under control for decades thereby providing a refuge for international investors' money as needed. Furthermore, fiscal stability, facilitated by the debt brake rule, federalism, and direct democracy, helped maintain a strong currency.[58] Fourth, for institutional reasons noted earlier, the Swiss political system is pragmatic, predictable, and conservative. This involves an arms-length approach to regulation, including much self-regulation in banking and finance, which is consistent with Swiss liberalism.[59] This is made possible as well by the fact that Switzerland is not a member of the EU or the Eurozone, and thus not obliged to conform to their regulations.[60] Finally, increased global competition caused some Swiss banks to expand. To that end UBS was created in 1998 by the merger of two other banks. Two years later it acquired the U.S. brokerage firm, PaineWebber, which vastly increased its business in the American market. By 2003 UBS was the fourth-

---

52 Swiss Bankers Association 2010, pp. 13–16.

53 OECD 2010, 2009b, pp. 32, 59.

54 Federal Department of Finance 2010.

55 FINMA 2009, p. 36; Swissinfo.ch 2014.

56 Interview with Wolf Linder, University of Bern.

57 Low Tax 2015. In 2009, however, responding to EU pressure, Switzerland loosened its notoriously opaque rules on bank secrecy.

58 Breiding 2013, pp. 135–36; Christoffersen et al. 2014, pp. 4, 127; Jordan 2012; Swiss Bankers Association 2010, p. 17.

59 Banking self-regulation has two parts. Nowadays, under "autonomous self-regulation" the SBA passes codes of conduct on its own initiative, which the state recognizes and enforces. Under "mandatory self-regulation" the state requires the banks to establish self-regulatory rules governing their conduct, such as anti–money laundering rules (OECD 2009b, p. 79; Swiss Bankers Association 2010, pp. 60–61).

60 Christoffersen et al. 2014, chaps. 5 and 7.

largest bank in the world, envisioned by its leader, Marcel Ospel, as one of the world's great investment banks.[61]

Switzerland is one of the richest countries in the world, but that is not to say that it is without challenges. The 1970s were especially difficult, as the strong franc made it difficult for domestic industry to survive. That crisis was surmounted by exporting migrant labor, outsourcing, and seeking innovation in threatened industries such as watchmaking, largely funded by Swiss banks acting partly in service to the national interest (much like the Danish pension fund, ATP, during Denmark's financial crisis). While consensus and cooperation remained pronounced, the ways in which this had happened changed during the thirty years leading up to the financial crisis. The pressures of Europeanization gave rise to a shift in the balance of power among political parties, with the People's Party moving to the far right and gaining influence. A new axis of political conflict emerged—acceptance or not of Europeanization. Corporatism also changed as the interests of domestic and export-oriented industries gradually diverged thanks to economic globalization. Trade unions and employer peak associations are in most cases not as powerful now as they once were. As a result, the informal pre-parliamentary phase of policymaking, which involved consultation with expert commissions, interest groups, and stakeholders, is not quite as crucial in policymaking as it used to be, although it remains important.[62] Finally, the end of the Cold War led to the relative demilitarization of society and, as a result, Swiss firms became less likely to recruit elites from the military. This coupled with the fact that the big banks and other multinational companies were becoming ever more internationalized meant that the economic elite was less firmly rooted in traditional Swiss culture.[63]

Despite all this, Switzerland's thick institutional portfolio remained intact. Administrative institutions were well developed at several levels of government. Politically inclusive checks and balances (e.g., proportional representation, referenda) were in place and guarded against the abuse of political power or the domination of politics by narrow interests, differing from what we saw in Ireland. The civil service and bureaucracy were professionally oriented, well trained, and equipped with considerable expertise, particularly in the SNB. The parliament relied heavily on input from expert commissions and corporatist interest groups. The commissions, the debt brake, and the SNB provided important organizational capacities for macroeconomic management and, as we shall see, crisis management. Negotiation, compromise

---

61 Interview with Fabio Wasserfallen, University of Zürich; FINMA 2009, p. 17; Schubert 2011.

62 Sciarini et al. 2015, chaps. 1–3.

63 Interview with Fabio Wasserfallen, University of Zürich.

and the politics of reciprocal consent were still the norm, as in Denmark. Moreover, the elite dedication to the national interest was still reinforced if not always by military socialization then certainly by their acute awareness of Switzerland's vulnerability to external forces, including Europeanization and global competition. Finally, the level of trust in Swiss institutions was very high and their legitimacy was never in question. These institutions served Switzerland well during the financial crisis. However, the institutional terrain of any country is uneven. Where institutions were thinner they contributed to the Swiss financial crisis in the first place.

Origins of the Crisis

The 2008 financial crisis hit Switzerland hard. The crisis in Denmark and Ireland involved the collapse of housing bubbles, but in Switzerland, where more people rent than own their homes, the problem resulted from the country's two largest banks, UBS and Credit Suisse, investing overseas, particularly in U.S. subprime mortgages.[64] As finance is a central pillar of the Swiss economy, crisis experienced by its two biggest banks posed systemic threats to the financial system and the economy in general.[65] Hence, observers argue that Switzerland's financial crisis was just as severe as that in other countries, even though its housing market did not collapse.[66]

The seeds of trouble were already being sown in the 1980s. First, large institutional investors aggressively brought pressure to bear on Swiss banks to increase their returns, leading banks to begin making riskier investments. As a result, in 2005 UBS established a subsidiary hedge fund, Dillon Read Capital Management (DRCM). Second, Swiss banks also began to shift from a partnership model to a corporate stockholder model, which insulated directors and top managers from financial liability were the firm to get into trouble. In 1900 there were 700 Swiss banks organized on the partnership model; by 2008 there were a little over a dozen.[67] This shift encouraged managers to take more investment risks.[68] In light of the crisis, one former UBS executive lamented, "We should make investment banks partnerships again. Then they would think twice, three times, and four times before they would do [things that got them into trouble]."[69] Third, banks started hiring people from abroad

64 The Swiss toughened domestic mortgage lending regulations following a domestic housing market crisis in the early 1990s, which helped them avoid a housing bubble in the 2000s (OECD 2009b, chap. 3).

65 Commission of Experts 2010, p. 14.

66 Porten et al. 2009.

67 Breiding 2013, pp. 133, 143–45.

68 Breiding 2013, p. 133.

69 Breiding 2013, p. 133; interview with former Managing Director, UBS.

who were less interested in conservative wealth management than the more lucrative if riskier investments then coming into vogue—mortgage-backed securities, collateralized debt obligations, and credit default swaps. Furthermore, because the traditional military networks for elite recruitment were weakening, newly hired Swiss managers were less likely to have experience in the military, where they would have developed some sense of serving the nation; it became more likely that they would operate in their own self-interest, making money by dealing in risky investments.[70]

The upshot was that the large Swiss banks in general began moving into riskier investments. For instance, Marcel Ospel bought a cutting-edge Chicago derivatives boutique for UBS. He and other top managers encouraged more aggressive investment banking. At one point Ospel complained in a senior leadership meeting that UBS was moving too slowly in this area—"growing cobwebs," as he put it. According to a participant at that meeting, "If you hear the chairman say something like that, you say, 'Okay, then lets rumble! Let's do something about it.'"[71] Accordingly, banks started borrowing heavily to leverage these investments. According to the Swiss Financial Market Supervisory Authority (FINMA), by 2008 "the large Swiss banks, primarily UBS, had extremely low capital bases and extremely high levels of debt both in absolute terms and by international comparison." UBS and Credit Suisse borrowed these vast sums of money from two sources. One was internal from the traditionally conservative wealth management side of their own organizations. The other was the interbank lending market. As a result, UBS and Credit Suisse acquired large positions in the U.S. securitized residential mortgage market, whose collapse triggered the world financial crisis.[72] UBS was so highly rated that it could get money short-term at very cheap rates, particularly given the vast amount of money available in international credit markets. "People would throw money at us," said one former UBS manager.[73] This made it particularly easy to engage in far more speculative and risky investments than had been the case previously when the banks were primarily in the wealth management business. Part of the risk was that if it suddenly became difficult or expensive to borrow, then refinancing the banks' short-term debt would be hard. Prophetically, as early as 2002 UBS risk managers in Zürich worried that the bank's investments in the U.S. mortgage market—$20 billion by then—were going to be hard to unload if the housing market crashed.[74]

70 Interviews with Wolf Linder, University of Bern; Georg Kris, University of Basel; Klaus Armingeon, University of Bern; Jacob Tanner, University of Zürich.

71 Interview with former Managing Director, UBS.

72 FINMA 2009, pp. 14, 27, 35; OECD 2009b, chap. 3.

73 Interview with former Managing Director, UBS.

74 Schubert 2011.

Risk-taking was enabled by the fact that the Swiss authorities regulated the banks with a light touch—lightened even more in the late twentieth century thanks to neoliberalism.[75] This meant that banks shouldered much responsibility for managing their own affairs, including making sure that they were well capitalized against risk. The Swiss Federal Banking Commission (SFBC) placed great trust in UBS and Credit Suisse. When the SFBC raised concerns with UBS about its exposure in the U.S. mortgage market, the bank told them that it was in good shape—an assurance that SFBC accepted at face value, failing to realize that the figures it was being shown omitted the significant exposure of UBS to the risky derivatives held by DRCM and other off balance sheet operations.[76] According to our interview at the SBA, many people now believe that the SFBC lacked sufficient expertise and organizational capacities to adequately regulate the banks.[77] Like parliament, it was structured as a militia body where only the chairman worked full-time. None of the twenty-five member staff assigned to watch various big banks had comprehensive professional experience in the financial sector. Moreover, the SFBC had relied on bank self-regulation for a long time. A subsequent investigation into the crisis confirmed that SFBC relied too much on UBS's own internal analysis.[78] However, investigators added that the conservative nature of the Swiss political system was also to blame:

> The SFBC thus underestimated the risks arising from the deficiencies identified and as a result had too little power in implementing its requirements. In the deregulated environment of the time, a heavy crackdown would most likely have been construed as bureaucratic, anti-competitive and detached from reality and would not have received political backing.[79]

This is not to say that the SFBC simply sat on its hands and did nothing. It imposed tougher capitalization requirements on Swiss banks following a domestic credit crisis in the 1990s and then again in 2007 after new international guidelines (the Basel II Capital Accord) were passed. This was not a popular move in Switzerland particularly in the face of growing neoliberal worries about over-regulation. But the Swiss requirements were still stricter than the international guidelines.[80]

The banks may not have had enough expertise either. One indication was that they thought they were not overexposed in the subprime market.

75 Breiding 2013, pp. 143–44. Christoffersen et al. (2014, chap. 5) discuss the general Swiss propensity for arms-length regulation.

76 FINMA 2009.

77 Interview with Martin Hess, SBA.

78 FINMA 2009, pp. 19–22, 38, 48.

79 FINMA 2009, p. 39.

80 FINMA 2009, p. 18.

Another was that after the crisis when the state's crisis management team asked UBS how much the bank's toxic assets were worth, it took several days for UBS to provide an answer, a surprise to the team insofar as it suggested that UBS actually did not know.[81] Why might expertise at UBS be inadequate? In addition to the new recruitment protocol noted earlier, promotions were still often based on seniority and social or military connections rather than achievement or expertise.[82] Compounding the problem, ironically, was the fact that UBS's risk management system, which was reputedly among the best in the world, not only gave the impression that it was a risk-averse bank but also created considerable hubris inside it. People never questioned their investment and risk assessment models. Even the quantitative risk modelers believed that their models were accurate. Everyone suffered from risk-management groupthink. Besides, people assumed that simply because the bank's balance sheet was so huge they were more or less immune from serious trouble.[83] Even when warning signs were spotted they were not always made known to management. A UBS report to stockholders in March 2008 and a subsequent report to the SFBC acknowledged that there were weaknesses in reporting subprime risk exposure to senior management, inadequate control of the bank's trading in securitized assets, and insufficient attention by senior managers to the risks involved.[84]

It is worth mentioning that this form of groupthink was much more narrowly circumscribed than it was in either Denmark or Ireland. But it was related, as in these other cases, to the country's more general historical development. Had it not been for Switzerland's relatively thin regulatory institutions, which relied heavily on self-regulation not just in finance but also in many sectors of the economy, regulators might have shown greater skepticism to the banks' assessment of their risks. Moreover, as discussed later, the Swiss viewed their banking system with a certain amount of awe, assuming that it could do little wrong because it was just about the backbone of the economy. Less awe and more skepticism might have militated against such overconfidence in the banks' risk assessment claims.

Serious strains on the Swiss financial system began to appear in 2007 as the value of asset-backed securities based on U.S. subprime mortgages deteriorated. In May 2007 UBS announced that it was dismantling DRCM, which had suffered big losses in that market. A few months later Credit Suisse reported that it might suffer similar losses. When Lehman Brothers went

81 Interview with Peter Siegenthaler, former Head of Federal Finance Administration and Chair TBTF. A former Managing Director at UBS said that it actually took the bank about a year to figure out what their losses were.

82 Breiding 2013, p. 143.

83 Interview with former Managing Director, UBS. See also FINMA (2009, p. 21).

84 OECD 2009b, p. 63.

bankrupt in 2008 and credit markets froze, it was revealed that UBS and Credit Suisse had invested billions of dollars in toxic U.S. subprime mortgages. Both suddenly faced potentially catastrophic losses. The crisis was worse for UBS, which heading into the crisis had $2 trillion of highly leveraged assets on its books—its debt-to-equity ratio was more than 40 to 1. In the third quarter of 2008 alone, investors withdrew nearly $75 billion of assets from UBS. Eventually, Credit Suisse's losses were less than UBS's in part because it had realized late in 2006 that it was heavily exposed in the subprime derivatives market and quietly began to sell these assets. Nevertheless, by 2010 asset write-downs for these banks relative to the size of their capital base were larger than that of most of their U.S. and EU peers who survived the crisis. In the end, Swiss bank write-downs were larger as a percentage of GDP than that of any other OECD country except Iceland, which went broke![85] Switzerland's smaller banks were sound, having avoided these risky investments.[86]

The Swiss have long held their banks in very high regard—not just as places to do business but also as pillars of society. This was likely another reason why the regulators trusted them. So when the crisis hit, people were outraged. They launched a petition, which stated in part that "the standing and credibility of Switzerland as a democratic nation are compromised and imperiled," thanks to the banks' bad behavior. In other words, not just the banks but also Swiss national identity had suffered a serious blow.[87] In addition to raising red flags about the dominance of finance, and especially UBS and Credit Suisse, the crisis exposed thin spots in Switzerland's institutions: insufficient expertise among the militia regulators and thin organizational capacities insofar as arms-length regulation was concerned. Furthermore, big banks had nearly all abandoned the partnership model for the corporate alternative, and everyone, including the regulators, had trusted the banks as national paragons of social responsibility. The question then was how to handle the situation. At this point the thickness of Switzerland's institutions shifted into gear. But before explaining this, we need to review the crisis management package.

Crisis Response: Bank Bailouts

When the crisis hit the immediate problem was that UBS and—though to a lesser extent—Credit Suisse were seriously undercapitalized and loaded with toxic assets, especially from the U.S. subprime mortgage market. The great

---

85 OECD 2009b, pp. 11, 58, 62.
86 FINMA 2009, p. 15; Gow 2008.
87 De Quetteville 2008.

fear was that these banks were so big that they posed a systemic risk to the rest of the economy. In short, the banks were deemed too big to fail. There was no choice but to rescue them.[88]

Crisis management had a private and public component. On the private side, Credit Suisse turned down an offer from the government for assistance to restore liquidity in favor of CHF 10 billion ($9.4 billion) from Qatar's sovereign wealth fund and the Olayan Group, a long-standing shareholder. Similarly, UBS recapitalized in 2007 and 2008, eventually selling an 8 percent share of the company to the Singapore Investment Corporation. But given the size of its losses, this was not enough to resolve its capitalization shortfall.[89] It tried to attract additional private investors but failed.[90] On the public side, the state went into action very quickly. It started in 2008 with the government providing a CHF 6 billion ($5.6 billion) capital injection to UBS in exchange for a 9.3 percent stake in the firm. At about the same time the SNB established a special purpose company—StabFund—a so-called "bad bank" with a maximum life of eight years (extendable to twelve). StabFund would take over UBS's illiquid toxic assets to reduce the firm's liabilities, mitigate its liquidity problems, and restore its health. After things settled down, Stab-Fund would try to sell those assets with the SNB taking the first $1 billion of any profits from the sale and then splitting the rest evenly with UBS.[91] Stab-Fund was prepared to spend up to $60 billion—an enormous amount about the size of the Swiss federal budget—but ended up only spending $38.7 billion. UBS was forced to take a 10 percent loss on the value of the assets transferred to StabFund—a haircut designed to reduce the risks of moral hazard later. In effect, this was a loan from the SNB that StabFund would repay with interest. In addition, if the loan was not repaid fully upon termination of StabFund, the SNB would receive partial compensation in UBS equity shares.[92] The amount of money involved in purchasing UBS assets was huge, even for the central bank, and so it quietly borrowed $14 billion from the U.S. Federal Reserve Bank through its existing swap lines with the Fed. The SNB guaranteed that it would provide more later if that proved to be necessary.[93]

---

88 Breiding 2013, p. 128.

89 Swiss RE, a large insurance company, also invested in the U.S. subprime market, required capital injections and received them from Berkshire-Hathaway (OECD 2009b, pp. 63–64).

90 Breiding 2013, p. 149.

91 Gow 2008.

92 Kirkup and Waterfield 2008; OECD 2009b, pp. 67–68; Swiss Bankers Association 2010, pp. 9, 20.

93 Interviews with Aymo Brunetti, University of Bern; Peter Siegenthaler, former Head of Federal Finance Administration and Chair TBTF; former Managing Director, UBS. See also U.S. Federal Reserve (2015, p. 37).

Switzerland also took steps to attenuate the recessionary effects of the international financial crisis. First, in August 2007 when interbank lending was just beginning to tighten, the SNB was the first central bank to provide more liquidity to the banks through repo auctions.[94] In 2008 it slashed overnight interest rates nearly to zero. The fact that the franc was not pegged to the euro gave the SNB the organizational capacity to do so. Second, Keynesian automatic stabilizers kicked in, another element of organizational capacity made available thanks to the debt brake rules. Third, Parliament passed economic stimulus packages in 2008 and 2009 worth CHF 2 billion ($1.8 billion). Fourth, in March 2009 the SNB purchased foreign currency to relieve upward pressure on the Swiss franc, which stemmed from the demand for Swiss francs by foreigners seeking a safe haven for their money. The strong franc was hurting Swiss exports. This move was another reflection of the bank's thick organizational capacities, enabled this time by its long-standing history of supporting a strong currency. Further, in August 2011 the SNB dramatically increased Swiss franc liquidity to combat the strong franc. Finally, in September 2011 the bank set a minimum exchange rate for the Swiss franc against the euro, again to defend against an overvalued Swiss franc.[95] Such adjustments were revealing—and signs of Switzerland's institutional resilience during the crisis.

In November 2009 the Federal Council established the Commission of Experts—more commonly known as the Too Big To Fail Commission (TBTF). As its formal name indicated, this was a group of experts in financial matters. Its mandate was to define what too big to fail meant in Switzerland; analyze the benefits of such large companies to the economy and the consequences if one of them failed; and determine how the risks and consequences of failure could be minimized.[96] Its focus was largely on the systemic risk that the big banks posed for the economy, but analysis was also offered on the vexed question as to whether their sheer size meant that they enjoyed an implicit state guarantee if they got into trouble again. The commission made two broad sets of recommendations. First, the bigger banks needed better capitalization, less leverage, better liquidity, more risk diversification, and other buffers on their balance sheets to avoid systemic risk. Second, they should be

---

94 OECD 2009b, chap. 2. The repo market is one in which one bank buys securities from another bank agreeing that the first bank will repurchase them later with an interest payment. This was another way the SNB could lend money to the banks. The SNB's policy all along was to accept only very high-quality securities in its repo agreements. This created robust interbank lending that kept interbank credit lines open throughout the Swiss crisis (Danthine 2011).

95 Danthine 2011; Jordan 2012, 2014; OECD 2009b, p. 29; Porten et al. 2009; Swiss Bankers Association 2010, p. 9.

96 Commission of Experts 2010.

organized so that it would be easier to dismantle them if they got into trouble, notably by separating their systemic business from other types of business.[97] The government decreed that a second expert commission would later review whatever policies had been implemented as a result of the TBTF recommendations to see if they were working as intended, and to make further recommendations as necessary.[98]

In the end, Switzerland's crisis response worked. By 2010 Credit Suisse and UBS were again profitable and among the top twenty private banks in the world. UBS had become the world's largest private bank, managing $1.7 trillion for its clients. Although not a goal of the crisis response, UBS had market capitalization equivalent to 12 percent of Swiss GDP.[99] A former UBS manager summarized the bailout's effect: "In the end it was a good package.... We needed it; they gave it to us."[100] Furthermore, the banks' capitalization ratios were now higher than prevailing international standards, which put them on a safer financial footing than before the crisis. Even so, the OECD worried that they were still among the most systemically important financial institutions worldwide and probably unable to absorb major losses without help. Additionally, the government sold its stake in UBS for a CHF 1.2 billion ($1.1 billion) profit. The Swiss recession was less severe and ended faster than anywhere else hit by the crisis.[101] Finally, in November 2013 the SNB sold StabFund to UBS for a $3.8 billion profit, not including the $1.6 billion in interest it had already made on the initial loan to UBS.

Switzerland dealt with the crisis effectively. Swiss resilience is explicable in terms of the thickness of its institutions. Switzerland has long been vulnerable to global competition, and this has taught the Swiss to cope with good times as well as bad. Some claim that the SNB is "the best-managed central bank in the world"; certainly it was prepared to take decisive steps when necessary.[102] Furthermore, according to the OECD, "Past prudent fiscal policy provided room to implement fiscal stimulus in 2009 and 2010."[103] This was due in part to the debt brake rule, which, as noted, had kept the federal budget almost perfectly balanced during the years preceding the crisis and kept public debt much lower than in the Eurozone, Britain, or the United States.[104]

---

97 Interview with Peter Siegenthaler, former Head of Federal Finance Administration and Chair TBTF; Commission of Experts 2010.

98 Federal Department of Finance 2010; OECD 2009b, p. 71.

99 FINMA 2009, p. 36; OECD 2009b, pp. 32, 59; OECD 2010; Swissinfo.ch 2014.

100 Interview with former Managing Director, UBS.

101 Danthine 2011; OECD 2011, pp. 51–52; Swiss Bankers Association 2010, p. 20.

102 *Newsweek* 2014.

103 OECD 2010.

104 Interview with Andreas Huber, CCFM.

Third, unemployment remained relatively low thanks to the combined effect of Switzerland's very low level of employment protection and its use of immigration policy—another important organizational capacity the Swiss had used routinely in the past.[105] But the process by which Switzerland responded to the crisis with such resilience is complicated and requires explanation.

Crisis Response: The Process

Managing the crisis in Switzerland was largely a matter of insulated experts making decisions that eventually received widespread support. Considerable planning for a major bank failure had already happened by the time the crisis hit, which helped facilitate a resilient response from decision-makers. But in contrast to Ireland, whose insulated process was dominated by politicians, in Switzerland it was experts in whom everyone was confident who dominated the process, thereby infusing crisis management with great legitimacy.

Our previous cases showed that beyond simply creating a particular institutional portfolio, crisis management was influenced by taken-for-granted assumptions and cognitive frameworks. The same was true in Switzerland. First, decision-making was automatically entrusted to experts, particularly those in the Swiss National Bank. The Swiss have long held professionally trained experts in the civil service in high regard not only because most politicians are part-timers but also, as with politics in general, because everybody knows that political decisions may be subjected to referenda later if they trigger significant political dissatisfaction. As a result, people trust technocrats. Second, the decisions taken both in the immediate moment of the crisis and thereafter were endorsed by virtually all stakeholders as well as by the general public—a clear manifestation of the long-standing consensus-oriented nature of Swiss culture and politics. The fact that the Swiss National Bank took it upon itself to educate the public about its crisis management strategy showed how seriously technocrats take the need for consensus. Third, much of this was indicative of Switzerland's history of national solidarity in the face of vulnerability, especially insofar as in emergency situations the need for rapid and effective decision-making is recognized and therefore turned over to a small handful of experts. Finally, once the crisis had passed, representatives from a wider circle of stakeholders were brought into important national commissions, established to ensure that nothing like this would happen again—a move reflecting Switzerland's corporatist and consociational institutional structure as well as people's willingness to learn in ways that would facilitate adaptation going forward, much as it had earlier in ways that helped prepare them for the crisis at hand.

105 Baur et al. 2013.

INSTITUTIONAL PREPARATION

During the 1990s Switzerland experienced a real estate bubble that made people wonder what would happen to big banks if real estate prices suddenly fell sharply. As a result, SFBC and the SNB planned what to do if something like this caused a big bank to fail; they delivered their plan to the Federal Department of Finance in 1998. A few years later, concerns about Credit Suisse surfaced in the early 2000s when its insurance branch was performing poorly. Coincidentally, the demise in 2002 of Swissair, the national airline, put everyone on notice that a major national champion could fail.[106] So that same year a small group of experts from the SFBC and elsewhere began to consider what to do in the event of a major bank failure. They discussed their thinking in summer 2006 with UBS and Credit Suisse, and in January 2007 created a team of top officials from SSFBC, SNB, and the Federal Finance Administration, which launched projects to evaluate risks and rescue scenarios at large banks. The scenarios involved private as well as government assistance and yielded blueprints for future crisis management should they be needed.[107]

Peter Siegenthaler, who was part of the team, told us that as a result of their efforts, "We were well prepared" when the financial crisis hit.[108] This was confirmed by a leading analyst during the crisis at the Federal Department of Economic Affairs, who said that this planning was "extremely important" in handling the UBS case:

> Luckily, there was a preparation where the government was involved, the [central] bank, and the financial regulation supervision authority. But basically we prepared for a case like UBS. And when it came [the plan] was readymade.[109]

He explained as well that the people involved drew lessons from the ways in which the Swedish government had handled their own financial crisis in the early 1990s by guaranteeing all bank deposits, by creating a bad bank that took over toxic bank debts to be resold later, and by nationalizing troubled banks. Pre-crisis preparation also involved the fortification of Keynesian institutions. Switzerland experienced a severe recession in the 1990s that made the government realize that it needed to revamp the unemployment insurance system and reorganize the public budget, which was then running worrisome deficits. Two institutional changes resulted. First, the federal debt

---

106 Interview with Fabio Wasserfallen, University of Zürich; Georg Kris, University of Basel.

107 FINMA 2009, p. 31.

108 Interview with Peter Siegenthaler, former Head of Federal Finance Administration and Chair TBTF.

109 Interview with Aymo Brunetti, University of Bern.

brake rule was proposed and passed in 2001 by an overwhelming majority of the voters and cantons. Second, automatic stabilizers were reinforced. According to those involved in managing the financial crisis, "This was basically the framework that was in place when the crisis hit. And our argument was to very much let these automatic stabilizers play, and not spend more, except if we would have really been in a depression-like recession."[110] These organizational capacities diminished the impact of the Great Recession.

The point is that as a small vulnerable country, Switzerland was open to learning from past experience, a sure sign of institutional resilience. This is a normal part of Swiss politics.[111] Just as traditional was the fact that this was done by a small, insulated group of experts who were far more pragmatic than ideological.[112] As one interviewee noted, "The elites in this country are a very smart elite, I think. They are not very ideological, and they are very pragmatic, and very rational. So they sit together and say, 'We have a problem, and we have to solve it.' And they [have been] used for that for decades. It's nothing new."[113]

IMMEDIATE CRISIS MANAGEMENT: INSULATED EXPERTS AND THE SNB

When the crisis hit experts were again responsible for much decision-making, particularly during the early stages. Much of it happened in private with few participating. Some people told us that this was in keeping with the fact that the Swiss have tremendous trust in their experts, technocrats, and bureaucrats; this is one reason why their decisions were accepted by politicians and the public. More important, the SNB was always very independent from government and parliament, and the credibility of its leaders and experts was rarely contested. The SNB took the lead in handling the crisis by directing both emergency monetary policy and the bank bailout. During late October 2008 the SNB moved independently and of its own volition to preserve liquidity in the Swiss banking system by engaging in swap agreements with other central banks and cooperating with the European Central Bank to provide Swiss franc liquidity. The size of the U.S. dollar liquidity provision was expanded. The SNB staff gathered information from the Swiss banks, largely to determine what their liquidity situations were, and made suggestions to the three-member Board of Governors, which made all the decisions with complete autonomy from outside forces.[114]

---

110 Interviews with Peter Siegenthaler, former Head of Federal Finance Administration and Chair TBTF; Aymo Brunetti, University of Bern.
   111 Interviews with Wolf Linder, University of Bern.
   112 Interview with former Managing Director, UBS.
   113 Interview with Klaus Armingeon, University of Bern.
   114 Interview with senior official, SNB.

When it came to rescuing UBS, decision-making was again expert based and insulated. As the crisis began to unfold in 2007, the director of the SFBC, head of the SNB, and representatives from the Federal Department of Finance began meeting privately. The Minister of Finance wanted to let a bank go under if necessary to avoid future moral hazard problems. Discussion became more urgent in spring 2008 as the crisis worsened. After the summer holiday the Minister of Finance suffered a heart attack. He was replaced temporarily by his deputy, who was more open-minded about the possibilities of helping the banks and who left preparation of the decisions to the experts. By mid-October 2008 the decision had been made to implement a two-part plan: the government would provide capital injections and the SNB would create StabFund to remove UBS's illiquid assets from its books. The plan had been worked out behind closed doors by a small elite rescue committee consisting of a few top officials from the SNB, SFBC, some of their staff, and three members of the seven-member Federal Council. But the SNB's Governing Board made the final decisions on the StabFund in consultation with their staff and the SFBC. Once done, the package was presented to the government and announced publicly the same day.[115]

Politicians had little input or control over this process thanks to two other institutions that facilitated the country's resilient response. The constitution grants the Federal Council authority to make legislative decisions without parliamentary approval during a national emergency.[116] Similarly, the small parliamentary Finance Committee can approve emergency spending without further parliamentary approval if necessary—which it did in allocating the CHF 6 billion ($5.6 billion) capital injection to UBS. The Finance Committee took this action, however, in consultation with the experts at the SNB, SFBC, and Finance Department—rubber-stamping the experts' plan. But beyond that, the politicians were not involved. The SNB was fully responsible for setting up the StabFund and providing the $60 billion to finance it. The bank's decision required no government approval. Parliament was informed about it only after the fact.[117] Although in typical corporatist fashion the Swiss Business Federation and unions have seats on the SNB's advisory board, which meets monthly, they were never consulted separately during the UBS rescue. A representative from the SBF told us that they did not mind because "this was the proper way to handle the crisis; it [was] not possible to involve more people without causing disturbances" in the financial markets, a point made as well by others in our interviews, and one that underscores the legitimacy the SNB enjoyed.[118]

115 Interview with Peter Siegenthaler, former Head of Federal Finance Administration and Chair TBTF.

116 Interview with Wolf Linder, University of Bern.

117 Interview with senior official, SNB.

118 Interviews with senior official, SBF; Martin Hess, SBA.

Compared to that of Denmark, the Swiss crisis management process was closed and insulated. In Denmark a more inclusive set of voices was involved, either formally or informally, in the discussions, including the views of the Danish Bankers Association. In Switzerland, input from the banks was comparatively limited. They provided information to the rescue committee, notably about the magnitude of their liquidity problems so that the SNB would know how much money the StabFund would need.[119] UBS also helped establish and manage the StabFund. Beyond that, the bank had no influence. "We knew the business, but it was up to the government to decide what to do and how to do it. They were pretty tough."[120] The SBA was not involved.[121] Nor were the cantons, because banking regulation and monetary policy were exclusively the domain of the federal government. The cantons' Conference of Finance Ministers was informed of the UBS stabilization plan only after the decision was made, less to facilitate consensus than as a courtesy so they would not hear about it first in the media. However, they did not mind because they too realized that the situation had to be handled quickly and discretely in order to avoid a run on the bank or a sharp decline in its share price.[122] Indeed, one reason the rescue committee was kept so small was to prevent leaks.[123]

Consensus prevailed most of the time throughout the process. The experts agreed on both the government's capital injections and the SNB's StabFund plan. Furthermore, almost nobody in parliament objected once they were informed of the rescue package. Those who did object were concerned primarily with the amount of money involved rather than with the principle of the plan itself—the CHF 6 billion ($5.6 billion) capital injection was equivalent to about 10 percent of the Swiss federal budget. However, these concerns were laid to rest quickly because the public finances were in good shape, thanks to the debt brake rule, and the Minister of Finance convinced them that a bold move was necessary given how fast the crisis was unfolding. Finally, some of the political parties grumbled about the StabFund plan but realized that because the SNB was a fully independent entity they could not interfere.[124]

To be sure, when the plan was announced publicly there was some concern. Such a massive intervention into the private sector rubbed most Swiss the wrong way given their conventional liberal values. Furthermore, most

119 Peter Siegenthaler, former Head of Federal Finance Administration and Chair TBTF.
120 Interview with former Managing Director, UBS.
121 Interview with Martin Hess, SBA.
122 Interview with Andreas Huber, CCFM.
123 Interview with Martin Hess, SBA.
124 Interviews with senior official, SNB; Peter Siegenthaler, former Head of Federal Finance Administration and Chair TBTF.

people did not understand at first that the SNB would eventually get back at least some of the money the StabFund would spend on the UBS bailout. As a result, the central bank had to do a lot of explaining publicly to clarify the situation and to explain how the plan would operate. Once they understood, most people fell into line perceiving the process to have been legitimate.[125]

It might be surprising how little political opposition there was within the rescue committee, parliament, or even in the long run publicly. Why was this? First, everyone knew this was a crisis and realized, as one economist said, "We are a small state. We have to survive in a very hostile environment."[126] Second, ideology took a back seat to Swiss pragmatism; liberalism was replaced by state intervention. As one respondent explained, "Swiss liberalism is not as clean and clear as we would expect from economics. What happens is typical pragmatic [sic].... Let's forget our principles. Let's survive for the next days and find a solution that works."[127] Several people told us that such pragmatism is rooted deeply in Switzerland's history of small nation-state vulnerability.[128] Third, people trust their experts, especially in a crisis:

> It was clear this is good for the country; this is done by experts. No one is really shouting against it.... [It] is very telling that you have no politicization of the process. You have no real politics involved.... We obviously had people running that really well. And we had like very well-informed, smart people at the SNB who saw the risk, who knew what they were doing, and who did their job.... The politicians basically didn't know anything about it.[129]

Indeed, when really serious economic problems arise, politics is often set aside and the experts take over because the militia parliament does not have the necessary expertise.[130] Not even a potentially cantankerous political party like the populist People's Party raised a fuss over the rescue package.

Despite the closed and insulated nature of crisis management, it was clear from our interviews that Swiss technocrats managing the crisis were not averse to consulting with outside experts. The Ministry of Economy, for instance, did so with an informal advisory commission of academics. This sort of thing is common in Switzerland, as indeed it is in Denmark.[131] But recall that it stands in stark contrast to Ireland, where the secrecy laws prohibited

125 Interview with senior official, SNB.
126 Interview with Klaus Armingeon, University of Bern.
127 Interview with Klaus Armingeon, University of Bern.
128 Interviews with senior official, SBF; former Managing Director, UBS; Klaus Armingeon, University of Bern.
129 Interview with Fabio Wasserfallen, University of Zürich.
130 Interview with Fabio Wasserfallen, University of Zürich.
131 Interview with Aymo Brunetti, University of Bern.

government decision-makers from consulting outside experts during the crisis. So Switzerland enjoyed an element of organizational capacity that was absent in Ireland.

The effect of direct democracy may have also influenced Swiss crisis management. We were told off the record that UBS and Credit Suisse were among the first banks in the world to write down their assets. Our respondent said that some banks in other countries, such as J.P. Morgan and Deutsche Bank, were slower to do so and "miscalculated" the true value of some of their assets. The Anglo Irish Bank actually lied about it, as we noted earlier. He speculated that the Swiss banks were more honest not only because they were under a bright public spotlight but also because they might be subject to the public's wrath through a referendum campaign if they were caught cooking the books or lying—another indication that institutional inclusiveness was an important source of institutional legitimacy. The threat of direct democracy is always in the background and everybody knows it. Besides, he added, the banks "cannot afford to do some monkey business," because the state's experts would catch them.

THE TOO BIG TO FAIL COMMISSION AND BRUNETTI GROUP

Resilience involves not only expert and consensus-oriented decision-making but also learning and flexibility. Nowhere was this more evident in the Swiss case than in the Too Big To Fail Commission. Two things led to its formation. First, there was general recognition that some of the Swiss banks remained very large relative to the size of the Swiss economy. As we learned in one interview, "that's a big problem, a very big one.... Even today UBS and Credit Suisse are too big to be saved by the Swiss government. They are just too big."[132] Secondly, the sheer magnitude of the UBS bailout generated a lot of public discussion. Given direct democracy in Switzerland, everyone realized that there could be a political backlash if steps were not taken to try to prevent something similar from happening again someday. Put differently, learning was politically imperative. This was made abundantly clear in our interview at the Swiss Business Federation:

> And especially in Switzerland where you have a direct democracy ... it's not only the question if we [the business community] are happy with the situation, it's [also] the question are the people happy with the situation. Because if they're not, there will be some reaction. So that's why I mentioned this combination with the too big to fail strategy, where the responsible parties or the involved parties realized we have to change something. We have to do some regulation or at least to think on different actions.

132 Commission of Experts 2010; interview with Aymo Brunetti, University of Bern.

So the commission was formed and comprised fourteen experts from the public and financial sectors, including people from the Swiss Financial Market Supervisory Authority (FINMA), which replaced the SFBC in 2009; the Department of Finance; SNB; the secretariats for Economic Affairs and for the Competition Commission; two universities; and seven financial firms, including UBS and Credit Suisse.[133] It was more inclusive than the original rescue committee. Its mandate was to make recommendations to avoid failure of a bank that could topple the entire financial system. The commission made several recommendations that were presented to the Minister of Finance, who submitted them to parliament where they were passed in record time.[134]

The chair of the commission told us that this was the first expert commission he knew of whose recommendations were all written into law. Initially the regulators wanted tougher regulatory changes than did the banks. But in typical Swiss fashion a compromise was reached and in the end everyone on the commission agreed to the TBTF recommendations, including UBS and Credit Suisse, who promised not to oppose them later. In fact, according to the SBA, all Swiss banks welcomed the TBTF legislation. Even though everyone subscribed to a liberal economic philosophy and did not want excessive regulation, nobody wanted another crisis.[135] The results of the commission's discussions were reported publicly and, as a result, the banks faced considerable public pressure to go along. Furthermore, both the left-wing and right-wing members of parliament agreed to the recommendations even though the left wanted more state intervention and the right wanted less. In the end, this was a moment of great consensus. There were several reasons for this, which by now should sound familiar. First, the issues involved were very technical so that no politician was knowledgeable enough to object to the experts. Secondly, there was a clear sense that these things needed to be dealt with quickly. Finally, the compromises reached within the commission were so finely tuned that parliament, which often fiddles with proposals from expert commissions before enacting them, did not dare change the legislation as it was proposed to them.[136] But although politicians were not involved in the commission, they did have indirect influence in ways that were typically Swiss. Commission members were cognizant of the political parties' opinions on the matter and took them into consideration during their deliberations. This was an example of the blocking power that often frames political decision-making in Switzerland.[137] In any case, FINMA and the SNB supported

133 Commission of Experts 2010.

134 Interview with senior official, SNB.

135 Interview with Martin Hess, SBA.

136 Interviews with Peter Siegenthaler, former Head of Federal Finance Administration and Chair TBTF; Aymo Brunetti, University of Bern.

137 Interview with Aymo Brunetti, University of Bern.

the commission's recommendations noting that they were "a result of a broad-based consensus within the [Commission] of Experts [TBTF]."[138]

The commission's enabling legislation provided for a review of its recommendations after three years. This was done partly at the behest of the banks. They worried that since Switzerland would be the first mover internationally in beefing up regulations after the crisis, they might suffer a competitive disadvantage until the rest of the world caught up. They wanted a review to make sure that other countries were following suit.[139] This resulted in the Brunetti Group, named after its chair, Aymo Brunetti, an academic economist with government experience. The group sought to investigate whether the TBTF legislation was working as intended or whether it required revision.[140] The group included top officials from the SNB, FINMA, the Federal Department of Finance, and the banks. No politicians were involved, and all meetings were conducted privately. When we interviewed Brunetti, the group had not yet finished its work or reported any findings to the government. It was still in the process of determining how much of the TBTF legislation had actually been implemented, comparing the TBTF legislation with the ways in which other countries were handling the too-big-to-fail problem in order to see if their policies were better than those of the Swiss. This was another example of institutionalized expert learning and flexibility. Brunetti told us that his group's work was important because Switzerland remains very exposed to the too-big-to-fail problem.[141]

Whether the Brunetti Group report will spark controversy or be accepted by consensus like the TBTF recommendations was unclear at the time of our interviews. Brunetti speculated that the banks would oppose any suggestion of further regulatory toughening. But he suspected that the politicians would be more compliant. Those on the left would be happy to rein in capitalism further. Those on the right would see tougher regulations as "saving the nation" from further disaster.[142] The latter is another example of nationalism affecting politics. As it turned out, the Brunetti Group's report called for two things once it was published. First, stringent leverage ratio requirements for banks were recommended, which mostly affected UBS and Credit Suisse, where banks would have to increase the amount of capital set aside to cover losses should their investments turn sour. Second, the report urged the government to initiate preliminary talks with the EU on the scope of a possible

---

138 FINMA 2010.

139 Interview with Martin Hess, SBA.

140 The group's official name was the Express Group for the Development of the Swiss Financial Market Strategy.

141 Interview with Aymo Brunetti, University of Bern.

142 Interview with Aymo Brunetti, University of Bern.

financial services agreement whereby EU and Swiss banking regulations would be aligned, thus assuring Swiss banks fluid access to the EU market. Drawing upon these talks, the commission suggested that the government could then decide whether pursuing such an agreement made sense. These moves were embraced by the SBA, representing Switzerland's internationally oriented banks, but opposed by a consortium of cantonal and smaller regional banks— an indication of the growing divide between internationally and domestically focused sectors of the economy.[143] But overall the TBTF Commission and the Brunetti Group were additional examples of Swiss institutional strength. Both were established to revisit prior legislative and regulatory action. Hence, they institutionalized learning, adjustment, and flexibility. This was not unlike Denmark's series of six bank packages, where it was often the case that one package was designed to compensate for the shortcomings of a previous package.

INTERNATIONAL EFFECTS

Crisis management played out in an international context, which had several effects on decision-making. First, as noted, the SNB borrowed $14 billion from the Fed in order to finance the initial purchase of UBS's illiquid assets. As a small country whose central bank's financial resources were limited relative to the size of its troubled banks, Switzerland was constrained in terms of its capacity to give bailouts, unless it received outside assistance. The Fed agreed to help both because it did not want another debacle like Lehman Brothers and because it realized that UBS did so much business in the United States that its demise would exacerbate the already dire financial crisis in America. Second, Swiss decision-makers studied what other countries and international organizations were doing to manage the crisis. Notably, the Brunetti Group kept an eye on changing EU and U.S. banking regulations. The TBTF Commission watched the Basel Committee on Banking Supervision and the G20 countries' Financial Stability Board, which were working to find ways to reduce systemic risks to the world's financial system. In fact, all countries today tend to follow the guidelines issued by these international organizations.[144] But there was apparently little overt international pressure on Swiss regulators from these organizations. Although the TBTF Commission delayed its final report to see what the Basel Committee recommended, in the end Switzerland's new regulatory regime was tougher than the international conventions in terms of capitalization, leverage, and other requirements.

---

143 Group of Experts 2014; Swissinfo.ch 2015.
144 Interview with former Managing Director, UBS.

The Swiss also adopted various cross-border agreements, including regular information exchanges with the United States, Britain, and the EU.[145] Overall, the Swiss were leaders not followers. They did not succumb to international pressure. As noted earlier, Switzerland did not belong to the Eurozone, thereby allowing them greater control over their currency.

Finally, there was the issue of corporate inversion—reincorporating a Swiss firm overseas, which would reduce the tax revenue accruing to Switzerland from that firm. Prior to the crisis the SFBC questioned UBS about their subprime investments and was satisfied with UBS's response that everything was fine. This turned out to be a serious mistake. Peter Siegenthaler, head of the TBTF Commission, told us that the SFBC had discussions with both banks about increasing their capitalization to hedge against these potentially risky investments. But both banks refused and reminded everyone in meetings that they could relocate their operations to New York, London, or somewhere else if the regulators persisted. The threat of corporate inversion was clearly a constraint on how far the regulators were willing to go—and how far politicians were willing to go because, according to Siegenthaler, the "political influence of the two big babies [UBS and Credit Suisse] was really very, very high." Of course, the threat of corporate inversion may have been a bluff. But even if it was just a bluff, it would have been effective because, as one respondent told us, politicians do not even want such a possibility discussed publicly.[146] Nor do they want banks saying publicly that tougher regulations will hurt their business and therefore undermine Swiss competitiveness and the national interest.[147] However, perceptions changed when the crisis hit. Trust in the banks deteriorated sharply. As one respondent explained, "They never thought that the Swiss banks would be as vulnerable as that.... This was a shock for politicians, for the government, [and] also for all the economists and bankers."[148] The banks' reputation as pillars of society was now in tatters. Not surprisingly, then, parliament moved very quickly to implement all of the TBTF Commission's recommendations for tougher bank regulation, because the threat of corporate inversion had lost much of its effect. The general point to be made is that the capacity for resilience is neither unlimited nor constant—the international constraints in play ebbed and flowed. We learned at the Swiss Business Federation that there is a delicate balance involved. On the one hand, people understand that capital may leave if regulations and taxes become prohibitive. On the other hand, the business commu-

---

145 Commission of Experts 2010; OECD 2011, pp. 57, 60; Reuters 2010.

146 Even if the banks were bluffing, the Swiss are sensitive to the possibility that multinationals may leave, for example, in pursuit of lower tax rates (interview with Andreas Huber, CCFM).

147 Interview with Amyo Brunetti, University of Bern.

148 Interview with Wolf Linder, University of Bern.

nity is aware of the power of voters thanks to Switzerland's direct democracy. Our contact at the SBF put it this way:

> There is a sensibility which is arising more and more now in our organizations and with our members that we need to reflect on the effect [of our actions] on society ... [but] there are effects on society if you put narrow regulations on business. There are effects on both sides and you have to reflect on that. If you don't do it, you get the bill at the end when there is voting on the situation.[149]

Conclusion

Switzerland is a country of contrasts. Its complex institutional web of cultural affiliations might have fractured the country had not extreme vulnerability led to the creation of a strong national identity. A thick institutional portfolio resulted leaving decision-makers with formidable capacities for resilience that served the country well during the financial crisis. The legitimacy of crisis management was largely unquestioned because trusted experts were in charge, operating within inclusive democratic institutions. Furthermore, there had been considerable learning and preparation for a major bank failure, which when the time came, benefited the experts who were able to put policies into practice that gained public support. Furthermore, steps were taken quickly to ensure that learning and further adjustments would continue to be made as necessary once the initial bailout package was launched. Not one but two expert commissions were established to ensure this. Resilience in the face of crisis was impressive.

Still these capacities had not been thick enough to prevent the crisis in the first place so the Swiss, in common with the Danes and the Irish, beefed up the state's regulatory capacities after the crisis hit, an exercise in institutional thickening. This too was done in a very consensus-oriented way. For instance, with little opposition the SFBC imposed a new capital regime on UBS and Credit Suisse, including tougher capitalization, leverage, and liquidity requirements to be phased in by 2013 after the crisis was over. Today the SNB's capitalization requirements for Swiss banks are among the toughest in the world.[150] The Brunetti Report recommended in 2014 that capital requirements should be tightened further to ensure that Switzerland would remain among the leading countries in this regard.[151] As noted earlier, a new organization, FINMA, for which planning had started in the late 1990s, opened in 2009 and replaced the SFBC. It was one of the first regulatory agencies in the

149 Interview with senior official, SBF.
150 Breiding 2013, p. 155; Commission of Experts 2010, p. 9.
151 Correspondence with senior official, SNB.

world to address weaknesses in the supervision of systemically important banks.[152] FINMA has "supreme authority" for regulating the financial securities industry.[153] It moved quickly, imposing stress tests for banks, engaging in better supervision and, unlike its predecessor, enjoying functional, institutional and financial independence from the Federal Department of Finance (FDF)—reporting instead directly to the Federal Council.[154] It also imposed more stringent liquidity and corporate governance requirements on the banks.[155] FINMA was among the first national financial regulatory agencies to set guidelines for employee compensation to discourage risk-taking.[156] It also hired more staff with expertise in finance to deal with the new regulatory requirements and the enhanced supervisory scrutiny that followed the crisis.[157] Recruitment at all levels was more self-consciously based on professional and/or academic experience and expertise than it was before at SFBC.[158] This was also a move to create more distance between the regulators and the banks than had been the case with the SFBC.

Nevertheless, a problem of expertise remained, as it has elsewhere, because, as one person told us, "The resources are immense within the banks compared to the resources of the FINMA ... [and so] they will always be behind." This is why some people insist that the banks need more capitalization, lower leverage ratios, and the like. Having these structural checks on banking behavior helps compensate for FINMA's comparative disadvantage in expertise.[159] Recall that we heard something similar in Ireland. However, in Switzerland plans to improve the state's regulatory capacity by establishing FINMA began well before the crisis hit. In this regard, Switzerland's greater proclivity for resilience is clear; the Swiss were being proactive, whereas the Irish were merely reactive.

In some ways these changes did not deviate from Switzerland's traditions. For example, FINMA's primary remit is micro-prudential supervision, as it was for its predecessor, ensuring that the organizations it supervises are solvent, that sufficient risk controls are in place, and that business is conducted in a prudent manner. SNB still has a mandate to help stabilize the financial sector and plays a key role in macro-prudential policy.[160] Despite this division

152 OECD 2009b, p. 11.

153 Swiss Bankers Association 2010, p. 23.

154 OECD 2009b, pp. 12, 78.

155 Interview with Andreas Huber, CCFM; FINMA 2009, pp. 42–47; Swiss Bankers Association 2010, pp. 23, 57.

156 Federal Department of Finance 2010; FINMA 2009, pp. 40–42; OECD 2009b, p. 76.

157 Interview with Martin Hess, SBA.

158 New regulations as of 2012 also required more stringent requirements for professional expertise in supervising Swiss pension funds (OECD 2011, pp. 63–64).

159 Interview with Aymo Brunetti, University of Bern.

160 OECD 2009b, p. 81.

of labor the FDF, SNB, and FINMA signed a Memorandum of Understanding in January 2011 to improve the exchange of information. They agreed to meet biannually to discuss financial stability and financial market regulation, and to exchange information about the macroeconomic environment, the condition of the financial markets and banks, and national and international regulatory initiatives. The Finance Department also created a working group to further review macro-prudential regulation and supervision.[161] Importantly, FINMA still recognizes the utility of self-regulation, and so the Swiss tradition has not been completely abandoned—a vestige of Switzerland's liberal corporatism.[162] In some cases, the SBA still passes codes of conduct on its own initiative, which FINMA then recognizes and enforces. These private codes are in effect public standards where infringements are subject to sanctions under the banking law. In other cases the state requires the banks to establish rules governing their conduct, notably rules to prevent money laundering.[163] Self-regulation is common in corporatist systems where the state off-loads regulatory responsibility to the industry but stands ready to enforce the industry's standards when necessary. The state stands as the "Damocles sword of threatened direct state intervention" that makes self-regulation work.[164]

Was Swiss crisis management a normal decision-making process or not? It certainly was not normal insofar as it was not corporatist at the start. Even Denmark's crisis management, which was insulated and elitist, was more inclusive than it was in Switzerland. On the other hand, the Swiss response was very normal insofar as it was pragmatic rather than ideological, run by an elite group of highly trusted expert technocrats rather than politicians with little expertise, and influenced by an awareness that there could always be push back through the institutions of direct democracy. The Swiss response was also surprisingly quick compared to other countries. It was a regulatory front-runner in the too-big-to-fail era.

Yet again it is time to step away from a picture that might seem perfect in order to acknowledge looming difficulties. All of these revolve around the ever-greater impact of Christian Blocher's People's Party. Blocher's own period on the Federal Council was dramatic, in that he broke the convention of silence about key decisions, thereby politicizing Swiss politics. But an upstart entity has become "something else" as it is now the largest party in Switzerland with two seats on the Federal Council. Its rise is based on a desire to keep immigrants out, whether from the EU or from other places. This poses

161 OECD 2011, pp. 66–67.

162 FINMA 2009, pp. 42–47; Swiss Bankers Association 2010, pp. 23, 57.

163 OECD 2009b, p. 79; Swiss Bankers Association 2010, pp. 60–61.

164 Streeck and Schmitter 1985, p. 20. See also Offe (1981).

two threats to the Swiss economic model. The first was particularly apparent while we were doing our fieldwork. Trade treaties with the EU would have lapsed if Switzerland had managed to prevent the free movement of labor agreements to which it is party. That would have caused immense problems as Swiss industries depend upon educated labor from the EU, especially from Germany. In the event, Switzerland caved into the determination of the EU not to make any concessions on the free movement of labor, although legislation was passed encouraging Swiss firms to try harder to hire Swiss nationals. Small nation-states in Europe have often had to cave in, as was famously true both of Denmark and Ireland, and the fact that Switzerland has done so represents a remarkable piece of evidence supporting our general argument. Still, we detected a good deal of nativist sentiment; it may yet rear its ugly head again. Secondly, the rise of the party is not only based on anti-immigrant sentiments, and on Islamophobia in particular. Just as important is a new sense—resulting from the insulated, expert-led support given to the troubled banks—that benefits accrue to the elite much more than to the people at crucial moments. National identity is being contested once again. If this continues the possibility exists that the consensual nature of Swiss politics may yet fray, with consequences that are hard as yet to envisage.

5

Conclusion

Vulnerability can increase national solidarity allowing institutions to be built that work for a country's collective benefit, allowing it to stay afloat when a squall hits. The Danish case exemplifies our argument about the paradox of vulnerability. And the Irish and Swiss cases do too, albeit with interesting nuances. Switzerland shows that the potentially deleterious effects of difference can be muted if institutions provide sufficient voice to prevent ethnic difference from becoming politicized; the strong national identity accordingly went hand-in-hand with loyalty to the linguistic, religious, and cantonal cultures. The Irish case is complex and the most interesting, and it is very important to us because it supports our argument both negatively and positively: when independence was absent or a measure of sheltering was present, institutional thickening was stymied, when vulnerability was felt it flourished. We begin this conclusion by reviewing the cases for a final time, sharpening analysis by the summary comparisons in table 5.1.

Denmark's protracted history of military defeats reduced the country's size and made it extraordinarily homogeneous; the perceived vulnerabilities that resulted increased national solidarity, leading to continual institutional development. As a result, Danish institutions were quite thick when the crisis hit. The Danes had considerable technocratic expertise on hand to which politicians deferred for purposes of crisis management. The decision-making process was rooted in long-standing corporatist traditions that had led to the inclusion of the banks, the regulatory agency, the central bank, and eventually a large pension fund—as well as other interests represented through informal backchannel communications. Nearly everyone felt that the process was legitimate and therefore acceptable because of the trust they placed in the experts running it. Moreover, the experts had a set of crisis management

TABLE 5.1. The Three Cases Compared

Key Variables	Denmark	Ireland	Switzerland
Perceived Vulnerability of the State	**High** 1864 defeat by Prussia Geopolitical dangers Trade openness	**Mixed** Low during British rule (no state to be vulnerable) High during civil war Low during British shelter High during stagflation High during financial crisis	**High** Geographic location Geopolitical dangers Trade openness
Perceived Vulnerability of the Nation	**High** 1864 defeat by Prussia Geopolitical dangers Trade openness	**Mixed** High during British rule High during civil war Low during British shelter High during stagflation High during financial crisis	**High** Geographic location Geopolitical dangers Trade openness
Sense of National Identity and Solidarity	**High** Cultural homogeneity Fortified by folk schools Fortified by internal front Fortified by welfare state Fortified by proportional representation	**Mixed** Cultural homogeneity High during British rule Low during civil war Low during post–civil war High during stagflation High during financial crisis	**High** Respect for cultural difference Fortified by canton pacts Fortified by constitution Fortified by proportional representation

	Thick	Thin	Thick
Institutions			
Expertise	High: Reliance on technocrats	Low: Lack of technocrats	High: Reliance on technocrats
Inclusiveness	Open: Strong corporatism; proportional representation	Closed: Weak corporatism; proportional representation yet single-party dominance, patronage & clientelism	Open: Strong corporatism; consociationalism; proportional representation; federalism; referenda
Legitimacy	High: Much trust & consensus in policymaking process	Low: Limited trust & consensus in policymaking process	High: Much trust & consensus in policymaking process
Organizational capacities			
General	Strong: Early institution-building	Weak: Late institution-building	Strong: Early institution-building
Crisis specific	Strong: Automatic stabilizers; crisis blueprints; PCA funds; division of labor for crisis management; state access to bank portfolios	Weak: Regulators' inability to assess bank portfolios; no effective crisis preparation; barriers to outside expertise	Strong: Debt brake; monetary policy flexibility; immigration policy; crisis blueprints; constitutional emergency powers
Resilience in the Face of Crisis	**High** Expert-run response State bank guarantee Private funding 6 bank packages Continuous policy adjustment	**Low** Politician-run response State bank guarantee Public funding Fiscal crisis and Troika rescue Little policy adjustment	**High** Expert-run response UBS bailout Public funding TBTF and Brunetti commissions Continuous policy adjustment

blueprints devised in the wake of earlier troubles, and so they had both the general and crisis-specific organizational capacities for dealing with the situation in a resilient manner, notably with a series of bank packages that exemplified the capacity for continuous policy learning and adjustment.

The Irish story is more complicated and best classified as "mixed" in the sense that perceptions of vulnerability and a sense of national unity vacillated at particular historical junctures. Colonial subjugation ruled institutional growth out of court. After independence the shelter provided by the former metropole delayed the moment at which Ireland had to face the vulnerabilities so well known to the Danes and Swiss. Moreover, despite its nominally homogeneous population, the national question remained unsettled after independence—and still is insofar as it is a crucial legacy dividing Irish politics, particularly in allowing Fianna Fáil a near-hegemonic role. As a result, Irish institutions remained thinner than in the other two cases, which meant that Ireland's response to the crisis was also less resilient and effective. Expertise was in remarkably limited supply; decision-making excluded virtually all interested groups; and many people were suspicious and distrustful of the entire process given the inside deal-making, patronage, clientelism, and cronyism that had long marked Irish politics. Finally, Irish organizational capacities were limited compared to those of the other two countries. There had been little preparation for anything like the financial crisis, while institutional obstacles prevented policymakers from consulting experts outside the state—with the authorities lacking the means to assess the severity of the crisis until it was too late.

In Switzerland, perceptions of extreme geopolitical and economic vulnerability led to a number of early agreements among the cantons that prevented the politicization of religious and linguistic differences, thereby allowing for the creation of a strong national identity albeit one based on respect for cultural differences. The institutional thickening that followed, particularly the formation of very inclusive political processes, not only helped reinforce that identity but also facilitated a resilient response to the financial crisis. Experts in the central bank managed the crisis. This was a closed and insulated process that might have raised serious legitimacy questions in other countries but that was accepted in Switzerland due to the considerable trust people put in state technocrats. Indeed, consensual politics very early on made institutional provisions to turn over policymaking authority to the experts in emergency situations. As in Denmark, the Swiss also had the advantage of crisis-specific organizational capacities, including crisis blueprints created earlier that anticipated the possibility of a major bank failure. Swiss resilience was especially evident in the institutionalized learning of the much more inclusive TBTF commission and Brunetti group, both of which were set up to monitor earlier crisis management moves and make adjustments as necessary.

We have insisted on the need to grasp critical historical features of these cases in order to understand why they responded to the crisis as they did.

These historical influences go beyond simply establishing the institutional portfolios with which decision-makers worked in the moment of crisis. They also created the cognitive frameworks and assumptions that guided decision-making. For example, one cannot understand why the Danes and the Swiss were so trusting of the experts who handled the crisis without understanding that their long histories of nation-state vulnerability had caused political groups to cooperate for the national good. Conversely, one cannot understand why in Ireland experts were not called upon to the same degree without acknowledging the legacy of British-style generalist education or the long history of political patronage and clientelism, itself the outgrowth of long-standing nationalist conflicts. In short, the big, slow-moving processes of history mattered a great deal in our cases.

Expanding the Cases

Our theoretical claim is large, but the sample of cases we have provided to support it is small. This raises two methodological issues. First, one might object that we have more variables than cases and, as a result, have not provided a definitive test of our theory. It is important to remember, however, that our aim has been process tracing rather than conventional theory testing. Process tracing seeks less to determine the most significant variables than to determine how they interact with each other over the *longue durée*.[1] Second, studies based on a small number of cases are disadvantaged in not being able to generalize their findings with confidence to a larger set of cases. For this reason we now turn briefly to additional cases to see whether our argument can withstand further scrutiny. We could pick cases that have enjoyed considerable success for reasons that seem to easily confirm our ideal-typical model, such as Uruguay, the Czech Republic and Slovakia after their velvet divorce, or the Baltic countries. But we turn instead to Greece and Iceland because they appear to present further challenges to our argument. After all, both were small and homogeneous countries that suffered massively in the financial crisis.

GREECE

Greece is a small nation-state of about eleven million people. Our general argument might seem to be undermined by the fact that during the financial crisis this small and homogeneous country received the largest bailout in postwar Europe, thereby becoming the exemplar in the eyes of many of a failed state with virtually no institutional resilience. Although it did not suffer

---

1 Bennett and Checkel (2015a) discuss the trade-offs between process tracing in a small number of cases and developing theoretical generalizations in a large number of cases.

a banking crisis per se, the fiscal crisis of its state was worse than that of Ireland. Accordingly, attention must be given to Greece to see if its difficulties disprove our main arguments. Let us note immediately that this is not the case. To the contrary, the Greek case is explicable through the use of the variables on which we have relied throughout.

The best way to approach Greece is to note that it resembles Ireland. On the one hand, both countries escaped empires so as to become independent, and then moved from poverty into the heart of the developed capitalist world. Yet the greatest resemblance between Ireland and Greece lies in factors of weakness, though these factors are greatly amplified in the Greek case. For a very long time political-economic development in both countries was seriously hobbled. In Ireland this was due in large part to the relative weakness of institutions that did so much to explain the stumbling nature of its response to the financial crisis. The country is young, with the legacy of its civil war and residual nationalist divisions creating clientelist politics that contributed so much to the housing bubble that brought the economy to its knees. Greece in a key sense is even younger and its political divisions massively greater. Crucially, national identity has been contested continually and viciously. This lack of agreement played an enormous role in consolidating and expanding the clientelist character of the political economy that lay behind both its economic difficulties and the nature of its response to the financial crisis. Finally, as in Ireland, there are nevertheless moments in Greece when the paradox of vulnerability can be seen at work—that is, when the benefits of small-nationhood can be seen to have driven social and economic life forward. But such moments have been relatively rare.

This last point requires some explanation because it cuts to the heart of our basic argument about the paradox of vulnerability. The problem is simple. Greece has been very vulnerable geopolitically throughout its modern history yet this has not created the sense of solidarity and in turn institution-building that our theory would expect. External powers and geopolitical catastrophes have long dominated Greek development. Geopolitics has entered into the heart of its society, thereby setting one fragment of the nation against another. In this sense Greece is significantly different from our other cases. A precondition for the success of small nation-states is the independence of the country. Such independence has very often been lacking or at least seriously compromised in the Greek case. External powers insisted on more than one occasion on a monarchical presence, with more direct interference during the Cold War. A flagrant example of the latter can be seen in the decision of November 1952 to accept an American diktat, in the face of the threatened loss of U.S. aid money, to change the electoral system from proportional to majoritarian representation—a move away from relatively more inclusive and consensus-oriented politics—designed to benefit the political right and American foreign policy interests.[2] In a nutshell, Greece has suffered for most of its modern history from repeated episodes of dependence.

The fact that Greece gained its independence from the Ottomans in 1832 seems at first sight to undermine the claim just made, that the country is younger than Ireland. But there are considerations that lend sense to this statement. To begin with, the nationalist movement that sought independence was far weaker than that which achieved secession in the Irish case. Most of the key nationalist leaders were members of what would become the diaspora, above all the merchants situated in cities such as Odessa. The initial rising took place in what is now Romania, where it failed badly. Bandits led more sustained fighting in the lower part of the Peloponnese, but their aims were very different—less about nationalism, more about self-interests. Fighting eventually broke out between these two groups, testifying to the lack of a shared sense of national identity. Put differently, nationalism was an ongoing project rather than the outcome of any sort of firmly established identity. In the end, independence depended on the external intervention of the Great Powers, many of them driven ideologically to support the "fountain of modern liberty." The Treaty of 1832 did not, revealingly, receive a Greek imprimatur.

The task of building the new country was immense, as the elite sought to move society—or, rather, very different regional societies—from an oriental empire to a modern and occidental nation-state. One might say that the country was an early "late modernizer" and thus very different from our other cases, all of which had some elements of historical continuity with which to work.[3] Some moves toward institutional thickening were made in the nineteenth century, notably the introduction of a Western legal system, land reform consolidating an egalitarian peasant social structure, and the creation both of a schooling system and the nationalizing of the church. But there were considerable difficulties as well. Perhaps most notable is the fact that democracy (in the form of complete male suffrage) came so early, in 1843. In other countries state-building has been most successful typically when bureaucratic forms were established under an old regime before the introduction of democratic demands. In the Greek case, because this did not happen "the state assumed a disproportionate importance as a source of employment, and the proportion of bureaucrats to citizens was far higher than in Western Europe."[4] This expansion did not denote efficiency but rather rent-seeking to which was added the traditional clientelism of daily life. "Laws, which parliament . . . spewed out in large quantities, were there essentially to be got round

---

2 Clogg 2013, p. 144.
3 Kalyvas 2015, p. 1 and passim. We are heavily indebted to this brilliant account.
4 Clogg 2013, p. 59.

rather than obeyed."[5] Since then, attempts to streamline, rationalize, and increase the effectiveness of the bureaucracy have often been the result of external interference rather than of national development. The basic point is simple: Greek institutions were and still are thin, at times extremely so.

Nevertheless, the key feature of the society, or rather of the members of its elite, was the desire in the nineteenth century to expand the country's size so as to incorporate the two-thirds of the Greek population living outside the initial territorial boundaries. Bluntly, the urge to expand meant that Greece did not perceive itself to be a small and vulnerable nation-state in any way whatsoever. Very much to the contrary, its dreams included the conquest of Istanbul and the replacement of the Ottomans by a Greek Orthodox entity—one bound to be imperial as it would incorporate many Muslims into the country. Such dreams of greatness distorted the development of the state's organizational capacities, most obviously by directing more than half of all state expenditures toward the military. To be sure, there was some expansion of the nation-state in the nineteenth century, most notably the acquisition of Thessaly in 1881 as the result of a Great Power arrangement to cut Bulgaria, Russia's ally and Greece's powerful new enemy, down to size. Furthermore, there was a period of serious infrastructural development at the end of the century, during the premierships of the great modernizer Kharilaos Trikoupis. But this was followed by the state's default on its debt in 1893, and much worse by decisive defeat at the hands of the Ottomans in 1897.

But even then the dreams of grandeur did not die away; in fact it became both more complex and more urgent as other Balkan states sought to gain territory from the Ottomans, mostly in Macedonia. Two Balkan wars saw Greece increase its territory by a further 70 percent, at the expense of the Ottomans in 1912 and of Bulgaria in 1913. But even this was not enough. The elite split in 1914 between royalists leaning toward the Central Powers, who favored neutrality, and the republicans, led by Eleftherios Venizelos, who sought to join with the Entente, convinced that British control of the Mediterranean would allow Greece to gain still more territory. Rival governments and rival armies were set up so that the "national schism" was absolute. The way in which the war ended seemed to have justified Venizelos's Republican camp, because Greece was granted, in complex formulae, extensive territories in Asia Minor. However, the resurgence of Turkey under Kemal Ataturk led not just to the loss of territories gained by Greece in 1920 but also to a mass population exchange in the years that followed. Greece was forced to absorb over a million and a quarter mostly Orthodox Christians, fully 30 percent of the population at that time, with most of them choosing to settle in the areas of northern Greece previously inhabited by the Muslims who had

5 Clogg 2013, p. 61.

been expelled. The war ended with executions, bitterly resented. The disaster as a whole "shaped politics for decades to come by defining the character of the Greek party system, forging the political identities of Greeks, and politicizing the military. Most importantly, it infused politics with a degree of nationalist intensity never seen before, reinforced by reciprocal purges of public administration and the military."[6]

This was the moment when Greece finally perceived itself to be a small and vulnerable nation-state. Megalomaniacal dreams were set aside given the end of irredentist politics. Furthermore, the country benefited from the dynamism of the population that had arrived. But attempts made to modernize and adapt failed rather quickly, given that the divisions within the nation did not just continue but actually increased in the maelstrom of the international politics of the twentieth century. A period of fascism-lite under Ioannis Metaxas was followed by entry into the Second World War despite desperate attempts to avoid entanglement. German victory and vicious occupation by the three Axis powers during the war morphed into a civil war between the communists, heavily based in northern Greece and with strong allegiance to the Soviet Union, and the more conservative royalist forces. The brutality of the civil war is legendary, not least because "the unfinished business of national integration" fed into civil strife.[7] British and American involvement prevented Greece from disappearing behind the Iron Curtain, not least through the generosity of the Marshall Plan, but the memories of the conflict remained visceral. The Communist Party was banned in 1947, with the democracy established at that time being heavily influenced by the American unofficial protectorate. Furthermore, conflict between left and right in the 1960s provided an excuse for discontented younger officers in the military to mount a coup and thereby to rule by military means until 1974.

A moment of recapitulation is in order. For nearly a hundred years after gaining its independence Greece neither perceived itself to be nor acted like a small vulnerable nation-state. Despite gaining formal independence in the nineteenth century, Greece was far from independent in a meaningful sense for much of the twentieth century thanks to its geopolitical entanglements. All of this hampered the development of a unified national identity, solidarity, and in turn the institutional thickening that one might have expected otherwise of a small and vulnerable nation-state.

Nonetheless, the Greek economy and society took major steps forward in the postwar years. The annual economic growth rate in the late 1950s rose to 4.4 percent and soared between 1961 and 1973 to 7.4 percent. By 2008 Greece had moved up to rank twenty-sixth in the world Human Development Index.

6 Kalyvas 2015, p. 71.
7 Kalyvas 2015, p. 96.

It is easy to explain the change: the war was over, allowing Greeks to grab—eagerly—the opportunities before them, in which task they were aided by the sensible anti-inflationary policies that were put in place. But many problems remained. The temptation to play with the electoral rules persisted, while fiscal extraction was low—especially before elections. Geopolitical tensions, above all over Cyprus, continued to occupy much of the elite's attention, with military expenditures accordingly still crowding out those that would have facilitated industrial development and productive institutional thickening. Moving closer to the EU, first through an associate membership, then through entry in 1981, and eventually through joining the Eurozone in 2001, caused great difficulties for Greek industries that had hitherto benefited from protective tariffs. Finally, it took a considerable time to defeat urban terrorism. Nonetheless, during this period Greece had finally begun to act like a small vulnerable nation-state seeking to control its own destiny, learning now to act flexibly in a hostile world.

Let us recall again Ernest Renan's perceptive comment that a strong nation depends upon the ability to forget, so as to change its national identity to suit new circumstances. The danger of excluding any group from daily political life is that the desire to get its own back or to make up for what one has missed will overrule any sense of discipline and restraint. In 1974 the ban on the Communist Party was lifted, but this did not lead to any general political settlement. The lack of discipline based on resentment most certainly characterized PASOK, the socialist party led by Andreas Papandreou, which dominated Greek politics in the years after 1981. In many areas there were quite simply vast handouts. There has always been clientelism and patronage in Greece, but these were massively exacerbated by PASOK. State employment shot up during PASOK's first decade in power, yet the quality of output was poor and the associated costs were escalating.[8] Public workers were often hired for life due to their social or political connections rather than their qualifications and expertise. Rules and regulations were often passed and implemented at the behest of influential constituents. Politicians often engaged in brazen corruption and were shielded from investigation and prosecution. Transparency International ended up ranking Greece as the most corrupt country in the EU, another sign of thin organizational capacities. Furthermore, government statistics and reporting were neither systematic nor necessarily accurate. For example, in order to qualify for Eurozone membership, the government understated the size of its deficits for years. Tax evasion was rampant, often helped by tax collectors on the take. Roughly a quarter of all economic activity went unreported, well above the EU average. As a result, the Greek pension system was underfunded and the public school system was

8 Kalyvas 2015, p. 144.

in such bad shape that parents had to pay for private tutors in order for their children to get into a university.[9] Not surprisingly, trust in the government was extremely low by EU standards. According to the World Economic Forum, just before the financial crisis the quality of Greece's political-economic institutions ranked fifty-eighth in the world, much worse than that of Denmark, Switzerland and Ireland, which ranked third, fifth, and seventeenth, respectively.[10] In short, "Greece entered the crisis as a dysfunctional state with an impaired economy."[11]

Crucially, the government had begun to borrow massively once entry into the Eurozone made it possible to do so at remarkably low interest rates.[12] Public sector wages and pension payments were increased, and the 2004 Olympic Games were sponsored. Borrowing helped spur growth that had suffered during the 1990s: from 2001 to 2008 it ran at nearly 4 percent annually.[13] But this was not based on genuine economic development. What was most noticeable was a consumption boom and the fact that spending on public administration as a percentage of total public expenditures was higher in Greece in 2009 than in any other OECD country. Accordingly, Greek debt skyrocketed. By 2006 the government's debt was about 110 percent of GDP— ten times larger than Ireland's. When Lehman Brothers collapsed and the 2008 financial crisis hit, Greece was badly exposed. The availability of credit inside the capitalist world tightened for all countries, massively so in the case of Greece. As the underlying economic fundamentals were so weak, Greece's credit rating was downgraded in 2009—the first of many downgrades that eventually pushed Greek debt to junk bond status. As a result, borrowing costs to service debt and keep the government running soared. The yield on ten-year Greek bonds jumped to 18 percent by 2011. Projected government deficits, initially forecast to be about 3.5 percent of GDP, ultimately exceeded 15 percent. This was a catastrophic fiscal crisis of the state. As its borrowing costs climbed so did unemployment as the economy went into free fall. Despite efforts to stem the hemorrhaging, by 2015 the economy had contracted by 25 percent and the unemployment rate stood at about 28 percent.[14] As one observer concluded, Greece's institutions, both political and economic,

9 Angelos 2015, chaps. 1 and 2.

10 World Economic Forum 2008.

11 *The Economist* 2014a.

12 In late 1993 the yield on ten-year Greek bonds was over 24 percent—more than twice as high as Irish, Italian, Spanish, or Portuguese bonds, and higher still than French, German, or British bonds. By the time the euro was introduced, the yield on Greek bonds had dropped to about 6 percent, only a few points higher than bedrock German bonds (U.S. Congressional Research Service 2011).

13 Angelos 2015, chap. 1; Blyth 2013, pp. 47, 80.

14 Angelos 2015, chap. 1.

could not handle the opportunities—and dangers—associated with joining the Eurozone. The result was the great Greek financial crisis of 2009.[15]

It was soon crystal clear that the government did not have the capacities to cope with the situation, so almost immediately the Troika stepped in much like it would in Ireland. The Troika worried that a disorderly default on Greek public debt would cause panic among investors about other high-debt Eurozone countries, thereby triggering a major sell-off of bonds from all of them and causing extraordinary losses for banks holding the debt. Many feared that the fate of the Eurozone hung in the balance.[16] The Troika agreed to provide Greece with assistance but only if the government embarked on an austerity program that cut government spending to the bone, jacked up taxes, reduced public pensions, and privatized a number of state-owned enterprises. In May 2010 Greece received a €110 billion loan from Eurozone countries and the IMF, the first of several loans it would receive. Eventually, even private bondholders had to take a haircut of about 75 percent on the value of Greek debt plus write-offs of roughly €100 billion.[17] In addition, the ECB provided liquidity support for Greek banks totaling €98 billion by May 2011, roughly 40 percent of Greece's GDP, because the banks not only were caught in the credit crunch but also suffered from depositors pulling their money out in anticipation of bank failures. By 2015 Greece had received €245 billion in bailout assistance—the largest debt restructuring in history and more than three-and-a-half times the size of the Irish bailout. Underscoring the thinness of Greek institutions, the Troika also demanded public sector reform: upgrading the public bureaucracy, firing 150,000 civil servants by 2015 who lacked appropriate skills and qualifications, and slashing pay for those remaining by as much as 35 percent. The idea was to improve government efficiency, stimulate economic growth, begin paying off the government's debt, and reduce the budget deficit by 11 percent of GDP bringing it down to below 3 percent of GDP by 2014.[18] As a member of the Eurozone with no discretion over monetary policy and with few other organizational capacities Greece had little choice but to bend to the Troika's will.

Riots and demonstrations erupted and became commonplace as the public suffered the consequences. Whatever legitimacy the government may have had was eroding badly. All of this fueled the rise of extremist political parties—the neo-Nazi Golden Dawn party on the radical right and Syriza on

15 Kalyvas 2015, p. 193.

16 U.S. Congressional Research Service 2011.

17 The Troika was extremely reluctant to impose haircuts in Greece. The reason why they eventually pushed for them in Greece but not Ireland is likely because the Greek state was bankrupt and totally discredited whereas the Irish state was not.

18 Angelos 2015, chaps. 1 and 4; Blyth 2013, pp. 71–73, 80; U.S. Congressional Research Service 2011.

the radical left. Both achieved electoral success in part by playing the nationalist card, pledging to put the nation above all else and proclaiming that Greece had been victimized by foreign lenders with little regard for the disastrous consequences for the Greek population. Syriza came in first in the 2014 European parliamentary elections and Golden Dawn came in third. In January 2015 Syriza won the Greek legislative election, but with a majority of only two seats. It also won a snap election eight months later.[19] It was easy for these parties to appeal to nationalist sentiments. After the Second World War the Germans had not been obliged to pay Greece any reparations. So during negotiations with the Troika when Germany demanded austerity in exchange for a bailout, most Greeks were incensed—Germany was plundering Greece again. Moreover, capitalizing on the long history of Ottoman rule, Golden Dawn fanned the anti-Turkish flames by warning that foreigners were trying to take over the country—warnings that evoked hatred of and violence toward immigrants of all sorts. Once again perceptions of extreme nation-state vulnerability had spilled over into nationalism of the worst kind.[20]

Greece demonstrated little resilience in the face of the crisis. It simply did not have the capacities to handle the situation, which is why the Troika stepped in so quickly. But the Troika rescue plan fell far short of its goals. Although Greece avoided default and eventually reduced its deficits, the economy suffered a severe recession and high unemployment. There were several reasons for this, including among others the Troika's wildly unrealistic expectations for reform, its initial refusal to restructure Greek debt, its insistence on austerity policies, panicky financial markets, and uncertainty within the EU about exactly what direction things should take. But one reason was particularly important: the shortcomings of the Greek political system, notably interest group politics, bureaucratic inertia, insufficient administrative expertise, the labyrinthine legal and regulatory framework, clientelism and patronage, and opposition from vested interests. Greece has done little to thicken its institutions since the crisis hit. Its patronage and clientelist political system is still a mess.[21] The government remains "frighteningly inexperienced" in dealing with Brussels given the size of the issues at hand and, as a result, has more than any other Eurozone country endured years of "outsourced governance" at the hands of the Troika.[22]

It is important to note that Greece was unlike Ireland in one very important respect—Greece did not develop hidden economic strength during the earlier period of growth that might have facilitated a fairly rapid recovery

19 *The Economist* 2014b.
20 Angelos 2015, chaps. 3 and 5.
21 Fukuyama 2014, chap. 6
22 *The Economist* 2015a, 2015b.

from the financial crisis. Greece's firms are on average smaller than those in other European countries, typically catering to domestic consumers and lacking management abilities to adjust quickly and innovatively to shifts in demand. Moreover, there are few incentives for creating new firms. Much of this economic weakness stemmed from decades of poor political and economic decisions and growing maladministration. In other words, for structural reasons that the Troika failed to recognize, Greece was and remains economically weak.[23]

This brings us to a final point. Some dictating from the outside may be a good thing, at least insofar as some of the Troika's demands for institutional reforms are slowly being heeded by the Greek government. In any case, one should not underestimate the Greeks. They have had multiple crises, often caused by overly ambitious elites. But they often managed to bounce back.[24] The same may be true again. Indeed, they were strong enough politically to resist leaving the Eurozone, which probably would have been a major setback. Whether the EU, after Brexit, will allow Greece a bit more fiscal slack and debt write-offs remains to be seen. The same is true for Germany's willingness to provide cheap funds to the Greeks. But one would expect the EU to be more forgiving of Greece in order to help shore up the EU project. At the time of writing, this progressive development has not occurred.

ICELAND

Iceland is extremely small—its population is slightly over 315,000 people—but it possesses its own language and it sustains a high culture. It is very homogeneous, marked by an egalitarian, social democratic tradition, and it accordingly has a very strong sense of national identity.[25] It was among the wealthiest countries in the world just prior to the financial crisis. Given our argument, it might be surprising, then, that the financial crisis hit Iceland so hard. The stock market plunged by roughly 98 percent, the foreign exchange market stopped working, the three biggest banks collapsed, and the economy witnessed the third biggest fall in output and the fourth biggest fall in employment of all OECD countries. Some have argued that this was the eleventh worst financial collapse in world history. Yet Iceland rebounded faster and more effectively than any other OECD country.[26] The explanation for both its crisis and the resilience of its rebound has much to do with Iceland's nation-building and state-building traditions, and its exceptionally small size.

23 Kalyvas 2015, pp. 177–82.
24 Kalyvas 2015, chap. 7.
25 Booth 2015, pp. 127–134.
26 Wade and Sigurgeirsdottir 2010, p. 5, 2012, p. 130.

Iceland has a long history of internal cooperation and consensus-making. In the tenth century it established what some consider to be the world's oldest parliament, where clan chieftains gathered to establish laws and agreements. Conflicts over religion were resolved by arbitration in the eleventh century in order to avoid civil war. Nevertheless, civil war did break out among clans in the thirteenth century, but over issues to do with power and influence rather than religion. Stability was restored when the chieftains signed a covenant establishing a union with the Norwegian crown. Since that time there has been virtually no serious internal conflict over issues concerning the nation—no civil wars and, as we shall see, no war to gain independence. Unlike Ireland and Greece, the national question was laid to rest long ago. So Iceland is an essentially harmonious country whose strong national identity has long been rooted in and reinforced by all sorts of myths and sagas about its initial discovery, early parliamentary formations and resilience in the face of a terribly inhospitable geography and climate.[27]

Iceland was a colony first of Norway and then—from 1262—of Denmark. In 1874 Denmark granted Iceland its first constitution, which established a modern parliament with legislative powers, although executive powers remained in Copenhagen with Icelandic legislation remaining subject to Danish approval. Home Rule was granted in 1904 in order to appease an emergent Icelandic independence movement. In 1918 Denmark recognized Iceland as a sovereign state and gave it another constitution but agreed to continue managing its foreign policy for the next twenty-five years. During the Second World War Britain occupied the country, turning it over to the United States in 1941 until the end of the war. In 1944 Iceland voted overwhelmingly to end its relationship with Denmark and become a constitutional republic. Full independence had finally arrived without a shot being fired. So unlike Ireland, Iceland experienced little nationalist animosity over the question of independence either before or after it was achieved. Iceland let the Americans maintain a military base during the Cold War, which they did until withdrawing in 2006.

All this had a profound effect on institution-building. On the one hand, like Ireland, Iceland is a very young nation-state. Again like Ireland, it was protected in many ways for centuries by a more powerful neighbor, which when coupled with its tiny size meant that it never required the construction of a sophisticated state bureaucracy. In particular, its regulatory apparatus remained very thin and its politics were subject to patronage and clientelism. On the other hand, some institutions were quite thick. Iceland inherited a long history of inclusive democracy and Scandinavian-style consensus-making. As a result, parliamentary democracy, proportional representation, and the

27 Jónsson 2009, chap. 1.

welfare state were well developed. Although left-wing parties were weak, unions were strong and the major economic sectors—agriculture and fishing —were well organized along corporatist lines.[28] Perhaps for these reasons Iceland's institutions before the crisis were ranked sixth best in the world according to the World Economic Forum, just one spot below Switzerland and three below Denmark.[29] But this overlooked some important elements of the social formation.

Lurking behind these formal political institutions was a handful of fourteen wealthy families—the so-called Octopus—whose tentacles controlled much of the economy, with very tight personal connections to a small clique of politicians and the media. In such a tiny country this created all sorts of opportunities for patronage, nepotism, cronyism, and corruption. Large financial contributions flowed from the bankers and other interest groups to the governing political parties. In particular, the business and agricultural interests supported the conservative Independence Party, formed in 1929 as the champion of the Icelandic independence movement, and the winner of the largest share of votes in every election from then until 2009. Given the patronage involved, the situation was reminiscent of Fianna Fáil's single-party dominance in Ireland![30] This generated something else similar to events in Ireland: the rise of groupthink and barriers to the expression of dissent— particularly in the Octopus-controlled media—over what bankers and policymakers were doing in the run-up to the crisis. Groupthink was exacerbated by the fact that in such a very small country like this there was a dearth of economists, which further hobbled meritocratic recruitment in the areas of finance, macroeconomic management, and financial regulation.[31] Groupthink and hubris marked the financial sector as it expanded quickly during the late 1990s and early 2000s into overseas markets.[32]

The financial competence of parliament and the regulatory apparatus was thin. The development of the Financial Supervisory Authority (FSA) failed to keep pace with the extremely rapid growth of the banking sector, discussed below. It was understaffed and weak; its staff lacked specialized knowledge about international banking.[33] As a result, the FSA relied heavily on the

28 Jónsson 2009, p. 10; Wade and Sigurgeirsdottir 2012, p. 132; World Economic Forum 2009.

29 World Economic Forum 2008.

30 Booth 2015; Boyes 2009, p. 51; Wade and Sigurgeirsdottir 2010, 2012.

31 Booth 2015, pp. 135–142; Boyes 2009; Wade and Sigurgeirsdottir 2010.

32 Jónsson 2009, p. 56.

33 Boyes 2009, p. 122; Jónsson 2009, pp. 138–43; Wade and Sigurgeirsdottir 2012, p. 135. In 2005 the British stationed a secret agent in Iceland to keep an eye on the financial system, because they feared that regulation was so lax that there were significant opportunities for money laundering by Russians and terrorists (Boyes 2009, p. 55).

banks for information. Regulatory capture ensued, exacerbated by the fact that regulators, top bankers, and politicians—notably Prime Minister David Oddsson—were enamored with Thatcherite free-market liberalism, which advocated a very light regulatory touch, the general liberalization of financial markets through the 1990s, including privatizing the banks, and the pursuit of speculative investment banking. Oddsson believed that this would help Iceland modernize by shifting its economic base from fish to finance.[34] Underscoring the lack of regulatory expertise in the state, Oddsson was appointed head of the Central Bank in 2008 even though he had no formal training in economics or finance, or any experience of working at a financial institution. In fact, appointments to all three of the recent Central Bank governorships had been former politicians.[35] This lack of expertise played a major role in the onset of the financial crisis.

Until the very late twentieth century Iceland's financial system consisted of a few small, conservative, state-owned commercial banks. The seeds of its financial crisis were first sown with the meteoric rise of three banks—Landsbanki, Kaupthing, and Glitnir—which grew from 1998 through privatization and mergers into world players with assets blossoming from 100 percent of GDP in 2000 to 800 percent by 2007. Their growth came from borrowing over $140 billion—ten times the country's GDP and fifty-six times its Central Bank's reserves. Two thirds of the money came from foreign sources. The money was used to engage in a wide variety of ill-advised mergers, acquisitions, and other investments, especially abroad and in businesses with which the banks had virtually no experience. This was a "cross-border, leveraged buyout frenzy."[36] They also lent money to each other and their own shareholders, who often used it to buy more shares in the banks themselves.[37] Warnings from foreign economists and from some Icelandic academics were ignored, and the prime minister closed the National Economic Institute in 2002 after it questioned what was happening. Although senior ministers established an ad hoc coordination group to plan in the event of a financial crisis, nothing came of it.

When Lehman Brothers collapsed the banks' massive debts were exposed as was the incompetence of the bankers and regulators. Interbank lending froze throwing the big banks into a severe liquidity crisis. Given the vast sums

34 Booth 2015, pp. 135–142; Boyes 2009, chap. 3; Jónsson 2009, pp. 38–42, 141; Wade and Sigurgeirsdottir 2010.

35 Jónsson 2009, pp. 30–31, 68, 142. They did, however, have a young, well-educated set of economists in the economic department during the early 2000s who were well versed in economic orthodoxy.

36 Jónsson 2009, p. 108. The banks did not, however, invest in the complex derivatives and subprime mortgages that brought banks down in other countries.

37 Boyes 2009, chap. 8.

required, the Central Bank and government were unable to cover the banks' debts and the currency quickly lost about half its value. Institutional thinness was the problem—the government never built up a sufficient infrastructure around the three rapidly growing banking giants.[38] Shortly after the crisis hit, the World Economic Forum downgraded Iceland's institutional ranking from sixth to thirteen.[39] Unemployment and inflation skyrocketed as did the cost of many Icelandic mortgages, many of which were indexed to foreign currencies and, therefore, suddenly underwater. Protestors took to the streets signaling a legitimation crisis, the Independence Party's coalition government was voted out of office. A Norwegian economist replaced Oddsson as the head of the Central Bank.[40]

Much of this sounds like a rehash of the Irish story—thin institutions, patronage, cronyism, neoliberalism, speculation, and lack of expertise run amok in a massive banking meltdown. However, the Icelandic response was very different. As the crisis began to unfold, it soon became apparent that the Central Bank was unable to act as lender of last resort because the big three banks' collective debt far exceeded its reserves. Help from the ECB was not forthcoming because Iceland was not in the Eurozone. As a result, Glitner was nationalized in September 2008. A week later parliament passed emergency legislation permitting the FSA to take over all the troubled banks. It did so, while refusing to socialize their debts and repay their foreign creditors. Instead, bondholders and creditors were forced to absorb the losses. Three new banks were established to take over the domestic accounts and healthy assets of the old troubled banks. The nonperforming assets were left in the old banks, where creditors could claim them if they wanted. So in stark contrast to Ireland, the government let the creditors—not the taxpayers—take the financial hit.

Meanwhile, in October 2008 the government asked the IMF to help stabilize the currency, which it did by providing a $2.1 billion conditional loan and arranging another $3 billion loan from other countries. With a strong push from the IMF the government also imposed capital controls, which are now credited with having prevented the outflow of $8 billion (roughly 50 percent of GDP) from the country. Eventually, the government pursued expansionary fiscal policy, increased and extended unemployment benefits, and adopted a more progressive tax code that included hefty tax hikes for the wealthy and relief for low- and middle-income families. It devalued the currency. It low-

---

38 Jónsson 2009, p. 138.

39 World Economic Forum 2009.

40 Booth 2015, pp. 127–160; Wade and Sigurgeirsdottir 2010, 2012; Woll 2014, pp. 21, 23–24.

ered household debt and mortgage interest payments and ruled mortgages indexed to foreign currencies illegal. As a result, although GDP dropped, unemployment was less severe than in Ireland and much of the rest of Europe, and Iceland rebounded from the crisis relatively quickly.[41] In addition, major financial sector reforms were launched, including the adoption of more sustainable banking models and implementation of a more effective regulatory structure.[42]

Commentators have noted that Iceland's heterodox crisis management stands in sharp contrast to the orthodox austerity responses of many other European countries.[43] There are several reasons for this. First, unlike Ireland, Iceland was quick to seek outside expertise. The government turned to experts from J.P. Morgan to advise how to handle the three big banks, cleanse their balance sheets, guarantee their depositors, and take over what was left— something J.P. Morgan knew about thanks to its earlier experience dismantling Washington Mutual in the United States. Iceland also quickly called the IMF for additional advice and assistance.[44] Second, Iceland was not subject to the Troika, because it was not in the Eurozone. This made it easier than it was in Eurozone countries to allow the banks to default at the expense of bondholders and creditors. Notably, in contrast to the Troika's insistence in Ireland in 2010 that the government refrain from giving bondholders haircuts, the IMF in Iceland supported the idea of letting the banks fail and issuing haircuts.[45] However, despite the IMF's proclivity for austerity, Iceland traveled the more heterodox path with Keynesian-style expansionary policies. In this regard, Iceland enjoyed more flexibility than the Eurozone countries. Crucial here was the fact that voters replaced the center-right Independence Party government with a left-leaning Social Democratic Alliance/ Left-Green Movement government.[46] Third, despite the initial decision to administer haircuts to foreign interests, parliament approved an EU request in October 2009 for the government to at least pay British and Dutch depositors €5.5 billion for the losses they suffered in their online bank accounts when the Icelandic banks collapsed. However, in an episode reminiscent of Switzerland's thick consensus-oriented political institutions, the president

41 Blyth 2013, pp. 235–40; Hart-Landsberg 2013; Jónsson 2009, p. 202; Wade and Sigurgeirsdottir 2010.

42 Matsangou 2015.

43 Armingeon and Baccaro 2012, pp. 164–65.

44 Jónsson 2009, pp. 169, 197.

45 We were told in an interview in Ireland that the IMF disagreed with its fellow Troika members over the issue of haircuts and favored administering them to bondholders (interview with David Begg, ICTU).

46 Matsangou 2015.

refused to sign it without a national referendum, which was held six months later and voted down. A new agreement was negotiated with the EU but rejected by another referendum in 2011.[47]

Although Iceland's thin bureaucratic, regulatory, and financial institutions were culpable in fomenting the crisis, the country's much thicker legislative and electoral institutions were pivotal in resolving it. Crisis management was consensus-oriented with an eye fixed squarely on the national interest—not the parochial interests of individual banks, bondholders, or creditors. Everyone realized they needed outside assistance and did not hesitate to ask for it. Indeed, all the major interest groups agreed that they needed to work together for the good of the country. Unions, business leaders, investment bankers, pension fund managers, and all the important politicians were willing to cooperate. Notably, much like the Danish pension fund ATP, the Icelandic pension funds were willing to sell half of their foreign holdings and exchange the proceeds for government securities to shore up Iceland's foreign reserves.[48] In this regard, Iceland benefited from its long history of institutionalized political consensus-making and the absence of internal nationalist conflicts. The benefits of a strong ideology of social partnership were obvious. But the country also benefited from a modicum of leeway thanks to the fact that it was not a member of the Eurozone and thus did not have to bend to the will of the Troika—or even to that of the IMF at least insofar as the pursuit of heterodox policy was concerned. In this regard Iceland had thicker organizational capacities than either Greece or Ireland.

Rigid Leviathans

As we begin to bring this book to an end, perhaps we might be allowed some speculative comments, essentially ad hoc in character, on a passing claim in the opening chapter—that large states may need to become more flexible if they are to remain successful within contemporary capitalism given the ease and speed of global interactions. This is no easy task. Japan, one of the most culturally homogeneous advanced countries in the world, has struggled since the 1990s to find solutions to its sluggish economic growth and deflationary tendencies. Italy and France seem to be just as incapable of reforming themselves and continue to struggle in the wake of the financial crisis. Britain cannot seem to get over having lost its empire, and has surely shot itself in the foot by voting to abandon the EU. The really interesting exception is Germany as it did a great deal to successfully modify its political economy in the 1980s and 1990s. But we should also remember that some states remain large

---

47 Hart-Landsberg 2013.
48 Jónsson 2009, pp. 149–54.

enough to still have options that others lack. This is true of Germany, the hegemon of Europe—whose prosperity in part results from that very position. Germany was able to protect its investors holding Irish bonds from suffering haircuts because of its substantial influence over the ECB. But the best-laid plans can go wrong. If Germany's insistence on austerity continues, it might yet lead to the collapse of the EU. Were that to happen, any new German national currency would become so strong as to adversely affect its capacity as an exporter.

But the most important case to consider is the United States, the world's hegemon. The American tradition of subscribing to a set of common norms and values contributing to a common national identity may be at risk.[49] Racial tensions remain and in some ways have grown worse since the 1970s, aggravated recently by concerns over immigration, persistent economic inequality the brunt of which is borne disproportionately by minority groups, and by gerrymandering of voting districts often designed to dilute the minority vote.[50] The result has been the worst political polarization and gridlock the country has seen since the Second World War, as well as the rise of right-wing populist nationalism within the Republican Party attacking Hispanics, Muslims, and other minority groups—nationalist trends that were exacerbated by and helped fuel Donald Trump's rise to the presidency. The country is now noticeably divided on ethnic lines, with the Republican Party becoming a redoubt of white voters. The United States has a long history of building state institutions that excluded African Americans and more recently newer immigrant groups from exercising political voice. The unintended consequence of this has been to undermine national unity. The Swiss used federalism to create a multi-ethnic nation-state, but the Americans used the same institutional matrix to protect states' rights in ways that exacerbate regional tensions, particularly between the North and South—and by extension racial animosities. The problem of divisiveness for the United States has been compounded by the massive influx of money into American politics that has enabled millionaires and billionaires, often with extremely conservative political agendas, to play an increasingly powerful if not always visible role in determining who runs for and wins high political office.[51] In this regard, the United States resembles Ireland insofar as patronage, cronyism, and corruption have become the order of the day at least in national electoral politics. This too undermines national unity. The current generation of policymakers may be either unwilling or unable to build thicker institutions better equipped to handle the vicissitudes and crises of globalization because they are unable

---

49 Hall and Lindholm 1999; Wilson 1996.
50 Edsall and Esdall 1992.
51 Mayer 2016.

to set aside their ideology and parochial self-interests and strive together for the benefit of the country as a whole.[52]

This was apparent during the 2008 financial crisis. When it began the Bush administration asked Congress to approve a $700 million emergency rescue package to save the banking system. But in September Congress voted down the request sending the financial markets into a tailspin. Most Democrats supported it but most Republicans opposed it. Eventually, the central bank, the Federal Reserve, intervened with a massive liquidity injection for the banks despite protests from some members of Congress, mostly Republicans. Moreover, institution-building in the form of new regulatory legislation —the Dodd-Frank Act—followed in 2010 but again with little bipartisan support. Wall Street had launched a massive lobbying campaign to kill it. But once it passed, Wall Street launched another attack to gut its implementation, the fate of which appears to hinge on the ability of an evolving set of small-group coalitions trying to defend the legislation—evidence that national unity and consensus have still not emerged in this case.[53] Whether the thickening of organizational capacities through Dodd-Frank will happen under the Trump administration is very much in doubt as of this writing. During the crisis, consensus-making and an ideology of social partnership in the national interest were sorely lacking. Politicians were for the most part not willing to step aside and let the experts handle things. The political parties were at odds with each other at almost every turn. Only the independent action of the Fed in cooperation with the Treasury and one or two executive branch agencies, such as the Federal Deposit Insurance Corporation, prevented the financial system from collapsing completely.

Of course, the United States survived and in fact bounced back fairly quickly from the crisis. In this regard, it did demonstrate resilience, but not the sort that we have been talking about. American resilience had much more to do with the fact that it was the world's hegemonic power. The special place that the United States holds in the international political economy affords it opportunities for action that no other country possesses. The fact that the dollar remains the world's dominant reserve currency allows the United States many privileges of seigniorage. Most immediately, the hegemon could print money at will thereby allowing the Fed to run its capital injection and quantitative easing programs, save the financial system and reduce the severity of

---

52 Tony Judt (2010) offers a powerful argument about why younger Americans in general have become so inclined to favor their individual self-interests over the collective interests of the nation—they have forgotten the lessons of the Second World War that gave rise to unifying institutions, notably the welfare state.

53 Ziegler and Wooley 2016.

the Great Recession that followed.[54] A good deal of the monies released were borrowed by emerging market economies. Such countries now suffer severely because the United States is starting to raise interest rates as its economy recovers, making their debt repayments difficult, thereby undermining their currencies. The crucial point to be made is that what suits the United States is not necessarily good for the world economy, something that might become dramatically worse should protectionist instincts be translated into policy. American economic policy is likely to become more haphazard, increasing the vulnerability of the small nation-states with which we have been concerned. There is no end of history in sight.

Looming Crisis

We have shown that to understand our three cases, and likely others, it is necessary to take the long historical view. But we do not assume that the situations in these countries are necessarily permanent. As it happens, change is not just possible but in fact likely. What lies ahead is not necessarily good news. The consensual politics on which Danish and Swiss success rested may be starting to crack. What matters here is not clashes internally between ethnic groups in Switzerland, something that is not possible in any case in Denmark given its remarkable homogeneity. What we see instead is the emergence of nativist sentiments largely based on social class, caused by concerns over immigration. The poorer members of these societies feel left out and accordingly are open to movements that demonize immigrants, especially if they happen to be Muslim. This is happening in other countries too, including in the United States, where Trump won the presidency; in Britain, where Brexit was partly a response to nativist sentiments; and in France, with the rise of the xenophobic National Front urging that the country follow Britain out of the EU. Such divisiveness may jeopardize the prospects in these countries for resilient responses to future crises.

The Danish People's Party played a pivotal role in national politics at least since the start of the century, and in 2014 it won the election with over 26 percent of the vote. It has successfully challenged the rights of legal immigrants to have the same access to the welfare system as Danish citizens. It also advocates limiting immigration to prevent Denmark from becoming a multiethnic society. The party's platform is premised on the notion that the influx of immigrants—actually rather small so far as a percentage of the general population—threatens to undermine traditional Danish culture. This threatens

---

54 Some have argued that if Iceland had such a privileged currency it too would have been able to save its troubled banks (Boyes 2009, p. 6).

national unity for sure, as nativist nationalism from below is not shared throughout the society. But something more serious may yet occur. We have seen that consensus in economic policymaking was disrupted when the People's Party supported the government of Anders Fogh Rasmussen, thereby allowing him to avoid consultation with other parties. That situation persists today as the People's Party has convinced the parliament to cut the university education budget and spend more on pensions, which benefit older Danes, an important part of the party's electoral base. This may well hurt Danish economic competitiveness by compromising human capital.

Something similar is happening in Switzerland. The Swiss People's Party, once only a junior partner in government, is now the strongest one with over 30 percent of the vote in the last election.[55] It has two of the seven seats in the Federal Council, and it has launched successful referenda limiting the construction of Muslim minarets, expelling criminal foreigners from the country, and in 2014 imposing quotas on immigration from the EU as well as non-EU countries—a move that violates Switzerland's bilateral agreement with the EU that granted trade openness in return for free movement of labor. In the final analysis, this last piece of legislation came to naught, as we have seen: this small-nation state caved in to the refusal of the EU to compromise. Britain is large enough to feel that it can manage without the EU, although the amount of illusion here is staggering; Switzerland is far too vulnerable to take such a risk. Still, our sense is that this issue may yet come to the fore again. In any case, it is certain that the rise of the Swiss People's Party has meant the emergence of genuine contention inside Switzerland, which causes some people to fret about the breakdown of its traditional consensus-making model.[56] Indeed, the party's rise might mean that national solidarity is coming to an end in a way that will affect resilience and economic prosperity. In a sense this would prove our general argument, making the description of Swiss success something of a eulogy for a world that is passing. Here it is important to note that Christian Blocher, the party's founder and leader, was a supremely successful businessman who made a fortune overseas, notably in China, before turning to politics. This means that he has a contradictory vision for the country—populism and nationalism for the lower classes but globalization and a modicum of Europeanization for the business community.[57] With respect to the latter, the Swiss People's Party does not resemble its Danish counterpart. More to the point, Blocher might still throw his weight behind moves to maintain, if not thicken, Switzerland's traditional institutions insofar as they utilize expert and consensus-oriented policymaking to help the

55 Christoffersen et al. 2014, p. 142.
56 Interview with Klaus Armingeon, University of Bern.
57 Interviews with Wolfgang Linder, University of Bern; Jacob Tanner, University of Zürich.

export sector, which of course includes much banking and finance. So for now it is not clear whether the rise of the People's Party will sound a death knell for the institutions necessary to either prevent or manage serious economic crises in the future.

The outbreak of nationalist political fervor cannot be reduced to shifts in nominal heterogeneity. Consider the numbers: In 2014 immigrants comprised 8.9 percent of the Danish population and 24 percent of the Swiss population—both involving only marginal increases over the past decade or so—and 12 percent of the Irish population. If political divisiveness along cultural lines was just a matter of numbers, then the politicization of immigration should have been greatest in Switzerland followed by Ireland and then Denmark. But controversy around the issue has emerged about as forcefully in Denmark as it has in Switzerland. And it has not emerged in Ireland, even though immigration contributed significantly to an increase in the Irish population, which jumped from 3.6 million to 4.2 million between 1996 and 2006.[58]

Why is it that in Ireland opposition to immigration did not increase like it did elsewhere? One interview in Dublin suggested that this was because immigration is "in our DNA," by which he meant that the Irish have a long history of emigration, know what it's like to be immigrants, and so are accommodating to immigrants when they arrive.[59] The political salience of immigration depends on historical experience as well as institutional factors. Certainly Ireland seems to have rebounded from the financial crisis rather well, having paid back the loans it received from the Troika and having benefited from an influx of foreign direct investment and intellectual property.[60] Now that the British have voted to leave the EU, Ireland's well-educated English-speaking population may prove to be an especially attractive magnet for foreign investment. The irony, of course, is that of our three main cases the one that fared the worst in the financial crisis may yet do very well.

58 Kirby 2010a, pp. 14–15.
59 Interview with Tony Donohoe, IBEC.
60 Boland 2016.

REFERENCES

Abulof, Uriel. 2015. *The Mortality and Morality of Nations*. Cambridge: Cambridge University Press

Alesina, Alberto, and Enrico Spolaore. 2003. *The Size of Nations*. Cambridge: Massachusetts Institute of Technology Press.

Anderson, Benedict. 1983. *Imagined Communities*. London: Verso.

Andeweg, Rudy. 2000. "Consociational Democracy." *Annual Review of Political Science* 3:509–36.

Angelos, James. 2015. *The Full Catastrophe: Travels among the New Greek Ruins*. New York: Crown.

Armingeon, Klaus, and Lucio Baccaro. 2012. "The Sorrows of Young Euro: The Sovereign Debt Crises of Ireland and Southern Europe." Pp. 162–98 in *Coping with Crisis*, edited by Nancy Bermeo and Jonas Pontusson. New York: Russell Sage.

BIS (Bank for International Settlements). 2008. *75th Annual Report, Part VII: The Financial Sector in the Advanced Industrial Economies*. Basel: BIS. http://www.bis.org/publ/arpdf/ar 2008e.htm (accessed January 2009).

Barnes, Lucy, and Anne Wren. 2012. "The Liberal Model in (the) Crisis: Continuity and Change in Great Britain and Ireland." Pp. 287–24 in *Coping with Crisis*, edited by Nancy Bermeo and Jonas Pontusson. New York: Russell Sage.

Bartlett, Thomas. 2010. *Ireland: A History*. New York: Cambridge University Press.

Barzel, Yoram. 1989. *Economic Analysis of Property Rights*. New York: Cambridge University Press.

Baur, Martin, Pierre-Alain Bruchez, and Barbara Schlaffer. 2013. "Institutions for Crisis Prevention: The Case of Switzerland." *Global Policy* 4 (Supplement 1, July):10–21.

Bell, Stephen and Andrew Hindimoor. 2015. *Masters of the Universe, Slaves of the Market*. Cambridge: Harvard University Press.

Bennett, Andrew, and Jeffrey Checkel. 2015a. "Process Tracing: From Philosophical to Best Practices." Pp. 3–39 in *Process Tracing*, edited by Andrew Bennett and Jeffrey Checkel. New York: Cambridge University Press.

———, eds. 2015b. *Process Tracing*. New York: Cambridge University Press.

Berg, Kasper Krone. 2015. "ATP Lap 240 Billion Kroner in Various Financial Crisis Tools." *FinansWatch*, April 9. http://finanswatch.dk/Finansnyt/article4946159.ece (accessed April 2015.)

Berger, Suzanne, ed. 1981. *Organizing Interests in Western Europe*. New York: Cambridge University Press.

Bernanke, Ben. 2015. *The Courage to Act: A Memoir of a Crisis and Its Aftermath*. New York: Norton.

Bew, Paul. 2007. *Ireland: The Politics of Enmity 1789–2006*. New York: Oxford University Press.

Bew, Paul, and Henry Patterson. 1982. *Sean Lemass and the Making of Modern Ireland*. London: Gill and Macmillan.

Bjerre-Nielsen, Henrik, and Jimmy Scavenius Lang. 2011. "From Bank Package to Exit Package." *International In-house Counsel Journal* 4(16):1–9.

Blyth, Mark. 2013. *Austerity: The History of a Dangerous Idea*. New York: Oxford University Press.

Boland, Vincent. 2016. "Ireland's 26% GDP Growth Met with Bafflement." *The Financial Times*, July 13.

———. 2015a. "Inquiry into Banking Crisis Struggles to Heal Ireland's Wounds." *The Financial Times*, July 31.

———. 2015b. "Fiscal Watchdog Warns Dublin Not to Repeat Spending Errors." *The Financial Times*, November 27.

Boland, Vincent, and Peter Spiegel. 2014. "Trichet Letters Show Bailout Threat Made to Ireland." *The Financial Times*, November 7.

Booth, Michael. 2015. *The Almost Nearly Perfect People: Behind the Myth of the Scandinavian Utopia*. London: Vintage.

Borrás, Susana, and Leonard Seabrooke. 2015. "Sources of National Institutional Competitiveness: Sense Making and Institutional Change." Pp. 1–20 in *Sources of National Institutional Competitiveness: Sense Making and Institutional Change*. New York: Oxford University Press.

Boyes, Roger. 2009. *Meltdown Iceland*. New York: Bloomsbury.

Brazys, Samuel, and Aidan Regan. 2015. "These Little PIIGS Went to Market: Enterprise Policy and Divergent Recovery in the European Periphery." Working paper 2015/7, University College Dublin Geary Institute.

Breiding, R. James. 2013. *Swiss Made: The Untold Story behind Switzerland's Success*. London: Profile Books.

Campbell, John L. 2011. "The U.S. Financial Crisis: Lessons for Theories of Institutional Complementarity." *Socio-Economic Review* 9:211–34.

———. 2004. *Institutional Change and Globalization*. Princeton: Princeton University Press.

———. 2003. "States, Politics and Globalization: Why Institutions Still Matter." Pp. 234–59 in *The Nation-State in Question*, edited by T. V. Paul, G. John Ikenberry, and John A. Hall. Princeton: Princeton University Press.

———. 2002. "Ideas, Politics and Public Policy." *Annual Review of Sociology* 38:21–38.

Campbell, John L., and John A. Hall. 2015. *The World of States*. London: Bloomsbury Press.

Campbell, John L., John A. Hall, and Ove K. Pedersen, eds. 2006. *National Identity and the Varieties of Capitalism: The Danish Experience*. Montreal: McGill-Queen's University Press.

Campbell, John L., and Ove K. Pedersen. 2014. *The National Origins of Policy Ideas: Knowledge Regimes in the United States, France, Germany and Denmark*. Princeton: Princeton University Press.

———. 2007. "The Varieties of Capitalism and Hybrid Success: Denmark in the Global Economy." *Comparative Political Studies* 40(3):307–32.

Campbell, John L., Charles Quincy, Jordan Osserman, and Ove K. Pedersen. 2013. "Coding In-Depth Semi-Structured Interviews: Problems of Unitization and Inter-Coder Reliability and Agreement." *Sociological Methods and Research* 42(3):294–320.

Cardiff, Kevin. 2016. *Recap: Inside Ireland's Financial Crisis*. Dublin: Liffey Press.

Carstensen, Martin. 2013. "Projecting From a Fiction: The Case of Denmark and the Financial Crisis." *New Political Economy* 18:555–78.

Carswell, Simon. 2010. "The Big Gamble: The Inside Story of the Bank Guarantee." *The Irish Times*, September 25. http://www.irishtimes.com/news/the-big-gamble-the-inside-story -of-the-bank-guarantee-1.655629 (accessed October 2010).

Central Bank of Ireland. 2015. "The Role of the Financial Regulator." http://www.financial regulator.ie/about-us/role/Pages/default.aspx (accessed June 2015).

Chari, Raj, and Patrick Bernhagen. 2011. "Financial and Economic Crisis: Explaining the Sunset over the Celtic Tiger." *Irish Political Studies* 26(4):473–88.

Christensen, Johan. 2015. *The Power of Economists within the State*. Unpublished manuscript, Department of Public Administration, University of Leiden.

———. 2013. "Economists and Neoliberal Reform." Ph.D. diss., Department of Politics, European University Institute.

Christoffersen, Henrik, Michaelle Beyeler, Reiner Eichengerger, Peter Nannestad, and Martin Paldam. 2014. *The Good Society: A Comparative Study of Denmark and Switzerland*. New York: Springer.

Clarke, Blanaid, and Niamh Hardiman. 2012. "Crisis in the Irish Banking System." University College Dublin Geary Institute Discussion Paper Series, University College Dublin. February.

Clogg, Richard. 2013. *A Concise History of Greece*. New York: Cambridge University Press.

Commission of Experts. 2010. *Final Report of the Commission of Experts for Limiting the Economic Risks Posed by Large Companies*. Bern: State Secretariat for International Financial Matters (SIF).

Coser, Lewis. 1956. *The Functions of Social Conflict*. New York: Free Press.

Country Economy. 2015. "Rating: Ireland Credit Rating." http://countryeconomy.com/ratings/ireland (accessed June 2015).

Crouch, Colin. 2011. *The Strange Non-Death of Neoliberalism*. Cambridge: Polity Press.

Dahrendorf, Ralf. 1957. *Class and Class Conflict in Industrial Society*. London: Routledge and Kegan Paul.

Danske Bank. 2012. *Danish Support Packages for the Financial and Corporate Sectors*. Copenhagen: Danske Bank.

Danthine, Jean-Pierre. 2011. "Swiss Monetary Policy in the Public Eye." Paper presented at the Money Market Event, Zurich, March 24, Swiss National Bank Zurich.

Dardanelli, Paolo. 2015. "Multi-lingual but Mono-national: Exploring and Explaining Switzerland's Exceptionalism." Pp. 295–323 in *Federalism, Plurinationality and Democratic Constitutionalism*, edited by Ferran Requejo and Miguel Caminal. Abingdon: Routledge.

Davies, Howard. 2010. *The Financial Crisis: Who is to Blame?* London: Polity.

Davis, Gerald. 2009. *Managed by the Markets: How Finance Reshaped America*. New York: Oxford University Press.

De Quetteville, Harry. 2008. "Financial Crisis: Why the Swiss Economy Is Still as Safe as—er—a Swiss Bank." *The Telegraph*, October 14.

Deutsche Bundesbank. 2013. *Deutsche Bundesbank Eurosystem*. http://www.bundesbank.de/Navigation/EN/Statistics/Time_series_databases/Macro_economic_time_series/its_details_value_node.html?tsId=BBK01.EU3312 (accessed September 2013).

DKM Economic Consultants. 2008. *Review of the Construction Industry 2007 and Outlook 2008 to 2010*. Dublin: DKM Economic Consultants. http://www.environ.ie/en/Publications/StatisticsandRegularPublications/ConstructionIndustryStatistics/FileDownLoad,18630,en.pdf (accessed December 2011).

Donovan, Donal, and Antoin Murphy. 2013. *The Fall of the Celtic Tiger*. New York: Oxford University Press.

Dorney, John. 2013. "A Short History of Freedom of Information in Independent Ireland." *The Irish Story*. http://www.theirishstory.com/2010/07/25/a-short-history-of-freedom-of-information-in-independent-ireland/#.VX66Fk3bLcs (accessed June 2015).

The Economist. 2015a. "Beware Greeks Voting for Gifts." January 31, pp. 18–20.

———. 2015b. "Charlemagne: Greece and Its Discontents." January 31, p. 47.

———. 2014a. "Greece's Return to the Markets: The Prodigal Son." April 12, pp. 69–70.

———. 2014b. "Greece's Protest Parties: Syriza and other Radicals." May 31, pp. 45–46.

———. 2010a. "Still Crazy after All These Yields." November 13, p. 85.

———. 2010b. "How Now Brian Cowen?" October 9, p. 72.

Edsall, Mary D., and Thomas Byrne Edsall. 1992. *Chair Reaction: The Impact of Race, Rights and Taxes on American Politics*. New York: Norton.

Eichengreen, Barry. 2008. *The European Economy since 1945*. Princeton: Princeton University Press.

Elster, Jon. 1989. *Nuts and Bolts for the Social Sciences*. New York: Cambridge University Press.

Esping-Andersen, Gøsta. 1984. *Politics against Markets: The Social Democratic Route to Power*. Princeton: Princeton University Press.

European Commission. 2013. "Ireland's Economic Crisis: How Did It Happen and What Is Being Done about It?" http://ec.europa.eu/ireland/economy/irelands_economic_crisis/index_en .htm (accessed May 2013).

———. 2008. "State Aid: Commission Approves Danish Liquidation Aid for Roskilde Bank." Press release, November 5, Brussels. http://europa.eu/rapid/press-release_IP-08-1633_en .htm (accessed April 2008).

Evans, Peter. 1995. *Embedded Autonomy*. Princeton: Princeton University Press.

Evans, Peter, and J. Rauch. 1999. "Bureaucracy and Growth: A Cross-National Analysis of the Effects of 'Weberian' State Structures on Economic Growth." *American Sociological Review* 64:748–65.

Evans, Peter, Dietrich Rueschemeyer, and Theda Skocpol, eds. 1985. *Bringing the State Back In*. New York: Cambridge University Press.

Federal Department of Finance. 2010. *Swiss Financial Market Policy*. Bern: Federal Department of Finance.

FDIC (Federal Deposit Insurance Corporation). 2005. "Consolidation in the U.S. Banking Industry: Is the 'Long, Strange Trip' about to End?" *FDIC Banking Review* 17(4)31–61. https:// www.fdic.gov/bank/analytical/banking/2006jan/article2/article2.pdf (accessed January 2015).

Finansforbundet. 2009. "On the Right Track: Finansforbundet's Proposals for Financial sector Regulation in Denmark." Copenhagen: Finansforbundet.

FINMA. 2010. "Committee of Experts on 'Too Big To Fail' Issue—FINMA and SNB Recommend Rapid Implementation Measures." Press release, October 4. http://www.finma.ch/e /aktuell/Pages/mm-schulssbericht-exko-tbtf-20101004.aspx (accessed August 2015).

———. 2009. *Financial Market Crisis and Financial Market Supervision*. Bern: Swiss Financial Market Supervisory Authority (FINMA).

Finn, Daniel. 2014. "Rethinking the Republic." *New Left Review* 90:45–76.

———. 2011. "Ireland on the Turn?" *New Left Review* 67:5–39.

Fligstein, Neil, and Jacob Habinek. 2014. "Sucker Punched by the Invisible Hand: The World Financial Markets and the Globalization of the U.S. Mortgage Crisis." *Socio-Economic Review* 12:637–65.

Fligstein, Neil, and Doug McAdam. 2012. *A Theory of Fields*. New York: Oxford University Press.

Fukuyama, Francis. 2014. *Political Order and Political Decay*. New York: Farrar, Straus and Giroux.

Gallagher, Michael, and Paul Mitchell. 2005. *The Politics of Electoral Systems*. Oxford: Oxford University Press.

Garvin, Tom. 2004. *Preventing the Future: Why Was Ireland so Poor for so Long?* Dublin: Gill and Macmillan.

Gellner, Ernest A. 1983. *Nations and Nationalism*. Blackwell, Oxford.

Gilardi, Fabrizio, and Fabio Wasserfallen. 2014. "How Socialization Attenuates Tax Competition." *British Journal of Political Science* 46:45–65.

Girvin, Brian. 2010. "Before the Celtic Tiger: Change without Modernization in Ireland 1959–1989." *Economic and Social Review* 41(3):349–65.

Goldberg, Linda, Craig Kennedy, and Jason Miu. 2010. "Central Bank Dollar Swap Lines and Overseas Dollar Funding Costs." Federal Reserve Bank of New York, Staff Report 429. http://www.newyorkfed.org/research/staff_reports/sr429.pdf (accessed April 2015).

Gorski, Philip. 2003. *The Disciplinary Revolution*. Chicago: Chicago University Press.

Goul Andersen, J. 2011. "From the Edge of the Abyss to Bonanza—and Beyond: Danish Economy and Economic Policies 1980–2011." *Comparative Social Research* 28:89–165.

Gourevitch, Peter. 1986. *Politics in Hard Times*. Ithaca: Cornell University Press.

Gow, David. 2008. "Switzerland Unveils Bank Bail-out Plan." *The Guardian*, October 16.

Grossman, Emiliano, and Cornelia Woll. 2012. "Saving the Banks: The Political Economy of Bailouts." Unpublished manuscript, Sciences Po, Paris.

Group of Experts. 2014. *Group of Experts on the Further Development of the Financial Market Strategy: Final Report*. Bern: Swiss Federal Council.

Habyarimana, James, Macartan Humphreys, Daniel N. Posner, and Jeremy M. Weinstein. 2009. *Coethnicity: Diversity and Dilemmas of Collective Action*. New York: Russell Sage.

Hall, John A., and Charles Lindholm. 1999. *Is America Breaking Apart?* Princeton: Princeton University Press.

Hall, Peter A., ed. 1989. *The Political Power of Economic Ideas: Keynesianism across Nations*. Princeton: Princeton University Press.

———. 1986. *Governing the Economy*. New York: Oxford University Press.

Hall, Peter A., and Michèle Lamont. 2013. "Introduction." Pp. 1–34 in *Social Resilience in the Neoliberal Era*, edited by Peter Hall and Michèle Lamont. New York: Cambridge University Press.

Hall, Peter A., and David Soskice, eds. 2001. *Varieties of Capitalism*. New York: Oxford University Press.

Hardiman, Niamh. 2012. "Conclusion: Changing Irish Governance." Pp. 212–31 in *Irish Governance in Crisis*, edited by Niamh Hardiman. Manchester, England: Manchester University Press.

———. 2010. "Bringing Domestic Institutions Back into an Understanding of Ireland's Economic Crisis." *Irish Studies in International Affairs* 21:71–87.

Hardiman, Niamh, Spyros Blavoukos, Sebastian Dellepiane-Avallaneda, and George Pagoulatos. 2016. "Austerity in the European Periphery: The Irish Experience." Working paper 2016/04. University College Dublin Geary Institute.

Hart-Landsberg, Martin. 2013. "Lessons from Iceland." *Monthly Review* 65(5), http://monthly review.org/2013/10/01/lessons-iceland/ (accessed January 2016).

Hedström, Peter, and Richard Swedberg. 1998. "Social Mechanisms: An Introductory Essay." Pp. 1–31 in *Social Mechanisms: An Analytical Approach to Social Theory*, edited by Peter Hedström and Richard Swedberg. New York: Cambridge University Press.

Helleiner, Eric, and Andreas Pickel, eds. 2005. *Economic Nationalism in a Globalizing World*. Ithaca: Cornell University Press.

Hirschman, Albert O. 1945. *National Power and the Structure of Foreign Trade*. Berkeley: University of California Press.

Hollingsworth, J. Rogers, and Wolfgang Streeck. 1994. "Countries and Sectors: Concluding Remarks on Performance, Convergence, and Competitiveness." Pp. 270–300 in *Governing Capitalist Economies*, edited by J. Rogers Hollingsworth, Philippe Schmitter, and Wolfgang Streeck. New York: Oxford University Press.

Honohan, Patrick. 2008. "The Financial Crisis: Ireland and the World." The Michael Littleton Memorial Lecture. Dublin: RTE.

Honohan, Patrick, Donal Donovan, Paul Gorecki, and Farique Mottiar. 2010. *The Irish Banking Crisis: Regulatory and Financial Stability Policy 2003–2008. A Report to the Minister for Finance and the Governor of the Central Bank*. Dublin: Central Bank.

Indexmundi. 2013. *World Factbook*. http://www.indexmundi.com/ (accessed September 2013).

Jensen, Jason, and John A. Hall. 2014. "The Decomposition of the Oldenburg Imperial Monarchy," *Nations and Nationalism* 20(4):742–59.

Joint Committee of Inquiry into the Banking Crisis. 2016. *Report of the Joint Committee of Inquiry into the Banking Crisis*, vol. 1. Dublin: Houses of the Oireachtas.

Jones, Erik. 2008. *Economic Adjustment and Political Transformation in Small States*. New York: Oxford University Press.

Jónsson, Ásgeir. 2009. *Why Iceland?* New York: McGraw Hill.

Jordan, Thomas J. 2014. "The Challenges of the Global Economic Crisis—Can Switzerland Master Them?" Zurich: Swiss National Bank.

———. 2012. "Monetary Policy in the Financial Crisis—Measures, Effects, Risks." Paper presented at the Swiss Banking Global Symposium, Zurich, November 16. Zurich: Swiss National Bank.

Judt, Tony. 2010. *Ill Fares the Land*. New York: Penguin.

———. 2005. *Postwar: A History of Europe since 1945*. New York: Penguin.

Kalyvas, Stathis. 2015. *Modern Greece*. New York: Oxford University Press.

Kang, David. 2002. *Crony Capitalism*. New York: Cambridge University Press.

Kapstein, Ethan. 1994. *Governing the Global Economy*. Cambridge: Harvard University Press.

Kaspersen, Lars Bo. 2013. *Denmark in the World*. Copenhagen: Hans Reitzels Forlag.

———. 2006. "The Formation and Development of the Welfare State." Pp. 99–132 in *National Identity and the Varieties of Capitalism: The Danish Experience*, edited by John L. Campbell, John A. Hall, and Ove K. Pedersen. Montreal: McGill-Queen's University Press.

Katzenstein, Peter J. 1985. *Small States in World Markets: Industrial Policy in Europe*. Ithaca: Cornell University Press.

———. 1984. *Corporatism and Change*. Ithaca: Cornell University Press.

Kenworthy, Lane. 2008. *Jobs with Equality*. New York: Oxford University Press.

Keohane, Robert, and Joseph Nye. 1977. *Power and Interdependence: World Politics in Transition*. Boston: Little Brown.

Kindleberger, Charles P. 1951. "Group Behavior and International Trade." *Journal of Political Economy* 59(1):30–46.

Kirby, Peadar. 2010a. *Celtic Tiger in Collapse*. New York: Palgrave.

———. 2010b. "When Banks Cannibalize a State: Analysing Ireland's Financial Crisis." Elanco Royal Institute working paper 178/2010. Madrid: Real Instituto Elcano.

Kirchgässner, Gebhard. 2013. "Fiscal Institutions at the Cantonal Level in Switzerland." Unpublished paper, Department of Economics, University of St. Gallen, Switzerland.

Kirkup, James, and Bruno Waterfield. 2008. "Financial Crisis: Switzerland Injects 'Bail-out' Billions into Banks." *The Telegraph*, October 16.

Kissane, Bill. 2007. "Size Matters? Small Size and Economic Performance in Finland and Ireland." Paper presented at the Conference on Small States, John Sloan Dickey Center, Dartmouth College, March.

Kluth, Michael, and Kennet Lynggaarad. 2012. "Explaining Policy Responses to Danish and Irish Banking Failures during the Financial Crisis." *West European Politics* 36(4):771–88.

Koch, Hal. 1952. *N.F.S. Grundtvig*. Antioch, Ohio: Antioch Press.

Korsgaard, Ove. 2006. "The Danish Way to Establish the Nation in the Hearts of the People." Pp. 133–58 in *National Identity and Varieties of Capitalism*, edited by John L. Campbell, John A. Hall, and Ove K. Pedersen. Montreal: McGill-Queen's University Press.

———. 2004. *Kampen om Folke*. Copenhagen: Glydendal.

Kriedte, Peter, Hans Medick, and Johann Schlumbohm. 1982. *Industrialization before Industrialization*. Cambridge: Cambridge University Press.

Kriesi, Hanspeter, and Alex Trechsel. 2008. *The Politics of Switzerland: Continuity and Change in a Consensus Democracy*. Cambridge University Press.

Lane, Philip. 2011. "The Irish Crisis." IIIS discussion paper no. 356. Dublin: Trinity College.

Lieberson, Stanley, and Freda Lynn. 2002. "Barking up the Wrong Branch: Scientific Alternatives to the Current Model of Sociological Science." *Annual Review of Sociology* 28:1–19.

Lieven, Dominic. 2000. *Empire: The Russian Empire and Its Rivals*. London: John Murray.

Lijphart, Arend. 1999. *Patterns of Democracy*. New Haven: Yale University Press.

Linder, Wolf. 2010. *Swiss Democracy: Possible Solutions to Conflict in Multicultural Societies*, 3rd ed. New York: Palgrave Macmillan.

Lindvall, Johannes. 2012. "Politics and Policies in Two Economic Crises: The Nordic Countries." Pp. 233–60 in *Coping with the Crisis*, edited by Nancy Bermeo and Jonas Pontusson. New York: Russell Sage.

Lounsbury, Michael, and Paul Hirsch. 2010. "Markets on Trial: The Economic Sociology of the U.S. Financial Crisis." *Research in the Sociology of Organizations* 30(Special issue, parts A & B).

Low Tax. 2015. "Switzerland: Related Information, Bank Confidentiality." Low Tax: Global Tax and Business Portal. http://www.lowtax.net/information/switzerland/switzerland-banking-confidentiality.html (accessed August 2015).

Mahoney, James. 2000. "Raising the Standard: New Guidelines for Designing Social Inquiry." Unpublished paper, Department of Sociology, Brown University.

Malešević, Siniša. 2014. "Irishness and Nationalisms." Pp. 10–21 in *Are the Irish Differerent?*, edited by Tom Inglis. Manchester: Manchester University Press.

March, James. 2010. *The Ambiguities of Experience*. Ithaca: Cornell University Press.

Marx, Anthony. 2003. *Faith in Nation: Exclusionary Origins of Nationalism*. Oxford: Oxford University Press.

Matsangou, Elisabeth. 2015. "Failing Banks, Winning Economy: The Truth about Iceland's Recovery." *World Finance*, September 15. http://www.worldfinance.com/infrastructure-investment/government-policy/failing-banks-winning-economy-the-truth-about-icelands-recovery (accessed January 2016).

Mayer, Jane. 2016. *Dark Money*. New York: Doubleday.

McAdam, Doug, Sidney Tarrow, and Charles Tilly. 2001. *Dynamics of Contention*. New York: Cambridge University Press.

McConnell, Daniel, and Tom Lyons. 2012. "Whistleblower's Dire Warnings Silenced by Senior Finance Chiefs." *The Irish Independent* April 22. http://www.independent.ie/opinion/analysis/whistleblowers-dire-warnings-silenced-by-senior-finance-chiefs-26845568.html (accessed July 2012).

McDonald, Frank, and Kathy Sheridan. 2008. *The Builders*. London: Penguin.

McGarry, John, and Brendan O'Leary, eds. 1993. *The Politics of Ethnic Conflict Regulation*. London: Routledge.

Min, Brian, Lars-Erik Cederman, and Andreas Wimmer. 2010. "Ethnic Exclusion, Economic Growth, and Civil War." Unpublished manuscript, Department of Sociology, University of California, Los Angeles.

Ministry of Business and Growth. 2013. *The Financial Crisis in Denmark—Causes, Consequenes and Lessons*. September 8. Copenhagen: Ministry of Business and Growth. https://sf.cbs.dk/jrangvid/report_on_financial_crisis_in_denmark (accessed May 2015).

Morgan, Glenn. 2008. "Market Formation and Governance in International Financial Markets: The Case of OTC Derivatives." *Human Relations* 61(5):637–60.

Mortensen, Jens Ladefoged, and Leonard Seabrooke. 2009. "Egalitarian Politics in Property Booms and Busts: Housing as Social Right or Means to Wealth in Australia and Denmark."

Pp. 122–45 in *The Politics of Housing Booms and Busts*, edited by Herman Schwartz and Leonard Seabrooke. New York: Palgrave Macmillan.

Newsweek. 2014. "How the Swiss Are Beating the Financial Crisis." July 1. http://www.news week.com/how-swiss-are-beating-financial-crisis-83429 (accessed April 2014).

Norris, Floyd. 2013. "In Ireland, Dire Echoes of a Bailout Gone Awry." *The New York Times*, July 5.

North, Douglass. 1990. *Institutions, Institutional Change and Economic Performance.* New York: Cambridge University Press.

OECD. 2014. *OECD Factbook.* Paris: OECD. http://www.oecd-ilibrary.org/economics/oecd -factbook_18147364 (accessed February 2016).

———. 2011. *OECD Economic Surveys: Switzerland 2011.* Paris: OECD.

———. 2010. "Economic Survey of Switzerland 2009: Getting Out of the Crisis." Paris: OECD.

———. 2009a. *OECD Economic Surveys: Denmark 2009.* Paris: OECD.

———. 2009b. *OECD Economic Surveys: Switzerland 2009.* Paris: OECD.

Offe, Claus. 1981. "The Attribution of Public Status to Interest Groups: Observations on the West German Case." Pp. 123–58 in *Organizing Interests in Western Europe*, edited by Suzanne Berger. New York: Cambridge University Press.

O'Leary, Brendan. Forthcoming. *Passages from Colonialism to Consociation.* New York: Oxford University Press.

———. 2005. "Debating Consociational Politics: Normative and Explanatory Arguments." Pp. 3–43 in *From Power Sharing to Democracy*, edited by S.J.R. Noel. Toronto: McGill-Queens University Press.

———. 2003. "What States Can Do with Nations: An Iron Law of Nationalism and Federation?" Pp. 51–78 in *The Nation-State in Question*, edited by T. V. Paul, G. John Ikenberry, and John A. Hall. Princeton: Princeton University Press.

———. 2001. "The Elements of Right-Sizing and Right-Peopling the State." Pp. 15–73 in *Right-Sizing the State: The Politics of Moving Borders*, edited by Brendan O'Leary, Ian Lustick, and Tom Callaghy. New York: Oxford University Press.

Ó Riain, Seán. 2014. *The Rise and Fall of Ireland's Celtic Tiger.* New York: Cambridge University Press.

———. 2007. "Competing State Projects in the Contemporary Irish Political Economy." Pp. 165–85 in *Contesting the State: Lessons from the Irish Case*, edited by M. Adshead, P Kirby, and M. Millar. Manchester, England: Manchester University Press.

———. 2004. *The Politics of High-Tech Growth.* New York: Cambridge University Press.

O'Rourke, Kevin. 2006. "Late Nineteenth Century Denmark in an Irish Mirror: Land Tenure, Homogeneity and the Roots of Danish Success." Pp. 159–96 in *National Identity and the Varieties of Capitalism: The Danish Experience*, edited by John L. Campbell, John A. Hall, and Ove K. Pedersen. Montreal: McGill-Queen's University Press.

Østergaard, Uffe. 2006. "Denmark: A Big Small State—The Peasant Roots of Danish Modernity." Pp. 51–98 in *National Identity and Varieties of Capitalism*, edited by John L. Campbell, John A. Hall, and Ove K. Pedersen. Montreal: McGill-Queen's University Press.

Østrup, Finn. 2010. "The Danish Bank Crisis in a Transnational Perspective." Pp. 75–112 in *Danish Foreign Policy Yearbook*, edited by Nanna Hvidt and Hans Mouritzen. Copenhagen: Danish Institute for International Studies.

O'Toole, Fintan. 2010. *Ship of Fools: How Stupidity and Corruption Sank the Celtic Tiger.* New York: Public Affairs.

Patsiurko, Natalka, John L. Campbell, and John A. Hall. 2013. "Nation-State Size, Ethnic Diversity and Economic Performance in the Advanced Capitalist Countries." *New Political Economy* 18(6):827–44.

———. 2012. "Measuring Cultural Diversity: Ethnic, Linguistic and Religious Fractionalization in the OECD." *Ethnic and Racial Studies* 35(2):195–217.

Pedersen, Ove K. 2006. "Negotiated Economy: Corporatism and Beyond." Pp. 245–70 in *National Identity and Varieties of Capitalism*, edited by John L. Campbell, John A. Hall, and Ove K. Pedersen. Montreal: McGill-Queen's University Press.

Pierson, Paul. 2003. "Big, Slow-Moving, and … Invisible: Macrosocial Processes in the Study of Comparative Politics." Pp. 177–208 in *Comparative Historical Analysis in the Social Sciences*, edited by James Mahoney and Dietrich Rueshemeyer. New York: Cambridge University Press.

Pierson, Paul, and Theda Skocpol. 2000. "Historical Institutionalism in Contemporary Political Science." Presented at the annual meeting of the American Political Science Association, Washington, D.C., September.

Porten, Elin, Fabian Peters, Maiko Messelken, and Marietta von Meien. 2009. "Comparison of the Governmental Actions Undertaken in Response to the Financial Crisis in Europe." Brussels: European Commission. http://baobab.uc3m.es/monet/monnet/IMG/pdf/Crisi09_Europe Responses-2.pdf (accessed August 2015).

Porter, Michael. 1990. *The Competitive Advantage of Nations*. New York: Free Press.

Posner, Daniel N. 2005. *Institutions and Ethnic Politics in Africa*. New York: Cambridge University Press.

———. 2004. "Measuring Ethnic Fractionalization in Africa." *American Journal of Political Science* 48(4):849–63.

Putnam, Robert, and Kristin Goss. 2002. "Introduction." Pp. 3–20 in *Democracies in Flux: the Evolution of Social Capital in Contemporary Society*, edited by Robert Putnam. New York: Oxford University Press.

Regling, Klaus, and Max Watson. 2010. "A Preliminary Report on the Sources of Ireland's Banking Crisis." Dublin: Government Publications.

Reuters. 2010. "Swiss Delay Report on Too-Big-To-Fail Solutions." August 26. http://www.reuters .com/assets/print?aid=USWEA568820100826 (accessed August 2015).

Rueschemeyer, Dietrich. 2003. "Can One or a Few Cases Yield Theoretical Gains?" Pp. 305–36 in *Comparative Historical Analysis in the Social Sciences*, edited by James Mahoney and Dietrich Rueschemeyer. New York: Cambridge University Press.

Samuels, Richard. 1987. *The Business of the Japanese State*. Ithaca: Cornell University Press.

Scharpf, Fritz W. 1997. *Games Real Actors Play: Actor-Centered Institutionalism in Policy Research*. Boulder, Colo.: Westview Press.

Scheller, Hanspeter K. 2004. *The European Central Bank: History, Role and Functions*. Frankfurt: European Central Bank. https://www.ecb.europa.eu/pub/pdf/other/ecbhistoryrolefunctions 2004en.pdf. (accessed May 2014).

Schubert, Justin. 2011. "Big Bank, Small Country: Switzerland, the Financial Crisis and the European Union." *Inquiry Journal*, Paper 16, University of New Hampshire Scholars' Repository. http://scholars.unh.edu/inquiry_2011/16 (accessed April 2014).

Schmidt, Vivien. 2002. *The Futures of European Capitalism*. New York: Oxford University Press.

Schmidt, Vivien, and Mark Thatcher. 2013. "Theorizing Ideational Continuity: The Resilience of Neo-Liberal Ideas in Europe." Pp. 1–52 in *Resilient Liberalism in Europe's Political Economy*, edited by Vivien Schmidt and Mark Thatcher. New York: Cambridge University Press.

Schwartz, Herman. 2001. "The Danish 'Miracle'? Luck, Pluck, or Stuck?" *Comparative Political Studies* 3(2)131–55.

Sciarini, Pascal, Manuel Fischer, and Denise Traber, eds. 2015. *Political Decision-Making in Switzerland. The Consensus Model under Pressure*. New York: Palgrave Macmillan.

Shaw, George Bernard. 1907. *John Bull's Other Island*. London: Constable.

Simmons, Beth. 1999. "The Internationalization of Capital." Pp. 36–69 in *Continuity and Change in Contemporary Capitalism*, edited by Herbert Kitschelt, Peter Lange, Gary Marks, and John D. Stephens. New York: Cambridge University Press.

Singh, Prerna. 2015. *How Solidarity Works for Welfare: Subnationalism and Social Development in India*. Cambridge: Cambridge University Press.

Smith, Anthony. 1991. *National Identity*. Las Vegas: University of Nevada Press.

Sørensen, Aage B. 1998a. "On Kings, Pietism, and Rent-Seeking in Scandinavian Welfare States." *Acta Sociologica* 41:363–75.

———. 1998b. "Theoretical Mechanisms and the Empirical Study of Social Processes." Pp. 238–66 in *Social Mechanisms: An Analytical Approach to Social Theory*, edited by Peter Hedström and Richard Swedberg. New York: Cambridge University Press.

Soskice, David. 2007. "Macroeconomics and Varieties of Capitalism." Pp. 89–121 in *Beyond Varieties of Capitalism*, edited by Bob Hancké, Martin Rhodes, and Mark Thatcher. New York: Oxford University Press.

Stats Monkey. 2015. "Top Countries with Most Fortune Global 500 Companies." https://www.statsmonkey.com/table/12694-top-10-countries-with-most-fortune-global-500-companies.php (accessed August 2015).

Steinberg, Jonathan. 1996. *Why Switzerland?* New York: Cambridge University Press.

Streeck, Wolfgang. 1997. "Beneficial Constraints: On the Economic Limits of Rational Voluntarism." Pp. 197–219 in *Contemporary Capitalism: The Embeddedness of Institutions*, edited by J. Rogers Hollingsworth and Robert Boyer. New York: Cambridge University Press.

Streeck, Wolfgang, and Philippe Schmitter. 1985. "Community, Market, State—and Associations? The Prospective Contribution of Interest Governance to Social Order." Pp. 1–29 in *Private Interest Government*, edited by Wolfgang Streeck and Philippe Schmitter. Beverly Hills: Sage.

Swenden, Wilfried. 2006. *Federalism and Regionalism in Western Europe*. New York: Palgrave.

Swiss Bankers Association. 2010. *The Swiss Banking Sector*. Basel: Swiss Bankers Association.

Swissinfo.ch. 2015. "Domestic Banks Reject EU Finance Fusion." Swiss Broadcasting Company, January 8. http://www.swissinfo.ch/eng/domestic-banks-reject-eu-finance-fusion/41205970 (accessed September 2015).

———. 2014. "Is Switzerland Really the Country of Bankers?" Swiss Broadcasting Company, September 18. http://www.swissinfo.ch/eng/by-the-numbers_is-switzerland-really-the-country-of-bankers-/40473658 (accessed August 2015).

Taleb, Nassim. 2012. *Antifragility: Things that Gain from Disorder*. New York: Random House.

Thelen, Kathleen, and Sven Steinmo. 1992. "Historical Institutionalism in Comparative Politics." Pp. 1–32 in *Structuring Politics: Historical Institutionalism in Comparative Analysis*, edited by Sven Steinmo, Kathleen Thelen, and Frank Longstreth. New York: Cambridge University Press.

Tilly, Charles. 1984. *Big Structures, Large Processes, Huge Comparisons*. New York: Russell Sage.

Trading Economics. 2015. "Ireland Government Debt to GDP." http://www.tradingeconomics.com/ireland/government-debt-to-gdp (accessed June 2015).

United Nations. 2007. *Human Development Report, 2007/2008*. New York: United Nations.

U.S. Congressional Research Service. 2011. "Greece's Debt Crisis: Overview, Policy Responses, and Implications." Washington, D.C.: Congressional Research Service.

U.S. Federal Reserve. 2015. "Minutes of the Meeting of the Federal Open Market Committee." October 28–29, p. 37. Washington, D.C.: U.S. Federal Reserve.

Wade, Robert, and Silla Sigurgeirsdottir. 2012. "Iceland's Rise, Fall, Stabilization and Beyond." *Cambridge Journal of Economics* 36:127–44.

————. 2010. "Lessons from Iceland." *New Left Review* 65:5–29.

Weiss, Linda. 1998. *The Myth of the Powerless State*. Ithaca: Cornell University Press.

Wilson, William Julius. 1996. *When Work Disappears*. New York: Vintage.

Wimmer, Andreas. 2013. *Waves of War: Nationalism, State Formation and Ethnic Exclusion in the Modern World*. Cambridge: Cambridge University Press.

————. 2011. "A Swiss Anomaly? A Relational Account of National Boundary Making." *Nations and Nationalism* 17(4):718–37.

————. 2002. *Nationalist Exclusion and Ethnic Conflict: Shadows of Modernity*. Cambridge: Cambridge University Press.

Woll, Cornelia. 2014. *The Power of Collective Inaction*. Ithaca: Cornell University Press.

World Economic Forum. 2009. *Global Competitiveness Report, 2009–2010*. Geneva: World Economic Forum.

————. 2008. *Global Competitiveness Report, 2008–2009*. Geneva: World Economic Forum.

Yahil, L. 1991. "National Pride and Defeat: A Comparison of Danish and German Nationalism." Pp. 99–124 in *The Impact of Western Nationalisms*, edited by J. Reinharz and G. L. Mosse. London: Sage.

Yeats, W. B. 1933. *The Winding Stair and Other Poems*. London: Macmillan and Co.

Ziegler, J. Nicolas, and John T. Wooley. 2016. "After Dodd-Frank: Ideas and the Post-Enactment Politics of Financial Reform in the United States." *Politics and Society* 44:249–80.

Zimmer, Oliver. 2003. *A Contested Nation: History, Memory and Nationalism in Switzerland*. Cambridge: Cambridge University Press.

INDEX

Princeton Studies in Global and Comparative Sociology

A NOTE ON THE TYPE

This book has been composed in Adobe Text and Gotham. Adobe Text, designed by Robert Slimbach for Adobe, bridges the gap between fifteenth- and sixteenth-century calligraphic and eighteenth-century Modern styles. Gotham, inspired by New York street signs, was designed by Tobias Frere-Jones for Hoefler & Co.